THE LAW ENFORCEMENT MEDICAL ENCYCLOPEDIA

MARTIN GREENBERG, MD

NAVIGATING MEDICAL CHALLENGES
IN A DANGEROUS WORLD

THE LAW ENFORCEMENT MEDICAL ENCYCLOPEDIA

MARTIN GREENBERG, MD

NAVIGATING MEDICAL CHALLENGES IN A DANGEROUS WORLD

MARTIN GREENBERG, M.D

Copyright © 2025 by Martin Greenberg, M.D.

All rights reserved. No part of this publication may be reproduced, distributed, or transmitted in any form or by any means, including photocopying, recording, or other electronic or mechanical methods, without the prior written permission of the copyright owner and the publisher, except in the case of brief quotations embodied in critical reviews and certain other noncommercial uses permitted by copyright law. For permission requests, write to the publisher, addressed "Attention: Permissions Coordinator," at the address below.

CITIOFBOOKS, INC.
3736 Eubank NE Suite A1
Albuquerque, NM 87111-3579
www.citiofbooks.com
Hotline:	1 (877) 389-2759
Fax:	1 (505) 930-7244

Ordering Information:

Quantity sales. Special discounts are available on quantity purchases by corporations, associations, and others. For details, contact the publisher at the address above.

Printed in the United States of America.

ISBN-13:	Softcover	979-8-89391-784-0
	eBook	979-8-89391-786-4
	Hardback	979-8-89391-785-7

Library of Congress Control Number: 2025913530

Table of Contents

Forword iii
Introduction vii
1. Nutrition Recommendations 1
2. Physical Training Recommendations.. 13
3. Self-Aid / Buddy-Aid..27
4. The Miracle of Sight 37
5. The Miracle of Hearing 59
6. Decisions, Decisions, Decisions… 73
7. Drug Related Risks 129
8. A Brief Ballistics Primer and Medical Ballistics 137
9. Heat Stress Injury 157
10. Cold Stress Injury.. 167
11. Law Enforcement Suicide 183
12. Dental and Facial Trauma 203
13. Radiologic/Nuclear Weapons of Mass Destruction 223
14. Biological Weapons of Mass Destruction................................. 237
15. Chemical Weapons of Mass Destruction 253
16. Explosions and Blast Injuries 269
17. Canine First Aid 281

Disclaimer and Terms of Use Agreement

The author and the publisher of this book, in any form, have made their best efforts to present an encyclopedic but not necessarily comprehensive discussion of the chosen topics. There is no warranty or representation regarding the accuracy, timeliness, completeness, or fitness of its contents. The presented information is strictly presented for educational purposes and as a basis for further, more guided research. If the reader decides to apply any of the recommendations made in this book, it becomes his/her full responsibility.

The author and the publisher disclaim any expressed or implied warranty or fitness of this book's contents for any purpose. The author and the publisher of this book will not be held liable to any party for any direct, indirect, special, incidental, punitive or other consequential damages derived from the direct or indirect use of any concept or recommendation made in this book. It is presented "as is" and without warranty. This includes any references cited in the text.

This book is © copyrighted and protected by Dr. Martin Greenberg under the US Copyright Act of 1976 and all other applicable local, state, federal and international laws with *all* rights reserved. No portion of this book may be copied or changed in any format without the expressed permission of Martin Greenberg, MD. Using the contents of this book in any manner represents an agreement with this disclaimer and the above enumerated terms of use.

FOREWORD

by Bill Lewinski, Ph.D.

I have been fortunate to have spent most of my life learning about critical incidents from those who have been there and with those whom I have shared them. Some were in person but most experienced vicariously through interviews or consultations. I have shared that experience with thousands of police and military officers through almost 50 years of professional interviewing, investigation and research. Most of the scientific research I have conducted was done to investigate or reveal information about these situations that would help others make better informed decisions, perform more effectively, and be able to investigate, explain or testify with greater clarity. This was directed toward situations where danger was imminent or immediate and the actions of the involved individuals were seriously consequential.

A fundamental truth that has been reinforced throughout my years of study is that the involved officer is a composite of many elements responding holistically to a incident. The implications of this are profound for all involved in the officer's professional behavior from the trainer to the adjudicator.

The holistic aspect is lost on most researchers, instructors, investigators and adjudicators, or they are ill informed by outdated concepts of perception, cognition and decision making, or their belief that human emotions are limited to fight, fright and freeze just as Walter Cannon observed in rats in 1932. Or, many believe that any behavior involving emotion is primarily driven by a part of the brain called the amygdala. Certainly the amygdala is involved but how do they explain that the same level of arousal drives the cognition and performance elements to two different interpretations and behaviors of threat or challenge. Two very different approaches to the same circumstance. Or they adhere to the concept of the triune brain (reptilian, limbic & neocortex) which is at odds with the work of modern neuroscience that demonstrates the extensive interconnectedness and overlap of brain regions. Simply, the brain and our body are now understood to be interconnected in many ways. Current research illustrates the interdependent nature of cognition and emotion and how they work together to make the brain more of a predictive than a reactive system. There is a need for more and relevant science of performance in the police and other professions.

The holistic aspect of human behavior is not lost on Dr. Greenberg. From our first meeting in a great Italian restaurant in Chicago until today, I continue to be impressed by his understanding of the depth, complexity, diversity and integration of human performance, particularly in dynamic tactical situations. His experience as a medical doctor, surgeon, SWAT doc, but most of all his curiosity have provided him with a wealth of understanding and insight. This work is entitled a Medical Encyclopedia, but it is more than that. It is an Encyclopedia of all the physiological and cognitive components of human performance at the edge, plus a range of medical information from nutrition for health and high performance to wound care when under assault. It is a compendium of the lessons learned by one who took an oath to heal, and another to protect and who lives both of those. It is his repertoire of the knowledge he has acquired and that he believes is important for those who serve - to know, understand and use. It is a vast expanse of the latest, relevant science supporting understanding and insight in the human being using "tools" in often, complex, dynamic and urgent circumstances.

This text is an amazing resource for those who work in any profession that requires high levels of performance under conditions that are at times of extreme stress or even duress. It is a must read!

I am grateful for Dr. Greenberg and his creation of this unique text.

Bill Lewinski, Ph.D.
Founding Partner & Co-Owner
Chief Research Officer
FORCE SCIENCE®

Introduction

We all have experienced medical problems requiring internet research. Without a knowledge base about any topic, we are left to randomly "google" the subject but we have no clear idea of what we find is accurate or important. This volume provides that knowledge base in many areas of interest to us all.

For law enforcement, each chapter's topics such as self-aid/buddy-aid, ballistics, visual and hearing impairment, nutrition and exercise have obvious relevance. These chapters provide important information to protect them in their daily activities. It also provides an in-depth knowledge base for law enforcement training at all levels.

For the medical community including students, residents and practitioners it presents a scientific and sound medical understanding including treatment options for many field medical problems including heat and cold injury, bleeding control, airway management and many other subjects they might not encounter in a standard training program.

The benefits of this information for the general public are multifaceted. The discussions are written in simple English. Medical terminology is always explained. Haven't we all wanted to avoid frostbite or heat stroke? We are surrounded by a violent society. Wouldn't we all want to know how to react should we become involved in such an event? We hear about nuclear weapon threats internationally and bioweapon threats, even possibly including the Covid-19 pandemic at home. Rather than blind fear, we can now learn about these threats and what can actually be done to mitigate them. Gaining insight into how we think and learn can help us to learn more effectively. Information about nutrition and exercise can lead us to live healthier lives.

Knowledge is power. With this sound information base, further studies and searches can be directed more intelligently. Important concepts in each chapter are presented in italics to highlight them. On a different note, over the past forty years of medical practice as an orthopedic surgeon and over twenty years as a tactical medic, I have many times heard "I'd like to be a fly on the wall" after folks hear about a medical or tactical scenario. Now you can really see "how the sausage is made." What did we learn in advance about these issues? What are our concerns? What decisions must we make to deal with them? How can we prevent or mitigate any of these problems? Now this is all laid out in an understandable scientific and medical format. I believe that this book will be a great benefit to those of us interested in the local, national and international world around us. Good luck on this adventure!

Nutrition Recommendations

Martin Greenberg, MD

The goal of this chapter is to review the controversial subject of nutrition. Few topics are as hotly debated as the elements of a healthy diet. Violent supporters and detractors of diametrically opposed dietary recommendations co-exist, publish volumes and sell their nutritional wares. The scientific basis of such nutritional claims is frequently lacking. We hope that this discussion will spark your curiosity to make your own healthy, informed nutritional choices.

The Goal of Nutrition
Since pre-historic times, ancient man survived a challenging environment without reliable heating, housing or medicines as his diet was enormously healthy including fresh water, fish, fowl, game, vegetables, fruit, and unprocessed grains. The "modern illnesses" of cardiovascular disease and diabetes were unknown. The goal of any diet should be to promote a vigorous, disease-free lifestyle well into advanced age. Does the modern diet promote a long, healthy life or does it sow the seeds of our "modern" diseases?

The History of Carbohydrates in the American Diet
Two hundred years ago, the per capita consumption of sugar was less than ten pounds. In the 1890s, cola soft drinks were

introduced to our nation. By 1928, each American citizen consumed an average of 120 pounds of sugar/year. In 1996, the figure rose to 152 pounds. (1) Also in the 1890s, the milling industry of wheat into nutritionally empty, white flour developed on a national scale. Flour is directly metabolized in our body to glucose (sugar). Sugar has no nutritional value and is in many ways harmful to health. In the 1800s, people ate large amounts of butter, lard, beef, pork, whole milk and eggs. However, the first heart attack (or coronary occlusion as it was called then) was not described until 1912. Dr. Paul Dudley White, President Dwight D. Eisenhower's personal cardiologist, stated that he did not personally see a heart attack patient until the 1920s. In the sixty years from 1910-1970, coronary heart disease grew from an unknown illness to the killer of fifty percent of our population. At the same time, our animal fat/red meat consumption dropped while America's carbohydrate intake increased sixty percent. (2) Regardless of our cultural differences with France, we should take note of their diet. They eat four times the amount of butter and twice the amount of cheese as we Americans and yet their rate of heart disease and obesity is sixty percent lower than ours. French women have the lowest rate of heart disease in the western world. Our diets are otherwise comparable except that the United States' per capita consumption of sugar is five and a half times that of France.

Insulin's Role in Metabolism
We have all heard of insulin as a hormone taken by diabetics to control blood sugar. "The insulin hormone is one of the most powerful and efficient substances that the body uses to control the use, distribution, and storage of energy."(3) We should view our body as an "energy machine." It never shuts down and it's powered by glucose. Blood glucose levels are maintained within a narrow normal range of about 60-110 milligrams/deciliter (mg. /100 ml blood). How does this occur? After eating, food

substances are digested and then absorbed in the small intestine. From carbohydrates, simple sugars are absorbed which then become glucose. Glycerol and fatty acids are absorbed from fats. Amino acids are absorbed from protein. Our body was designed in prehistoric times when refined sugar didn't exist. Its ability to deal with large quantities of excess refined sugar is limited. Here may lie the source of our problem.

Blood sugar sharply rises after eating most carbohydrates. Insulin controls the decision of how much glucose will be used immediately vs. how much will be diverted for storage. It is produced in the pancreatic *Islets of Langerhans.* As blood sugar rises, insulin converts some glucose to glycogen that is stored in muscle and the liver in limited amounts. When these areas are filled, excess glucose is converted to triglyceride and then to fat. Insulin usually works precisely to do this. Conversely, if insulin were absent, blood sugar levels would rise and the body would search for alternate energy sources. If insulin were present in excess, too much glucose would be processed and blood sugar levels would drop too low (hypoglycemia). In hypoglycemia, our body would release hormones to raise blood sugar including glucagon, ACTH, and adrenaline. Most officers are familiar with adrenaline's mostly negative effects in critical stress situations. Therefore, hypoglycemia's symptoms are not a good thing to experience from the officers' perspective. There is a direct relationship between what you eat and the amount of insulin released into your bloodstream. Both simple (sugar, honey, fruit, milk) and refined (flour, white rice, starch) carbohydrates readily convert to glucose and stimulate high levels of insulin release. Conversely, protein and fat consumption result in little or no insulin release.

As large amounts of insulin are constantly demanded by gargantuan glucose loads, our bodies become progressively less responsive to insulin's hormonal actions. Obese and diabetic individuals demonstrate an extreme degree of this unresponsiveness, hence the term *"insulin resistance."* It has been shown that high insulin levels actually can create or worsen this resistance. It is thought that bodily insulin cell receptors are blocked, preventing insulin from transferring glucose to the cell as an energy source. Inappropriately large amounts of insulin response to a carbohydrate load can also result in hypoglycemia. Symptoms of hypoglycemia include shakiness, tiredness, anxiety, irritability, depression and "brain fog." As insulin becomes less effective in using glucose as energy, it transfers more glucose into potentially unlimited fat stores. A worsening, vicious cycle is thus created where insulin is being secreted constantly and inefficiently in larger amounts to deal with large blood sugar loads. Its hormonal effect progressively diminishes and its overproduction causes intermittent hypoglycemia reactively stimulating more glucose release. Insulin receptors become worn out (high insulin level diabetes) and eventually the pancreatic islet cells stop producing insulin (low insulin level diabetes). The term *hyperinsulinism* describes the condition of having permanently high, yet ineffective, insulin levels.

Abnormalities of insulin metabolism are common and comprise a spectrum of disease. This continuum is described in five stages that are generally termed by Atkins the "Diabetes Related Disorder" or alternatively called "Syndrome X." Many of us are currently included in this spectrum without knowing it.

Stage 1: Insulin Resistance (IR) only;
Stage 2: IR + hyperinsulinism (HI);
Stage 3: IR, HI + abnormal glucose tolerance test;
Stage 4: Type II diabetes with high insulin levels;
Stage 5: Type II diabetes with low insulin levels.

A high insulin level creates a number of other problems. It increases salt and water retention leading to hypertension (high blood pressure). The problem is aggravated by higher levels of blood adrenaline as a response to the transient hypoglycemia we previously discussed. Insulin creates atherosclerotic plaques (hardening of the arteries). It can create sleep disorders by affecting brain neurotransmitters. It directly raises triglyceride and "bad" Low Density Lipoprotein (LDL) cholesterol levels. How can we get off this potential blood sugar "roller coaster"? Let us look at our current American diet more closely for some answers.

Twin Epidemics
Half of our nation is obese. Recently, there has been a one percent yearly increase in this percentage. Frighteningly, the fattening of America is projected to continue unabated. Although it is not 50%, the prevalence of diabetes in our country is also rising in a parallel manner. Why is this situation occurring and what can we do about it?

The American Medical Association (AMA) opines that the cause of obesity is that we eat too much fat and that we exercise too little. Reviewing their recommendations, The AMA wishes us to eat less saturated fat and exercise more. Actually, Americans have increasingly substituted carbohydrates for fat for the past 30 years.

In the years 1990-1997, total meat consumption increased thirteen pounds but red meat consumption decreased twenty-one pounds while poultry and fish intake rose thirty-one and three pounds respectively. During the same time, the fat content of beef decreased seventy percent per federal Food and Drug Administration requirements. Egg consumption decreased from 276 eggs in 1970 to 173 in 1997. During this twenty-seven-year period, Americans drank twenty-three percent less milk with whole milk intake dropping by two-thirds. Carbonated beverage use is now two and a half times the consumption of milk. In the same twenty-seven-year period, fruit and vegetable intake increased twenty-four percent, and grain consumption increased from 136 pounds to 200 pounds. Grain mixture intake (i.e., lasagna and pizza) increased one hundred fifteen percent. Snack food intake increased two hundred percent. Most interestingly, consumption of beverage (soda pop) sugar-based sweeteners increased from thirty-four pounds to a record 154 pounds since 1982! This two-fifths of a pound of added sugar per person per day equals forty-one gallons of regular soda pop consumption per year- up forty-seven percent just since the mid 1980s. Added dietary sugar alone accounted for eighteen percent of an individual's total caloric intake. Only about 6% of total calories were derived from naturally occurring sugars including fruits, vegetables, and milk lactose. From another perspective, in 1994 dietary carbohydrate calories including sugar increased to fifty-one percent (up four percent) while fat dietary calories dropped to thirty-eight percent (down four percent). Protein intake remained at a constant eleven percent. This data clearly shows that our population has been substituting carbohydrates for fat. (4)

At the same time that we have lowered our fat intake, obesity, diabetes, and heart disease have become epidemic problems. Two physiological facts help explain this. First, fat consumption triggers the central nervous system feeling of satiety (feeling full). Carbohydrate consumption does not have this effect and therefore promotes overeating. Second, as previously discussed, our body has a metabolic preference for burning alcohol, then carbohydrates and finally fat. Alcohol and protein are not stored in the body. Carbohydrates are metabolized to glucose and are stored in liver/muscle in limited amounts as glycogen. Beyond this, again, excess glucose is stored as body fat in potentially unlimited amounts. When carbohydrate intake is limited to less than 40g/day, fat is preferentially burned without muscle loss. Maximal satiety (feeling full) occurs when eating fat containing foods. This sensation does not occur when eating carbohydrates unless they are contained in a high fiber food. Because we don't feel full as quickly, we tend to eat more carbohydrates.

It seems intuitive that eating fat containing foods is unhealthy, but this is not the case. High carbohydrate diets all stimulate hyperinsulinemia (too high a blood insulin level), responsible for today's "most wanted" list of medical problems including diabetes, heart/cardiovascular disease, and atherosclerosis (hardening of the arteries including stroke and diabetic leg gangrene). Low carbohydrate (high protein/fat) diets have been wrongly accused of creating an unfavorable blood lipid (fat) profile. Dietary fat is the main source of High Density Lipoproteins (HDLs), the "good" cholesterol. Low Density Lipoprotein (LDL- the "bad" cholesterol) levels drop significantly while deleterious triglyceride levels dramatically drop up to 80% on a very low carbohydrate diet. Blood sugar levels are stabilized when added dietary glucose is eliminated and the carbohydrates converted in our body to glucose are limited.

A deadly combination of medical risk factors termed *The Metabolic Syndrome* includes obesity, hypertriglyceridemia, hypercholesterolemia, low HDL, hypertension (high blood pressure) and elevated blood sugar. These are also sequelae of the *Diabetes Related Disorder* described by Atkins. The risk of suffering a heart attack increases up to sixteen times in their presence. A low carbohydrate diet ideally addresses all these problems. Incidentally, a low carbohydrate diet may not necessarily contain more total fat than our current fat laden, high carbohydrate fare.

Your Ideal Weight
What is your ideal body weight? Your diet will be determined by whether you wish to gain, lose or maintain your body weight. In the low carbohydrate or keto approach, this means varying carbohydrate intake rather than counting calories. Carbohydrate intake varies by number of grams and the glycemic index of the carbohydrate. The Glycemic Index describes the insulin stimulating qualities of a particular food.

Refer to a Glycemic Index table for specific food values. Ideal body weight may be determined in several different ways. One method is the Body Mass Index (BMI). This is determined by a graph correlating height and weight. A BMI of 20-25 is healthy; 25-30 is overweight; 30 and over is obese. (5) Insurance companies also publish "desirable weight tables" as a part of the insurance evaluation process. The following example is excerpted from the Metropolitan Life Insurance Company Desirable weights for Men and Women aged 25 And Over in pounds according to height and frame in indoor clothing, and shoes. (6)

HEIGHT	SMALL FRAME	MEDIUM FRAME	LARGE FRAME
MEN (pounds)			
5'8"	132-141	138-152	147-166
5'9"	136-145	142-156	151-170
5'10"	140-150	146-160	155-174
5'11'	144-154	150-165	159-179
6'	148-158	154-170	164-184
6'1"	152-162	158-175	168-189
WOMEN (pounds)			
5'4"	108-116	113-126	121-138
5'5"	111-119	116-130	125-142
5'6"	114-123	120-135	129-146
5'7"	118-127	124-139	133-150

Simply put, we all have a "break point" of carbohydrate intake above which we will gain weight. This may range from about 50-100g/day and is unique for each of us. A diet below 40 carbohydrate grams/day will usually result in weight loss depending upon our individual insulin resistance (IR). The heavier we are, the greater the likely amount of this resistance. Carbohydrate Gram Counters are readily available at most nutrition stores, bookstores, at the library and on the internet. (7)

It's also very important to replace plant nutrients (phytonutrients) that are restricted in the keto diet with oral supplements. Ten servings of fruits and vegetables are recommended daily to provide these important nutrients. Green vegetables are generally considered low carbohydrate foods. Colored vegetables and all fruits are generally high carbohydrate foods. In the keto diet, fruit and vegetable supplements replace these restricted high carbohydrate items. There are a number of excellent commercially available fruit and vegetable supplements.

Vitamins and Nutrients
Vitamins are substances that allow the body to utilize the nutrients in foods. It is non-controversial that vitamin supplements are recommended. Vitamins A, D, E, and K are fat soluble. This means that they are stored in body fat stores and are not excreted through the kidneys in the urine. It is therefore possible to "overdose" taking these vitamins and develop serious toxic symptoms. Vitamins B and C are water soluble and are excreted in the urine. One cannot "overdose" taking too much Vitamin B and C. Other nutrients thought to be beneficial for metabolism include chromium picolinate (controlling cholesterol levels and stabilizing blood sugar levels) 200-600 mcg (micrograms) /day and niacin (cholesterol control) 500-1500mg /day.

Osteoporosis is also a common problem in our society originating in childhood with inadequate calcium intake. We generally think of osteoporosis as a geriatric problem but it starts in childhood. Bone calcium reaches its maximal level at age 24 after which it drops slowly. The higher the maximal bone calcium level reached in young adulthood, the higher it will be in later life. Bone loss occurs as a spectrum of disease. Mild to moderate loss is termed osteopenia. The goal of adequate calcium intake is to avoid vertebral compression, wrist, and hip fractures in later life. At least 1000mg calcium and 5000 IU (international units) of Vitamin D daily are currently recommended throughout life. A bone density study called a *dexascan* can clarify one's osteoporosis status and fracture risk and is recommended periodically for all of us. Despite calcium and vitamin D supplementation, we lose bone density after age 30 but this loss is minimized by maintaining appropriate calcium and vitamin D blood levels. Currently, 90% of Americans are vitamin D deficient due to use of sunscreen and increased device screen time. The ideal vitamin D serum level is in the 50s. This medically recommended level continues to rise as the understanding of its importance becomes better understood.

Dietary Recommendations

1. Drink eight "baseline" 8 oz. glasses of water/day. Heat and cold stress situations will demand added hydration requirements.

2. Take Calcium 1000mg/day and vitamin D 5000IU/day as a dietary supplement.

3. Consider limiting foodstuffs and beverages made with added sugar or processed flour especially if you are overweight.

4. Develop a healthy interest in studying nutrition to arrive at an independently researched decision about a healthy dietary lifestyle.

5. Call your physician to discuss obtaining appropriate blood tests including cholesterol, triglyceride, fasting glucose values, serum iron/total iron binding capacity for women, thyroid function studies and act upon your doctor's recommendations.

6. Review your daily exercise regimen and consider stress reduction techniques.

Good luck in your healthy dietary choices!

REFERENCES

1. Putnam and Allshouse, USDA Statistical Bulletin, No. 825, 1991 p.61
2. Beasley, J.-The Kellogg Report, 1989 p.144
3. Atkins, R.- Dr. Atkin's New Diet Revolution, Avon Books, 1999 p. 48
4. Kubik, C.-Chicago Medicine, vol. 106 no. 1, Winter 2003 pp. 32-34
5. https://www.weightwatchers.com
6. Metropolitan Life Insurance Company, New York, New weight standards for men and women. Statistical Bulletin 40.3, Nov.- Dec. 1959
7. Op cit. Dr. Atkin's New Diet Revolution pp. 413-419

Physical Training Considerations

Martin Greenberg, MD

"Exercise is the Fountain of Youth." (Covert Bailey)

The goal of this chapter is to explore the reasons why we need to exercise, to discuss some basic aspects of exercise physiology, and finally to make some specific exercise recommendations.

Why Should I Exercise?
Obesity is an epidemic in our nation. The Encarta Dictionary defines epidemic as "(a) rapid and extensive development or growth, usually of something unpleasant." In the last twenty years, obesity rates in adults have increased by over sixty percent. In 1999, over sixty percent of our population was at least overweight. This was true for both children and adults. Since 1980, the percentage of overweight children and adolescents have doubled and tripled respectively. Currently, twenty-one to twenty-four percent of children and adolescents are overweight and another sixteen to eighteen percent are actually obese. (1) Obesity is defined as a BMI (body mass index) above the 95th percentile as determined from the CDC 2000 sex specific BMI growth chart. Related medical conditions such as Type 2 Diabetes and its accompanying problems of high blood pressure, high blood cholesterol levels, heart and peripheral circulatory disease and are also increasing in a similarly

alarming manner. In the year 2000, the diagnosis of type 2 diabetes increased about fifty percent from its initial demographic levels. This type of diabetes is also called "non-insulin dependent" or "adult-onset" type diabetes. In this disease, the body produces the hormone insulin, but not enough or inappropriately released insulin to handle the body's dietary glucose (sugar) load. We will see that aerobic exercise improves the metabolism of glucose in many ways, fighting the "obesity epidemic" and its related diseases.

Equally important, fitness is our civic responsibility. Law enforcement officers take an oath to protect the public (and each other). Successful completion of our duties demands physical prowess. Ignoring our fitness responsibility places the public and our brethren in peril. Obesity also sets a bad example for the community in which we are role models and denigrates the symbols of government we represent including our agency, local, state and federal laws and even the Constitution of The United States.

Aerobic v. Anaerobic Exercise
Metabolism turns the dietary products of carbohydrates, fats and proteins into energy powering muscle cells. Delicate protein molecules called enzymes are crucial tools allowing the breakdown of these substances to efficiently occur. Enzymes are made by muscle cell DNA. Exercise stimulates muscle cells to produce enzymes. Glucose is broke down in 2 stages. In the first anaerobic (requiring little oxygen) stage, it becomes pyruvic acid. Pyruvic Acid is then aerobically (requiring oxygen) broken down to water and carbon dioxide in stage 2. Aerobic exercise occurs within the Training Heart Rate (THR) of 65-80% maximal heart rate. In this aerobic range, the heart and lungs can adequately supply muscle cells with oxygen. Both aerobic and anaerobic phases of metabolism can jointly occur and glucose is then completely metabolized. Beyond the THR, the cardiorespiratory system cannot keep up with muscle ox-

ygen demands and pyruvic acid is only incompletely metabolized. Exercise at >80% THR is called anaerobic exercise. In anaerobic metabolism, pyruvic acid becomes lactic acid that can even cause intense muscle pain. Once you catch your breath, "aerobic" enzymes may convert lactic back to pyruvic acid in aerobic metabolism. Fats at least partly require aerobic enzymes for metabolism. In aerobic metabolism (a THR of 65-80%) fats and glucose may be used as energy sources. With aerobic training, the body will also produce more of the needed enzymes to facilitate this process. Aerobic exercise will help to turn the body into a fat burning machine! Proteins can also be metabolized but this is a bad thing as they are our body's muscle building blocks. This may occur in a starvation state (really low calorie dieting) and should be avoided. Anaerobic metabolism may be further sub-divided into an *alactic anaerobic type* where the cycle is stopped at the pyruvic acid stage and a *lactic anaerobic type* where the metabolic cycle continues into lactic acid production. It makes sense that alactic anaerobic metabolism will be very short lived for less than 30 seconds of "explosive" effort such as weight lifting, jumping or sprinting. Lactic anaerobic metabolism would be utilized in short duration sports such as intermediate length running from about 200-1000m or 100-300m swimming. Aerobic exercise is defined by The American College of Sports Medicine as "any activity that uses large muscle groups, can be maintained continuously, and is rhythmic in nature." Examples of this type of exercise include cycling, cross country skiing, in-line skating, running, jumping rope and long distance swimming.

Exercise Physiology
Cardio-respiratory (CR) Fitness-Cardiorespiratory fitness is also called aerobic fitness or aerobic capacity. It is the physical state where the cardiovascular and respiratory systems work synergistically during exercise to supply oxygen to working muscles producing energy. Efficient system coordination is

needed for prolonged use of large muscle groups. The higher the level of cardio-respiratory fitness, the longer will be the sustained level of muscle performance.

Physiology of Aerobic Training- During aerobic exercise, increased oxygen must be delivered to large muscle groups. This occurs by increasing respiration (breathing) rate and depth, increased oxygen transfer to arterial blood, increased heart rate delivering more blood preferentially to large muscle groups and away from smaller ones and more efficient transfer of oxygen to and from muscle tissue. Continued aerobic training improves all of the above functions. Maximal oxygen consumption may be measured during maximal aerobic exercise as *VO2max or aerobic capacity*. This is the best indicator of cardio-respiratory fitness. During aerobic exercise, muscles use carbohydrate metabolic products to produce energy. Fats are utilized when carbohydrates are unavailable. With a low carbohydrate diet, aerobic exercise will develop and maintain a low percentage of body fat. Maximal aerobic exercise is needed to improve aerobic capacity.

Smoking is probably the single greatest factor decreasing aerobic capacity.

"FITT Factors" (Frequency, Intensity, Time, Type) - How frequently one exercises depends upon CR fitness levels. Aerobic workouts should be performed every other day. With training, the exercise program may be increased to five times /week. The more intense the exercise, the longer a recovery period will be needed. Intensity of exercise is the most important factor in improving CR fitness. The more muscle energy used, the greater the intensity of exercise. Ideal aerobic exercise at the Training Heart Rate (THR) occurs at 65-80% of the maximum heart rate (MHR) obtained from a recommended heart rate table (see below). The intensity of individual exercise is determined by the THR. For example, an unfit individual may attain his THR while walking whereas his fit counterpart of the same age may only obtain the same

THR by running briskly. Both people are experiencing the equivalent intensity of CR exercise at the same THR. Even in group exercise, aerobic training should be based on the individual group members' THR rather than running a set distance or a set speed. Taking one's wrist (radial) pulse and finding the proper running speed to maintain the THR for 20-30 minutes would be ideal. Of course, a distinction should be made between group aerobic training and physical fitness assessments where minimum performance levels must be demonstrated as a team qualification requirement. Men over 40 years of age and anyone with heart problems should obtain a cardiac evaluation possibly including a stress test prior to beginning an aerobic CR conditioning program. Several examples from a heart rate table are listed below.

Recommended Heart Rates during Exercise

(Resting heart rate of 72BPM for males and 80BPM for females; age in years) (2)

AGE	MAX HEART RATE	MAX ELITE TRAINING	65%–80% (THR)
5	195	166	130-160
30	190	162	124-152
35	185	153	117-144
45	175	149	114-140
50	170	145	111-136

Training Heart Rate (THR) may be determined by the % Maximal Heart Rate (MHR) method. Here, age is subtracted from 220 and then multiplied by the appropriate %MHR. For example, a thirty-year-old male or female would have a THR of 220-30=190 X .80= 152. The chosen THR varies with the CR fitness level. Measure the heart rate after five minutes of exercise. Use a heart rate monitor or measure your wrist (radial) pulse for thirty seconds and double it to obtain your heart rate. The chosen THR should be maintained for twenty to thirty minutes during each aerobic workout. The time elapsed during a workout is inversely proportional to its intensity. You might wish to train for twenty minutes at a new, higher training level but for thirty minutes at an established training level. It might require longer duration, more intense exercise for a fit individual to attain the same THR as his unfit counterpart. Exercise type may be described as primary or secondary. Primary exercises may be done alone (running, swimming, biking) and may independently maintain the THR while secondary exercises are done with others (singles tennis, full court basketball) and are not as effective in maintaining the THR.

Muscular Fitness- Two components of muscular fitness include strength and endurance. Strength is the greatest force exerted by a muscle in a single contraction. Endurance is the ability of a muscle to perform repeated sub-maximal contractions.

*Muscular Contractions-*The three types of muscle contractions are isotonic, isometric, and isokinetic. Isotonic contraction is a muscle contraction that causes a joint to move through a range of motion against a fixed resistance. Standard weight training is an example of isotonic contraction. Isometric contraction causes muscle contraction but no motion. Tensing a muscle or pushing against a wall is an example of isometric muscle contraction. Isokinetic muscle contraction causes a joint to move at a fixed speed. Varying force must be applied to the joint at different angles to accomplish this. Special weight training machines can create this type of muscular activity. Isotonic and isokinetic muscle contractions have a concentric positive phase and an eccentric negative phase. In the concentric phase, the muscle contracts while it returns to its resting length in the eccentric phase. A muscle can move more weight eccentrically than concentrically.

Principles of Muscular Training
Eight principles of exercise apply to endurance or strength training.

1. *Overload* - A muscle must be "overloaded" or exposed to loads greater than it normally experiences to be strengthened. A joint should be placed through a full range of motion to maximize strength training. *One maximal repetition (1-RM)* is a repetition performed against maximal resistance. Overloaded muscles adapt by strengthening. Fifty percent of 1-RM is needed to obtain strength gains. The maximum repetition (RM) method is used to calculate the training weight needed for maximum strength and endurance. Here, you find the weight that allows you to perform eight to twelve repetitions to momentary muscle failure.

   FITT factors for strength training using the RM method include three times a week frequency and 3-7 RM intensity.

   Endurance training includes three to five times a week frequency and 12-RM intensity.

   Strength and endurance training include three times a week frequency and 8-12 RM intensity.

   General overload principles include increasing resistance, increasing repetitions/set, increasing the number of sets while reducing the interval between them, and increasing speed in the concentric phase while decreasing it in the eccentric phase.

2. *Progression* - Weight should be increased five to ten percent when twelve repetitions can be done correctly.

3. *Specificity-* The muscle groups chosen for exercise should be identified by tensing them during slow performance of the exercise. In task related training, the exercise should closely mimic the task.
4. *Regularity-* Exercise should be performed three times a week to obtain maximal gains. Infrequent exercise can cause more harm than good by straining muscles. The same muscle groups should be regularly exercised. One might exercise every day but vary the exercised muscle groups so that each group is exercised three times a week.
   Group "team building" exercises should be done in the context of the individual members' exercise programs to avoid workout injuries. Team members must make the commitment to a personal exercise program. If no individual exercise program exists, group exercise becomes a risky proposition.
5. *Recovery -* Do not train the same muscle groups on consecutive days. Allow forty-eight hours to elapse after a strenuous muscle group workout. During a workout, the recovery time between sets should be one half to three minutes.
6. *Balance-* All major body muscle groups should be included in the overall exercise program. Opposing muscle groups should be exercised serially. For example, exercise elbow flexors, then exercise elbow extensors. Exercise large muscle groups before small ones. A good order would be the hips/legs, upper back/chest, arms, abdominals, low back, and finally the neck.
7. *Variety-* "Variety is the spice of life." Doing the same exercise indefinitely is boring. Varying

exercises while observing these principles will facilitate continued participation in the program.
8 *Timed Sets*- This exercise refers to performing a specific number of repetitions in a set period of time. The repetitions are then increased during an unchanging exercise and recovery time. This is frequently a good group exercise.

Workout Safety Factors
Using correct form during any exercise is crucial to avoiding injury. A spotter can observe and provide important feedback regarding form and also control weights during exercise muscle failure or during the performance of a dangerous or improper technique. The proper weight should be selected to conform to the 1-RM principle. This is the maximal weight that can be lifted one time. Weights must also allow proper exercise form for the proper number of repetitions at a lesser weight level. Don't hold your breath during strength training. Exhale during the concentric phase and inhale during the eccentric phase of exercise. For example, during a biceps curl exhale when bending the elbow and inhale when straightening it.

Phases of Conditioning
There are three phases of conditioning during any exercise program.
  Preparatory Phase- This phase lasts for about two weeks. During week one, the officer should use light weights to concentrate on proper exercise form and to decrease the risk of injury. During week two, heavier weights are used to determine the 1-RM level and the amount of weight allowing eight to twelve repetitions to failure.
  Conditioning Phase- Week three begins the conditioning phase. Here, the weight is increased to remain within the eight to twelve repetition range. The five to ten percent increment

rule is observed when increasing weight. One set/exercise is adequate if strength increases. If it does not, more than one set may be needed. Three sets are usually the maximum number of any single exercise.

Maintenance Phase- This phase is used to maintain a high level of fitness. Although peak performance is maintained with a three times a week frequency, one or two weekly exercise sessions may also suffice.

Warm Up and Cool Down- Warm up and cool down periods are integral parts of any exercise program. Warm ups prepare the body for the stress of exercise by increasing blood supply to muscles and joint range of motion including walking/jogging, muscle stretching for fifteen sec. intervals and joint rotation exercises. Progressive in-place aerobic exercises such as push-ups, sit-ups, jumping jacks and stair climbers (front/back leg alternations in a push-up position) are also popular before resistance training. Cooling down is important because it allows muscles to gradually decrease their circulatory demands allowing blood flow adjustments back to basal levels.

Common Exercise Related Injuries

Repetitive, resistive exercises of joints, muscles, and tendons may result in overuse injuries. The covering of tendons (paratenon) is the same tissue that lines joints (synovium). This vascular tissue can become irritated causing local pain and swelling termed *tendonitis* (an irritated tendon) or *synovitis* (an irritated joint). Ligaments connect joints and may partially tear or become strained. Knees and ankles are prone to this injury. Muscles may also partially tear and become strained and/or develop a collection of blood called a hematoma. Sacs normally present between muscle layers or under tendons may become irritated and swollen causing *bursitis*. The shoulder, elbow tip, hip, and knee are common locations for this problem. All these minor injuries may be treated at the outset with *Rest, Ice, Compression, and Elevation or R.I.C.E.* This may involve the use of crutches, a towel covering an ice bag on the affected area, a not-too-tight elastic bandage and elevation of the injured extremity above the heart level to decrease local swelling. *The heart is considered "sea level" for the body.* The extremity will drain above sea level but swell below it. Stress fractures (transverse breaks in long lower extremity bones) usually due to excessive running, are a more serious problem possibly requiring cast immobilization or even surgery. Of course, medical consultation is warranted for all persistent problems.

Overweight or Overfat?
Most of us look at an ideal weight chart to decide if we are overweight for our height. Some charts used by life insurance companies provide for small, medium, and large frame sizes to even more accurately predict the proper weight/height ratio. While this approach may accurately apply to Smith and Wesson firearms, it does not take into account the fatty replacement of unfit muscles and organs. Bailey (3) gives the example of a weightlifter who once had heavy but lean muscles. After discontinuing exercise, his muscles became soft and were partially replaced by fat. His total weight did not change but he became less fit and fatter. He was overfat, not overweight. Unfortunately, this process occurs to almost all of us as we age and become less physically active. We may be busier, but as time goes on, we generally perform less strenuous physical exercise. Like the weightlifter, our muscles also grow more fatty than when we were adolescents. Our weight may not have increased since then and will not increase until we become so overfat that fat deposits exceed muscle storage capacity and it is then deposited in subcutaneous tissues. Then, will body weight will rise. So, if you are five pounds overweight, Bailey hypothesizes that you are at least thirteen pounds overfat. Total body weight is not a fitness indicator.

Lean Body Mass (LBM) refers to the body's weight without added fat. Percent body fat can then be calculated and is a specific fitness indicator with males and females ideally at less than or equal to fifteen and twenty-two percent respectively. This is a percentage of LBM that is added to one's lean body mass (LBM) to obtain total weight for any desired percent body fat. Refer to an LBM table for LBM value ranges. (4) Some examples are:

Lean Body Mass (in pounds) For Men

Ht:	5'7"	5'8	5'9"	5'10"	5'11"	6'	6'1"	6'2"
LBM:	112–129	118–132	122–137	127–145	133–153	137–163	140–168	143–176

Lean Body Mass (in pounds) For Women

Ht:	5'5"	5'6"	5'7"	5'8	5'9"	5'10"
LBM:	83–99	86–102	90–105	93–109	95–115	98–119

Using the described formula, the ideal weight for a small frame 5'7" woman would be 90# (LBM) + (.22 X 90 = 20#) = 110#.

Team Building Exercises

Physical exercise that the team or group performs to improve team morale or bonding are termed "team building" exercises. Unless the team performs these exercises two to three times a week or incorporates them into the individual members' workout programs, they will not of themselves be physically beneficial. Therefore, most physical exercise that a part time team performs will primarily serve a team building function. Hopefully, team members will use these exercises as a basis for their personal home exercise programs. The group exercises may even be formally coordinated into personal fitness programs for the entire team. This would require individual team members to perform the same types of exercises at home on the same schedule. Although this level of coordination is rarely practiced, it is very possible to achieve. Exercise modifications based upon environmental conditions (especially in the heat) are crucial. Heat exhaustion/heat stroke are unacceptable occurrences in the training environment. 60% of all injuries occur during training. Any medical problem that can occur at work may also occur during training. Serious training injuries such as fractures (broken bones), joint dislocations and even non-exercise related problems such as gunshot wounds might occur. Pre-planning for their potential management is mandatory.

Planning a Lifelong Exercise Lifestyle
Commitment to fitness is a two-fold responsibility. We certainly have a clear responsibility to our team, agency, community, and nation to become and remain fit in order to fulfill our mission. Equally important is our personal responsibility to preserve our health to the best of our ability. "The body is the temple of the spirit." It is truly even a religious directive to care for one's body. Both the quality of our life and its duration will be directly related to our fitness choices. *Avoiding the Diabetic Syndrome epidemic, also known as Syndrome X including hypertension (high blood pressure), hypercholesterolemia (high blood cholesterol level), heart, and peripheral vascular disease is a conscious fitness and dietary choice.* Look at yourself and your colleagues. If you or they are overweight, you are already headed down this path. Now is the time to embrace health. Working as a team, you can succeed! Get together and seriously discuss the issue as a group. Develop an exercise program you all can live with and start working out. Incorporate "team building exercises" into the plan. Do it for your country, your agency, your team and your family. But mostly, do it for yourself!

REFERENCES

1. Bailey, Covert-The New Fit or Fat, Mariner Books, 8/12/91, p.6
2. Ibid. p. 46
3. Ibid. p. 20
4. Metropolitan Life Insurance Company, New York, New weight standards for men and women. Statistical Bulletin 40.3, Nov.-Dec. 1959

Self-Aid/Buddy Aid

Martin Greenberg, MD

Introduction
Much has been written about self-aid/buddy aid including what "aid" entails, where it should be appropriately administered and what gear will be needed. Self-aid/buddy aid could more specifically be termed field bleeding and airway management. This may be directed towards oneself or others. The Tactical Casualty Combat Care committee (TCCC) has published recommendations regarding the appropriate settings to provide this care. Here, we will discuss the medical threats of hemorrhage and airway compromise and their field treatment.

Vascular Anatomy of the Arm and Leg
Arteries and veins are the conduits carrying blood away from and back to the heart. Arteries are the thick-walled vessels carrying pressurized oxygen rich blood from the heart while veins are thin walled and carry low pressure oxygen poor blood back to the lungs and heart to receive more needed oxygen for the next circuit around the body. Since oxygen rich arterial blood is pressurized, an arterial laceration may appear to pump bright red blood. Alternatively, a venous laceration will release a constant flow of darker red blood. Incomplete arterial and venous lacerations will generally bleed more than

complete vessel lacerations. This is because the arterial wall muscle layer contracts around the zone of vessel injury. An incomplete laceration will be enlarged by this contraction while a complete laceration will tend to squeeze and shut the vessel's cut end. Small lacerations may therefore bleed profusely while large injuries or even limb amputations may only bleed minimally. The major artery travelling along the inner arm between the shoulder and the elbow is the brachial artery. The radial and ulnar arteries are the two major arteries of the volar or palm side forearm. There are many veins carrying blood back to the lungs from the upper and lower extremity. In the leg, the femoral artery is the major vessel travelling down the inner thigh carrying blood down the leg. It traverses the back of the knee as the popliteal artery and splits into the anterior and posterior tibial arteries in the leg. We describe the lower limb between the hip and the knee as the thigh. The area between the knee and the ankle is termed the leg. Again, many veins are present in the lower extremity carrying blood back to the lungs and heart.

Extremity Hemorrhage Control
Evaluating extremity bleeding requires some thought. First, is the bleeding minor or profuse? If profuse, is it pulsatile or constant? Both minor and non-pulsatile bleeding will likely be controlled with a pressure dressing. Pulsatile bleeding will likely require a tourniquet for hemorrhage control.

In the absence of pulsatile bleeding, I recommend applying a pressure dressing. This involves tightly packing the open wound with medical roller gauze or gauze pads and covering the wound with gauze pads or an abdominal (ABD) dressing and an elastic-type bandage if available. Using nitrile gloves is recommended if they are available. Sterility is not a concern applying a field pressure dressing. Lack of significant bleeding through the dressing means success. Helpful commercial products in pressure dressing application are the OLAES® and the Emergency Bandage®. The Emergency Bandage® was developed by the Israeli Defense Force and introduced to the civilian market in 1998. It combined the elastic dressing and a tourniquet in one dressing. It is available in multiple sizes and has extremity and torso variants. It is quite versatile and it can be applied as part of an extremity splint or even as a head wound dressing. The OLAES® Modular Bandage is a recent popular variant of this type of compression dressing. It is also available in multiple sizes and includes a pressure cup that can be used as an eye shield, a removable occlusive plastic sheet and three meters of medical gauze. It eliminates the windlass present of the Emergency Bandage and has several Velcro® control strips to maintain its integrity. It is currently available through Tacmed Solutions, Inc. (www.tacmedsolutions.com).

Hemostatic Agents: Exothermic v. Normothermic Agents
The first hemostatic agent to be used in field medical care was Quik Clot® produced by the Z-Medica company in 1984. The active agent was zeolite that promoted blood clotting via an exothermic (heat releasing) reaction. In its original form, the heat produced caused local tissue death and significant burns. This reduced its usefulness as it could not be used in conscious victims and it made later vascular repair more difficult. The active agent was then changed to kaolin, a silicate mineral also known as China clay. It is normothermic (does not produce heat) and is marketed commercially as Quik Clot Combat Gauze® and other products through multiple vendors. Another currently popular hemostatic agent is Celox®. Celox® is a normothermic hemostatic agent using chitosan, a natural polysaccharide. When exposed to blood, the chitosan granules swell, clot and eventually are metabolized. Celox® is marketed as a granular packet or as Celox-A® (an injectable applicator)

or Celox Rapid Ribbon® (a one inch wide gauze strip). In my opinion, the granular form of either product is ineffective as it will not stop arterial pulsatile bleeding and isn't needed for venous bleeds as a pressure dressing will suffice. Celox-A or Rapid Ribbon are capable of delivering Celox thru a gunshot entry wound to an arterial laceration when appropriately injected or packed in the wound.

Tourniquet Use/Recommended Tourniquets
The purpose of a tourniquet is to stop arterial blood flow to an extremity below the level of the tourniquet. There is historically a difference of opinion regarding when a tourniquet should be applied. About twenty years ago, the law enforcement literature uniformly stated that applying a tourniquet was consigning the involved limb to amputation. Even then, this seemed illogical to me when as an orthopedic trauma surgeon I had applied surgical tourniquets to arms and legs thousands of times for up to two hours with no adverse effects. Since then, tourniquet use has gained popularity and is frequently recommended as the primary treatment for any type of bleeding. Despite its benign nature when used for less than two hours, in my opinion a pressure dressing is preferable when treating non-pulsatile bleeding. If a pressure dressing is unavailable or fails to successfully stop what is felt to be non-pulsatile bleeding, then tourniquet use is appropriate. Even tourniquet application technique is somewhat controversial. It is frequently taught that the tourniquet should be applied "high and tight" meaning just below the shoulder or hip regardless of the level of injury and as tight as possible. Tourniquets should not be applied over joints as there is a bony impediment to their function. After exposing the wound, tourniquets should be applied several inches above the injury to avoid unnecessarily involving the uninjured parts of the extremity. They should be tightened until the bleeding ceases and no more. Unnecessarily high pressure may injure

local skin under the tourniquet. Once applied, the tourniquet may be left in place for up to two hours. The time of application is prominently written on the victim's forehead with an indelible Sharpie® marker or on the Combat Application Tourniquet® (CAT tourniquet) in my practice. Inadvertently leaving a tourniquet on, hidden under splints or dressings, beyond the two-hour time limit is a serious error. Hopefully, definitive medical care can be obtained during this two-hour timeframe. Personally accompanying the victim while the tourniquet is applied is strongly recommended if possible. There are many tactical tourniquets commercially available. Generally, positive tourniquet attributes should include ease of consistent application, width and resistance to failure with extremity motion. The most popular tourniquets have gone through several versions to improve their function and have been tested in multiple studies. They are the Combat Application Tourniquet® (CAT), the Special Operation Forces Tactical Tourniquet® (SOFT-T) and the Tactical Mechanical Tourniquet® (TMT). Applying the tourniquet one-handed on the opposite injured upper extremity is a degradable skill and requires periodic practice. The goal is to successfully apply the tourniquet to the opposite upper extremity in thirty seconds. The tourniquet should not be unbuckled during this application and should be stored in a folded manner to allow immediate application. Lower extremity self-application usually requires unbuckling the tourniquet and two-handed application is recommended. Facsimile (usually Chinese) tourniquets marketed as one of the popular brands are common and care should be taken to purchase the real product from reliable vendors. In a recent study, the CAT Gen. 7 tourniquet was the fastest to apply and the least subject to failure with active extremity motion compared with the SOFT-T (wide) and the TMT. (1) These are windlass type tourniquets relying upon windlass tightening for effective function. Other tourniquets include elastic, ratcheting and pneumatic types.

Tourniquets have even been integrally included in tactical operator's clothing. The CAT is recommended by the TCCC (Tactical Combat Casualty Care committee). The CAT and the SOFT-T (W) are the most currently accepted civilian tourniquets. Internet video application instruction is readily available by their distributors. I do not recommend elastic tourniquets in general due to their inherent variability in application and the increased possibility of local tissue damage due to excessively high pressure and possibly narrow application. One-handed application in the upper extremity is also difficult to impossible. I recommend purchasing a CAT or SOFT-T (W) tourniquet and practicing with it to achieve application proficiency. You are also most likely to receive one of these tourniquets if they are issued to you professionally or in an emergency. Having even more than one tourniquet readily available on either side of the body for easier one-handed application deserves consideration. Remember to use training items for training only. Do not carry training tourniquets operationally. Storing the tourniquet as part of an Individual First Aid Kit (IFAK) or "blowout" kit is highly recommended. The American College of Surgeons has developed an international course to train civilians and first responders to control hemorrhage called *STOP THE BLEED*®. This program was begun, as the American College of Surgeons notes on its website (www.stopthebleed.org), through a National Security Council federal initiative to raise public awareness of the problem of exsanguinating hemorrhage and to treat it. The American College of Surgeons was founded in 1913 and has more than 82,000 members. Its committee on trauma oversees the program that has two phases. In phase one, basic hemorrhage principles are outlined. This phase can be taken in person or online. Phase two is an in-person workshop practicing the skills of applying a pressure dressing and a tourniquet led by a STOP THE BLEED® instructor.

It emphasizes *the four steps of hemorrhage control:*
1. Call 911
2. Apply pressure with both hands
3. Pack the wound and press
4. Apply a tourniquet.

This course saves lives. The state of California and many municipalities have hemorrhage control kits available in public facilities similar to automatic external defibrillator (AED) availability. Hopefully, this action will gain increasing future popularity.

Airway Management Including Pneumothorax and Tension Pneumothorax

Airway management at the first responder level involves managing a patent airway. Simple obstructions in the mouth or upper pharynx (the back of the mouth) can be removed with a digital sweep maneuver. This involves placing the index finger deeply into the mouth and sweeping it from one side to the other. This is most successfully performed on unconscious victims. Other maneuvers to restore patency to the upper airway in a supine victim are the head tilt/chin lift procedure where the head is tilted slightly back and this may move the tongue away from the upper airway. The jaw thrust is a maneuver where the angle of the jaw is grasped on both sides with the index and long fingers. The posterior (back) of the jaw is then pushed up and forward while the thumbs are used to open the mouth if needed. These simple maneuvers may be performed simultaneously and they are taught in most basic first aid classes. Although they are simple, instruction and practice are recommended. The *adult recovery position* is also described as a way to maintain the chin lift in an unconscious victim in a mass casualty triage situation. Here, with a supine victim the near arm on "your" side is extended at 90 degrees to their torso. The opposite or far leg from you is bent at the knee and the victim is turned toward you. Their opposite or far hand is then placed under their extended chin. This helps maintain the patent airway and keeps secretions from draining down the airway when a victim cannot be continuously supervised. Again, practice is recommended.

A nasopharyngeal airway (NPA) is a latex tube placed in the nares (nose) of a semi-conscious or unconscious victim to help maintain a patent nasopharyngeal (nose and upper throat) airway. It has a collar on one end to prevent over-insertion and an angled tip. The recommended adult size is 28FR (French). It should be lubricated with an available lubricant and inserted with a back-and-forth rotating motion directed back and not up. The tip angle should be directed to the nasal septum (nasal midline). It should be fully inserted. Do not use this device in the presence of significant nasal/facial trauma and training is definitely recommended.

A pneumothorax or collapsed lung results from a loss of the vacuum seal keeping the lung "attached" to the chest wall. This is usually due in a trauma setting to a puncture wound or laceration of the chest wall. When we breathe, our brain sends a message to the diaphragm through the phrenic nerve. This nerve is innervated by the third, fourth and fifth cervical nerves in the neck. There is an old medical saying, "C 3, 4 and 5 keep the diaphragm alive." The diaphragm then acts like a bellows by increasing the space in the chest cavity. Because the lung is vacuum sealed to the chest wall and diaphragm, it expands and air is drawn in. We experience this as inhaling or breathing in. When the diaphragm relaxes, air is forced out of the lung as the chest cavity shrinks. We experience this as exhaling or breathing out. When the vacuum seal is broken by a puncture or laceration, the lung is no longer connected to the chest wall. It then no longer moves with the chest wall and diaphragm in respiration. Luckily, we can still breathe quite well with one intact lung. This is called a simple pneumothorax and it is not an immediate life-threatening field emergency. However, a complication may arise if the laceration or puncture wound acts as a one-way valve allowing air to enter the chest cavity on the involved side but not to exit. Then, an enlarging air bubble develops on one side of the chest cavity with every breath. The enlarging air bubble pushes the collapsed lung, the heart and great vessels and even the opposite lung away from it to the opposite side of the chest. This progressively compromises the opposite lung's function and obstructs blood returning from the body to the heart and lungs. Clinically, progressive dyspnea (difficulty with breathing) occurs. The neck veins protrude, and the neck and face may appear progressively cyanotic (red or bluish red). This emergent problem is called a *tension pneumothorax*. It may be prevented by applying a gauze or commercial chest seal dressing over the puncture wound. An established tension pneumothorax is treated by decreasing the size of the enlarging air bubble. This is done by inserting a 14G Angiocath® catheter at least three inches long through the chest wall into the air bubble. The recommended location for insertion is the fifth intercostal space in the mid axillary line of the thorax. In English, this means insertion between the fifth and sixth rib in the mid lateral line of the involved chest wall. If successful, a gush of escaping air will be heard through the catheter. Breathing will immediately improve. The Angiocath® catheter or commercial tension pneumothorax treatment needle is taped in place and left patent until definitive care is rendered. *Training is definitely recommended to perform this procedure but remember that it is a time sensitive, life and death problem!*

The Immediate First Aid Kit (IFAK) or "Blowout" Kit
Having a compact kit to control bleeding and simple airway problems is highly recommended for law enforcement professionals, armed citizens and the general public. The name and contents of this kit varies by vendor, but it is generally called an Immediate First Aid Kit (IFAK) or "Blowout kit." The kit is intended to be used on its owner. Larger kits called Mass Casualty Injury (MCI) kits are available for those events. Retired DEA agent Chuck Soltys has dedicated himself to

training as many law enforcement officers as possible in the use of his custom Blowout Kit that we will describe here. (2) The kit can be divided into basic and advanced items.

Basic Items:
- one Emergency Bandage® or Olaes® dressing;
- one pair of trauma shears;
- two pairs of nitrile gloves;
- one mini sharpie marker;
- one small Ziploc bag;
- one tactical tourniquet;
- eight strips of 2 or 3" duct tape;
- one roll of masking tape.

Advanced items:
- Two 14G Angiocath® needles at least 3" in length;
- one size 28FR nasopharyngeal airway (NPA);
- one hemostatic agent either Celox® or Quik Clot®. (The Celox-A® tampon is my personal choice).

The duct tape strips are buddy taped at their ends to allow for quick use. All the items are taped together with masking tape and can easily fit into a pants cargo pocket. Training in the use of all the kit's components is necessary and recommended. After appropriate training, keeping the kit on your person when in the field is crucial as one never knows when the need may arise. There is a famous law enforcement saying that "Guns are like parachutes. If you don't have one when your need it, then chances are that you won't ever be in need of one again." (3) In my opinion, the same may be said for the IFAK.

REFERENCES

1 Traeger et al., J Trauma Acute Care Surg. 2021
2 Soltys, C.-Assembling a blowout kit for patrol, Police One, 2009/2018
3 Rawles J.W.-Tools for Survival, Plume Books, (2009), p. 188

The Miracle of Sight

Martin Greenberg, MD

Scenario
A tactical team is called out to a remote area during the summer. "Shots fired and the building is on fire!" is the only intelligence received. Several team members choose to wear hats rather than helmets and goggles because of the extreme heat. An immediate entry is made because of the possibility of an active shooter. A clandestine drug lab is discovered. A crazed biker tosses a liquid in the face of the entry point man. He screams as the corrosive substance immediately blinds him. After subduing the perpetrator and clearing the building, the DEA is contacted and the injured operator is rushed to the nearest emergency department in a squad car. Thirty minutes has elapsed. In the E.D., the operator's eyes are copiously irrigated after a pH strip test determines that he has been injured with a caustic base. Because of the injury and the lack of prompt care, his sight is permanently damaged and his career is ended.

Introduction
We depend upon sight more than any of our other senses. Although other species see more sharply or may better distinguish even tiny movements, the human eye is unique as it is supported

by our large brain-computer and the eye sees in color. Light waves are decoded at multiple levels in the eye and in the brain. In poorly understood ways, this is done to "make sense" of images in light of our individual experience. So, no two people viewing the same object really see the same thing. Normal vision is mandatory for the tactical officer. A basic understanding of eye anatomy and function is needed to protect the eye from injury and to maintain healthy eye function. The goal of this chapter is to describe the eye's basic anatomy and physiology and to present some common eye problems and their treatment. Eye trauma and its avoidance/treatment are major tactical concerns that will be addressed.

The Human Camera/Computer
Think of the eye as an extremely adaptable camera and computer. Like a camera, light enters the eye through its front and passes through a lens called the cornea. Like a camera, the light reaching the lens passes through a diaphragm called the iris that may enlarge or constrict to control the amount of entering light. Also like a camera capturing an image on photographic film, light passing through the lens is bent so that an inverted, reversed image is produced upon the retina in the back of the eye. Instead of film, the retinal image is transformed into electrical signals transferred through the optic nerve to the brain's occipital lobe. Unlike a camera that focuses light by moving its lens, the eye focuses light by changing the shape of its lens. Rays of light entering the front of the eye are bent towards the center of the retina as they pass through the convex transparent lens that is thicker in its middle. This bending of light rays causes them to cross and invert and reverse the image cast upon the retina. In a complex way, the brain adjusts this image producing an accurate mental picture.

When viewing a distant object through a normal eye, parallel light rays pass through a flat lens with relaxed surrounding ciliary muscles and focus precisely upon the retina. With closer objects, light passing through the lens must be bent more to create the same precise retinal focus. The ciliary muscles then constrict causing the lens to thicken (become more convex) and restore focus. The process of clear viewing of both near and far objects is called *accommodation*. As we reach forty to fifty years of age, the lens becomes less pliable and our ability to accommodate dramatically diminishes. Since lengthening our arms is an impractical solution to this problem, reading glasses may be needed.

When viewing an object, our eyes move together so they will point directly at the "target." With a distant object, parallel rays of light pass from the object to the fovea, the point on the retina producing the sharpest image. Our eyes are spaced about two and a half inches (6 cm) apart. When viewing a close object, our eyes must "turn in" to allow light to strike the fovea. This process occurs automatically and is called *"convergence."* While children can converge (focus) on objects only three inches (7.5 cm) away, adults can focus clearly only to about five and a half inches (14 cm). Another benefit of our widely spaced eyes is *stereoscopic or binocular vision*. Each eye sees slightly different pictures overlapping in the brain's visual centers. Determining differences between the images allows a distance determination. Since each eye's "picture" overlaps, the brain receives an image in which the central or foveal part is made from both eyes and is therefore very clear and stereoscopic. The left and right eyes contribute solely to their respective sides of the brain's image. The entire image is called the visual field. Interestingly, the nose actually blocks a large part of each eye's visual field. (1)

Eye Anatomy
The retina is the lining of the back of the eye. It detects the upside-down, inverted image cast upon it and converts it into electrical signals transmitted through the optic nerve to the brain. The retina contains special photoreceptor (light sensitive) cells called *rods and cones*. There are about 125 million

rods and seven million cones oriented differentially with most of the cones packed into the centrally located fovea. Each cone or two connects to a nerve fiber in the fovea as compared to a nerve fiber per 300 rods in the rest of the retina. For this reason, the projected foveal retinal image is seen most clearly. Rods and some cones are otherwise dispersed over the remaining retina. Light hitting the retina must first pass through a plexus of only about 800,000 nerve fibers called *ganglion cells*. These nerves link the photo-processing cells in a poorly understood manner. Nerve fibers coalesce into the optic disc and leave the eye as the optic tract. The optic tracts combine to form the optic nerve. Since there are no rods or cones in the optic disc, it is called the *blind spot*. Blood vessels branch from the blind spot in a tree branch or arborizing manner. Viewing these blood vessels with an instrument called an ophthalmoscope gives important information about many medical problems. Rods, as their name suggests, are long, thin cells containing a purple-colored chemical appropriately called *visual purple or rhodopsin*. When visual purple is exposed to light, it is "bleached" and loses its color. An electrical signal is then produced and passed to a connecting nerve fiber. Rods respond best to white light and "see" in black, white, and gray. This is the anatomic basis for night vision. Rods are inactive in bright light. It takes twenty to sixty minutes for rhodopsin (and night vision) to regenerate. Cones are responsible for color vision. They contain chemicals responsive to red, yellow-green, or blue-violet. All other colors are variations of these primary colors. Cones outside of the fovea are not evenly spaced so color vision is not accurate when we are not looking directly at an object. To avoid bleaching a particular group of rods or cones, our eyes are always moving. Different sets of photoreceptors are being continually stimulated. Their shifting messages are translated by the retinal neuronal network and by the brain into a clear picture. Another benefit of this visual tremor is that we are kept from becoming aware of our blind spot that would appear as an empty hole in our visual field. The edges of the retina contain mostly rods that are stimulated by even small movements. Peripheral vision detects motion. The eyes reflexively swivel toward the moving object to center it onto the fovea for a clear picture. The received data is sent through the optic radiations and lateral geniculate nucleus to the brain's occipital cortex via the two optic nerves. Light from our right side is viewed by the left side of each retina and vice versa. Data from the left-hand side of each retina is transferred to the left side of the brain. Correspondingly, data from the right side of each retina is transferred to the brain's right side. To accomplish this, the inner or nasal optic tracts (half of each optic nerve) must cross. The crossover point in the brain is called the *optic chiasm*. The result of this arrangement is that light from the left side of each retina is always "viewed" by the left hemisphere of our brain and light from the right side of each retina is always sent to the brain's right cortical hemisphere.

Eye motion is controlled by six extra-ocular muscles. Through the action of these muscles, the eye may be moved 50 degrees up, 35 degrees down, 45 degrees externally, and 50 degrees internally. In a complex and poorly understood way, the brain allows both eyes to move synchronously by precisely contracting different extra-ocular muscles and calculating the speed of the tracked object. This complex feat is in itself a miracle of sight!

The brain allows both eyes to move synchronously by precisely contracting different extra-ocular muscles and calculating the speed of the tracked object. Tear glands above and lateral to each eye produce half a milliliter in tears each day. Tears are spread over the cornea by the eyelids every two to ten seconds through reflex blinking. They contain the agent lysozyme that destroys harmful organisms. Tears are drained into a small tear sac at the inner edge of each eye squeezed empty with each blink. They drain into the nasopharynx (the back of the throat) and are swallowed.

Basic Vision Problems and Solutions

Focus related problems result from defects in the shape of the eye. In the normally shaped eye, an image is sharply focused upon the retina. In *myopia,* or near-sightedness, the eye is too long from front to back or the lens is too rounded. The image of distant objects is formed in front of the retina making them blurry. Close objects, however, can still be seen clearly. In *presbyopia*, or far-sightedness, the opposite problem exists. The eye is too short or the lens isn't thick (convex) enough. The image is then formed behind the retina. While distant objects are seen clearly, closer objects are blurry. As we age, the lens becomes less compliant and is fixed in its flattened position. Irregularities in the shape of the cornea may distort the retinal image. This condition is termed *astigmatism.*

Problems related to abnormal eye shape or irregularities can be corrected by wearing glasses or contact lenses. In myopia (near-sightedness), concave lenses (thinner in the middle than at the edges) lengthen the focal distance of the lens appropriately to focus sharply on the retina. In presbyopia (far-sightedness), convex lenses increase the light bending power of the eye. In astigmatism, lenses may cancel corneal irregularities interfering with sharp visual focus. Bifocal lenses treat the decreased ability to accommodate with increasing age. The upper half of the corrective lenses have a distance prescription, while the lower half are convex so closer objects can be viewed when one looks down. Contact lenses work in the same way and may be either soft or hard types.

In the *Lasik procedure*, the shape of the cornea is changed to correct focal length problems. The benefit of the Lasik procedure is that it will make you eyeglass or contact lens free for distance or near vision but usually not both. Even if you could read well without correction prior to Lasik surgery, you will need optical lens correction for reading if you surgically correct distance vision. In other words, you may be reversing your visual deficit from near to far sightedness or vice versa.

The inability to distinguish colors to any degree is called *color blindness*. This inherited problem affects about eight percent of European and North American men. It is less common in other ethnic groups. The degree of disability resulting from color blindness relates to the color involved. A red-green deficiency would be more serious in our society than a yellow-orange deficiency. We can usually compensate for traffic control device related color deficiencies by experience. The green light, for example, is on the bottom position of a traffic control device. Specific traffic regulatory signs have specific colors and shapes. By experience, we know that octagonal stop signs are red. We actually may be unaware of minor color discrimination problems unless specific testing demonstrates it.

Ocular Hypertension (OHT) and Glaucoma

OHT affects three to six million people in the U.S. including four to ten percent of those over forty years of age.

We must be aware of the spectrum of diseases from OHT to frank glaucoma because precious sight is robbed silently: we become aware of a visual problem only after permanent, career-threatening visual loss has occurred!

Ocular Hypertension- The eye has a normal pressure of less than 21 mm Hg. (mercury). Intra-ocular pressure can be measured by a procedure called tonometry. Ocular hypertension describes a condition where intra-ocular pressure is greater than 21 mm, no loss of visual fields or optic nerve damage has occurred and no other eye disease is present to explain the OHT. This problem is a major risk factor for the development of visual field loss and optic nerve damage termed *glaucoma*. A person with intra-ocular pressure (IOP) of 28 mm Hg is fifteen times more likely to develop glaucoma than a borderline ocular hypertensive individual with a pressure of 22mm Hg. Multiple measurements of IOP are needed as there is a daily (diurnal) variation of 3-4mm Hg with pressures higher in the early AM and in the supine (lying down) position, and up to 10 mm in persons with eye damage.

Glaucoma Overview- In the year 2000, 2.47 million people in the U.S. had frank glaucoma and 130,000 were legally blind because of it. The glaucoma risk rises to forty-two percent for those with IOPs equal to or greater than 30mm Hg. Retinal artery blockages (vascular occlusions) will also occur in three percent of ocular hypertensives.

African Americans have three to five times the incidence of OHT/glaucoma as compared to the general population.

The retina has ten anatomic layers. In glaucoma, up to forty-percent of retinal "nerve layer" damage may occur before any visual field loss. It is a leading cause of blindness in our nation. Risk factors include people over forty-five years of age, those with a family history, people of African descent, those with OHT, diabetes, near-sightedness, steroid use, and previous eye injury. Obesity, smoking, and alcohol use are other concurrent risk factors.

Types of Glaucoma- We saw that the lens, iris, and cornea are bathed in a watery fluid called *aqueous humor* produced by the *ciliary body*. It then drains through the *trabecular meshwork,* a spongy drain one-fiftieth of an inch wide where the iris and cornea meet. An imbalance in the rate of production and drainage of this liquid leads to accumulation of aqueous humor and chronically elevated IOP and damage to the optic nerve. "The eye is like a sink where the faucet is always running, and the drain is always open." (2) Where drainage is inadequate, intraocular pressure rises and OHT results leading to chronic or *progressive open (or wide) angle glaucoma (POAG)*. Under high pressure, the eye is damaged at its weakest point-the optic disc. Here, the delicate optic nerve (made up of over a million nerve cells each several inches long but only 1/20,000th inch wide) forms and may be damaged or killed by elevated pressure. Chronic glaucoma is responsible for ninety percent of all cases. It appears in middle age and it may be inherited. Twenty percent of chronic glaucoma patients have a relative with the disease. There are only subtle symptoms of this serious problem including permanent loss of peripheral vision followed by "blank spots" in the central visual field. Teary, aching eyes, blurred vision and occasional headaches may also occur but are usually such non-specific symptoms that they are useless as warning signs. Because there are no obvious complaints associated with the gradual rise of intraocular pressure, glaucoma goes undetected until severe permanent loss of vision results. In POAG, there is no obvious defect in the trabecular meshwork and its dysfunction is the subject of current investigations. A subgroup of possibly up to one-third of POAG sufferers may not even have OHT!

Normal tension (aka low tension) glaucoma demonstrates optic nerve and visual field loss with normal intraocular pressure. This is thought to be due to poor optic nerve blood supply and is also the subject of current research.

Pigmentary glaucoma is a variant of POAG (Progressive Open Angle Glaucoma) that is more common in near-sighted young men in their twenties to thirties. It is an exfoliative problem that is the most common type of glaucoma in the world, but rare in America. Here, a concave iris with a wide iris-corneal angle causes the pigment layer of the iris to be abraded by adjoining structures and to shed pigment cells into the clogging trabecular meshwork. The IOP rises resulting in POAG or angle closure glaucoma (see below.) Not everyone with this problem develops glaucoma but if you have exfoliation syndrome, your chances of developing the disease are increased six times. A young person with disease in only one eye probably suffers from exfoliative glaucoma. This condition is treated with pupil dilating (mydriatic) eye drops. The accompanying visual blurring caused by pupil dilation may present a problem for the tactical operator. Extended release mydriatic eye drops may minimize this difficulty.

Acute, or narrow angle glaucoma (a.k.a. angle closure glaucoma) affects about a half million Americans. It preferentially strikes far-sighted Asian males and is heralded by sudden, severe eye pain, blurred vision, and dilated pupils. Even nausea and vomiting may occur. Recall that the trabecular meshwork sits anatomically in the angle where the cornea and iris meet at a forty-five-degree angle. As we age, the cornea enlarges. The closer the cornea is to the trabecular meshwork, the narrower this angle becomes, decreasing the meshwork's ability to drain aqueous humor. Increasing pressure further decreases the angle and creates a worsening, vicious cycle "…like putting a stopper over the drain of a sink." (3) Here, the eye becomes red and the cornea swells and clouds. Visual blurring and haloes may occur. Interestingly, this emergency problem occurs when the pupil dilates, such as in a darkened room like a theatre or when the operator is under stress, as pupils dilate during an adrenaline dump. Dilated pupils enlarge the iris and decrease the meshwork angle. These attacks may not always be full blown and may spontaneously resolve when the individual enters a well-lit room or goes to sleep (naturally constricting the pupil). This relatively rare form of glaucoma occurs in less than ten percent of cases but is an eye emergency demanding immediate medical attention. If untreated, it can cause optic nerve damage leading to permanent blindness in only a few days. Acute glaucoma is treated with eye drops to constrict the pupil and medication to lower IOP. When the IOP reaches a safe level, a laser procedure called an iridotomy is performed to create a drainage opening in the iris.

Secondary glaucoma is associated with another disease such as an eye injury, an eye tumor, or an inflammatory or exfoliative eye problem. Normal tension glaucoma may be included in this category.

Trauma related glaucoma may result from a blow to the eye, chemical or penetrating injuries. This is usually due to a mechanical change in the eye's drainage system. The operator sustaining eye trauma should obtain regular follow up eye care to monitor the eye for the development of OHT. Screening tests for glaucoma should be done on a yearly basis as a part of a regular eye exam. IOP measurements may be performed by an optometrist using air puff tonometry or by an ophthalmologist (an eye specialist MD) using a sensitive instrument called an applanation tonometer. Once again, if you have elevated IOP, the ophthalmologist will dilate your eyes and examine the optic disc for optic nerve damage and perform a visual field test to look for peripheral visual field defects. More frequent periodic monitoring is needed with mildly elevated IOP. There are several treatment options for the spectrum of problems from increased IOP to frank glaucoma.

Glaucoma treatment requires modification of the production and drainage of aqueous humor circulating through the eye and restoring normal intra-ocular pressure. Even before damage occurs, OHT should be treated if pressures exceed 28-30 mm Hg. with the goal being 24 mm or lower. Chronic glaucoma may not be discovered until late in the disease when permanent damage has occurred. This is why periodic eye exams are mandatory! Acute glaucoma will present with symptoms demanding immediate treatment. There are both highly successful medical and surgical treatments for glaucoma. They include eye-drops, pills, laser surgery, other eye operations, or a combination of the above. Inform your physician about any eye drops you use as they are absorbed into the bloodstream similar to medication taken orally. Close your eye for two minutes after drop insertion and press on the "nasal" side of your eyelid to maximize the local effect of the drop.

When drops are inadequate to control OHT, pills are prescribed. They work in the same manner as drops. Carbonic anhydrase inhibitors such as Acetazolamide (Diamox®) and Methazolamide reduce fluid flow into the eye. They may cause frequent urination, rashes and the uncommon complication of severe (aplastic) anemia. When drops and pills don't work, surgery may be recommended.

Laser surgery is a minimally invasive procedure for POAG called trabeculoplasty. Here, the laser is focused upon the trabecular meshwork and shrinks a portion of the meshwork that opens other meshwork areas allowing improved drainage. The IOP is checked a few hours later for improvement that may continue over a few weeks. This procedure may allow the POAG sufferer to avoid or delay traditional surgery. Medication may also no longer be necessary. In the classic surgical procedure, trabeculectomy, a portion of the meshwork is removed with the same goal as trabeculoplasty.

Eye Trauma
About 500,000 serious eye injuries occur in the United States annually. Eye injury is probably the most under-reported health problem in our nation. Eye injuries can dramatically limit physical function. The American Medical Association Guide to Evaluation of Permanent Impairment (6) equates complete loss of vision in one eye as a twenty-five percent loss of the visual system and an equivalent loss of function of the "whole man" (twenty-four percent). (4) Not many other body parts can make this impressive claim. More than one million Americans have permanent visual loss because of eye injury with about seventy-five percent suffering monocular blindness. In fact, eye trauma is the leading cause of monocular blindness in the United States and is only second to cataracts as the leading cause of national visual impairment. (5) These statistics are good reasons to understand the basic types of eye trauma. The following discussion includes some of the more common eye injuries the officer may encounter.

Ocular Burns - This injury may result in a laboratory setting or as the result of a battery explosion or intentional trauma. Severe swelling of all visible eye structures may occur. The conjunctivae may appear red (erythematous) or pale if blood flow is inadequate (conjunctival ischaemia). Often, the type of irritant is known. If it is not known, pH paper may be used to determine whether an acid or base is present. Acid burns usually damage the anterior chamber of the eye. Alkali burns may be more serious and affect the entire eye. As the pH rises (more base; less acid), the burn becomes more serious. Alkali combines with eye lipids (fats). Penetration of alkali into eye tissues may continue for long periods. With serious injury, the cornea may appear marbled or perforated. Retinal involvement may lead to complete blindness. The Hughes Classification of Alkali Burns to the Eye (6) gives a general prognosis based upon the initial evaluation of the injury.

Grade 1- Good Prognosis; No eye ischemia present;
Grade 2- Good Prognosis; Hazy cornea present; Ischemia involving less than one-third of the limbus (the circular part of the eye where the cornea meets the sclera or the outer white covering of the eye.)
Grade 3- Guarded Prognosis; Ischemia that is involving one-third to half of the limbus.
Grade 4- Poor Prognosis; Cornea is opaque; Ischemia that is greater than half of the limbus.

Chronic problems resulting from burns include inflammation of the iris and ciliary body (iridocyclitis), adhesions between the lens, iris (posterior synechiae) and eyelid deformity (ectropion). Acid burns may not require as much volume or time of irrigation as alkali burns. Severe alkali burns may require even twenty-four hours of irrigation.

Corneal abrasions- Here, the corneal epithelium is partially or completely abraded. Symptoms include pain, eyelid spasm (blepharospasm) and tearing. Fluorescein (a yellow-green dye) will be absorbed by the abrasion and can be viewed with or without magnification. The eye should also be evaluated for the presence of a foreign body including looking under the upper and lower eyelids. Determine whether the abrasion is "clean or dirty." When making this decision, consider the source of the abrasion. Contact lens related corneal abrasions are also common problems. Trauma to the eye while wearing a contact lens, a poorly fitting lens, an interposed foreign body between the eye and the lens, or contact lens overwearing are some common causes of contact lens corneal abrasions.

Foreign Bodies - Conjunctival foreign bodies may be removed by a physician using anesthetic eye-drops and a saline moistened cotton tip applicator. A careful search for foreign bodies under the eyelids should be performed. Corneal foreign bodies require the use of a magnifying "slit lamp" to gauge the depth of the injury. A "rust ring" is frequently present around a metallic foreign body that should be removed by an MD after about one day.

Ultraviolet Keratitis and Solar Retinopathy- UV (ultraviolet) light is the most common cause of eye radiation injury. The cornea absorbs UV radiation cumulatively (similar to skin exposure). Atmospheric ozone filters out UV radiation wavelengths less than 290nm (nanometers). Ultraviolet superficial punctate keratitis (SPK) is sunburn of the eye. It is also a nonspecific inflammatory condition in other eye disorders and here it is also known as "snow blindness." (7) UV exposure at noon is ten times greater than 0900 or 1500 hours. For example, if an un-tanned, fair-skinned person would require twenty-five minutes to develop sunburn at noon, it would take over two hours to develop a similar burn after 3:00PM (1500hrs). Although only one to two percent of UV radiation is reflected from grass, eighty-five percent may be reflected from fresh snow. The National Weather Service (NWS) and the Environmental Protection Agency (EPA) have developed a "UV Index" to predict the next day's outdoor UV levels on a 0 -10+ scale. You may obtain this information at www.epa.gov/sunwise/uvindex.html. According to the EPA, UV type A and B (100%) protective polarizing sunglasses should be worn with a UV Index of five or more. Skin cancer is also a risk, so from this perspective use at least an SPF 15 sunblock and attempt to avoid the sun between 1PM and 6PM if possible. Artificial light sources such as tanning beds or halogen desk lamps may also cause eye UV radiation exposure problems. Symptoms of UV keratitis typically occur four to eight hours after exposure to sunny, snow-covered areas. The eye will be painful and sensitive to light (photophobic). The conjunctiva will be red and swollen. Chronic UV over-exposure may cause cataracts. Usually, no permanent visual loss occurs after the burn resolves. Solar retinopathy denotes possible permanent visual loss from retinal scarring after sun gazing. Your mother was right. Don't stare at the sun!

Orbital Blowout Fractures- The bony socket of the eye is called the orbit. The thinnest part of the socket is the bottom, or floor followed by the medial (nasal) ethmoid sinus wall. This injury usually results from blunt, non-penetrating trauma such as a punch. Orbital fractures may be serious injuries as soft tissues surrounding the eye may become entrapped in the fracture limiting eye movement or causing double vision (diplopia). Eye infections may result from communication with the ethmoid sinus. Any signs of swelling, ecchymosis (black eye) or loss of eye motion following blunt eye trauma should be evaluated in the emergency department. If the diagnosis of a blowout fracture is made after a plain x-ray (Water's view) or CT (computed tomography) scan of the area, an ophthalmology (eye medicine) follow up is recommended.

Hyphema- refers to the collection of blood in the anterior chamber of the eye. In its fully developed form, the eye may look like an "8-ball." Re-bleeding may occur within five days and prompt emergency department referral is needed.

Subconjunctival hemorrhage- is a less serious problem where bleeding occurs within the white conjunctiva. Usually not a serious injury, it should be evaluated in the E.D. or urgent care facility as it may potentially hide a ruptured eye globe (eyeball).

Ruptured globe- is an eye emergency requiring immediate ophthalmologic consultation. Loss of vision is common because the force necessary to rupture the sclera or cornea is great enough to also cause serious internal eye injuries.

All eye injuries should be immediately evaluated by a physician, an urgent care facility, or in the emergency department.

Airbag Related Eye Trauma

Airbags inflate at about 200 MPH. Airbag inflation is really a small explosion that definitely saves lives but also can cause facial and eye injuries. Deaths in frontal equipped airbag vehicles reduce deaths by twenty-six percent among drivers and by fourteen percent among passengers compared to similar unequipped vehicles. Even unbelted driver and front passenger deaths were reduced by thirty-two percent and twenty-three percent respectively. Serious head injury risk is reduced sixty percent with lap belts and eighty-five percent with both lap belts and airbags. (8) As of 2003, the NHTSA (National Highway Transportation Safety Administration) estimated that airbags caused 220 deaths in low-speed crashes compared with 10,000 lives saved. Short drivers and those drivers sitting close to the steering column are most at risk. A four-level scale of eye airbag related injuries has been developed. (9)

Level one injuries were minor local skin abrasions.
Level two and three injuries included corneal abrasions and orbital fractures.
Level four injuries were most serious including optic nerve damage, globe injuries and retinal detachments.

3.1% of accident victims sustained eye trauma when exposed to airbags while only two percent not exposed to airbags suffered eye trauma. A Finnish study of a large number of accident victims revealed that the risk of airbag related eye injury was 2.5%. The serious eye injury risk was 0.4%. Eyeglass wear tripled the risk of airbag injury. No eyeglass use, however, increased the risk of chemical (propellant) airbag related injury (American Academy of Ophthalmology, 2003). Using lap-belts and moving the front seat(s) maximally back will decrease the incidence of airbag eye trauma. The use of "cage cars" (police vehicles with partitions) will limit backward seat adjustment and negatively impact eye safety. Modifying airbag technology to include seat positioners that monitor the driver's distance from the airbag, weight sensors that identify a small adult, airbags that deploy with dual force levels depending upon crash characteristics will further decrease potential eye injuries. (10)

The B.E.T.T. System
The *Birmingham Eye Trauma Terminology (BETT) system* is a standardized glossary of eye trauma terms that has been accepted by many eye professional organizations. It should be used whenever possible to allow for standardized reporting of eye trauma. Simply, injury is divided into open or closed globe types. Closed globe injury is either a contusion or a lamellar laceration. Open globe injury is categorized as either a laceration or rupture. Lacerations may be penetrating, intraocular foreign bodies (IOFB) or perforating trauma. Other specific terminology may then be used to describe the injury.

Eye First Aid
What specific first aid measures should be considered for common eye injuries? Seeking immediate medical care should occur simultaneously with the delivery of eye first aid. If you are alone in any of these situations, cover only the affected eye. Make a conscious effort to keep the normal eye quiet. Use a portable radio, cell phone or an appropriate hand signal to communicate distress.

"Clean" corneal abrasions are treated by instilling one cycloplegic (dilating) eye-drop of five percent homatropine to relax eye muscle (ciliary body) spasm, followed by the use of an antibiotic ointment polysporin, tobramycin or gentamicin. Don't use betadine ointment! Never use topical anesthetics in the treatment of corneal abrasions as they may eventually cause corneal ulcerations. Tape the eye shut; apply two eye pads. Oral pain meds may be needed. Promptly refer the officer to an ophthalmologist (eye specialist MD) or immediate care clinic for evaluation. A "dirty" abrasion requires the use of hourly antibiotic gentamicin, tobramycin, or ciprofloxacin (Ciloxan®) eye-drops, no patching, no ointments and immediate medical referral.

For foreign bodies penetrating the eye, don't remove the object or rub the eye. Wash your hands and cover the affected eye with a clean cup or object that will protect the object and eye but not touch the foreign body. If help is available, cover the unaffected eye with a clean dressing as it will keep the affected eye still. After a severe blow to the eye, close the eye and cover it with a cold compress or ice bag. Don't press directly on the eye. If possible, have the victim remain supine.

If a laceration to the eye globe or eyelid occurs, loosely cover both eyes with a sterile gauze dressing or eye pad. If possible, have the patient remain supine while seeking help.

When irritating chemicals get into the eye, flush the eyes with copious amounts of clean water. Turn the head to the side with the affected eye lower than the normal eye. In this position, the normal eye is not contaminated and the irritant will drain away from the body. Irrigate the eye(s) with warm water from the inside to the outside corner for at least ten to thirty minutes. Loosely bandage the eye(s) with a sterile dressing. Industrial eye irrigation solutions for specific contaminants may be available. Do not delay eye irrigation while searching for a special eye irrigation solution. Seek immediate medical attention.

The treatment for solar keratitis includes cycloplegic (paralysis of the ciliary muscles of the eye) drops (5% homatropine) and antibiotic ointment. Oral pain meds are recommended. Patching may be useful in the unlikely situation that exposure to the irritant light source cannot be limited.

If a severe allergic (anaphylactic) reaction occurs after an insect sting around the eye, you may see wheezing or shortness of breath. Severe eye swelling or swelling of "mucous membranes" such as the tongue or lips may occur. The lips may be blue and the victim may collapse. Elevate the legs and use an "epi pen" if available. Stabilize the airway as needed. Remember your first-aid "A, B, C s (airway, breathing, circulation)." Anaphylactic (allergic) shock is a life-threatening emergency!

Blood in the anterior chamber of the eye (a *hyphema*) requires atropine and steroid eye-drops and a metallic eye shield in a medical setting. A prompt emergency department referral is important as up to one-third of these injuries may re-bleed within five days. Anyone with a bleeding disorder may have more serious issues. This potentially serious problem requires immediate close follow-up by a physician.

Generally, blurred vision or prolonged eye pain also require prompt medical evaluation.

Once again, ALL eye injuries require immediate attention by a physician, urgent care or emergency room setting.

Defining Visual Impairment

Anyone with non-correctable, reduced vision is considered visually impaired. A great spectrum of impairment exists including visual field loss, color blindness, and depth perception vision defects. The most common assessment of visual acuity in employment exams and team qualifications is the ability to read a visual acuity chart as compared to a standard at twenty feet. The World Health Organization (WHO) defines visual impairment as follows:

Measurement of the better eye with the best possible glasses correction yielding-

20/30-20/60 (seeing clearly at thirty to sixty feet what a standard can see at twenty feet) = mild visual loss;
20/70-20/160 = moderate vision loss or moderate low vision;
20/200-20/400 = severe vision loss or severe low vision;
20/500-20/1,000 = profound vision loss or profound low vision;
<20/1,000 = near total blindness;

No light perception = total blindness (American Optometric Association-http://www.aoa.org.)
Legal blindness is defined in the U.S. as optimally corrected vision of 20/200 in the better eye or a remaining visual field of less than or equal to twenty degrees. (11)
All agencies have a visual acuity requirement at least at the entry level. Check your agency's entry and ongoing visual acuity requirements.

Eye Protection
The Occupational Safety and Health Administration (OSHA) is a U.S. Department of Labor agency charged with developing safety standards in many fields of industry. Standard number 1910.133 describes eye and face protection. The complete standard may be viewed online at www.osha.gov. Some salient features of these rules are that wrap around eye protection as well as eye protection over prescription lenses are mandatory if there is a risk of flying debris, chemicals, liquids, gases, or injurious light radiation. This certainly seems to describe the tactical environment. For reference, Standard 1910.133(b)(1) states "protective eye and face devices purchased after July 5, 1994 shall comply with ANSI Z87.1-1989" (replaced by American Society of Safety Engineers {ASSE} Z87.1-2003 titled "Practice for Occupational and Educational Eye and Face Pro-

tection") incorporated by reference through OSHA Rules section 1910.6. (12) The American National Standards Institute (ANSI) is a private, non-profit organization established in 1918 to administer and coordinate voluntary corporate compliance with the safety standards that it develops. It has a diverse membership of over 1000 private and public organizations. Standards are formed in a fair and equitable manner that strives for truly safe product development.

ANSI approved eye protection is wrap-around, shatter resistant, and resistant to being struck by a .22 caliber bullet. Many brands of polycarbonate eye wear are available that conform to this standard. It is inappropriate for this article to recommend a specific brand of eyewear although some brands do appear to be more durable and cheaper than others. It becomes the officer's responsibility to investigate the relative prices, durability, and warranties of these products. It is a good idea to check with other tactical teams to get an overview of a number of agencies' experiences with ANSI Z87.1 approved eyewear. Whether you choose glasses or goggles, it's important to wear your chosen ANSI approved eye protection at all times in the tactical and training settings. Selecting the appropriate shade of tint or an easily removable (or plastic rip-off tinted goggle) lens is another important consideration when moving from a light outdoor to a dark indoor environment. Check to ensure that 100% UV protection by polarized lenses is also offered by your eyewear.

Summary
1. The eye functions in many ways like a camera.
2. Eye anatomy and physiology work synergistically in poorly understood ways to translate a light source into a personally meaningful visual image-a miracle of vision!
3. Near sightedness, far sightedness and astigmatism can usually be well corrected by

the use of glasses or contact lenses.
4. Ocular hypertension and glaucoma are serious, under-recognized problems that, without regular evaluation, may silently rob our sight.
5. Eye trauma is the most underreported health problem in America.
6. Prompt, appropriate first aid and medical evaluation is important in the treatment of eye trauma.
7. Use ANSI Z87.1 approved, 100% UV protected eyewear at all training and other events!
8. Obtain regular eye exams including intraocular pressure measurements.

Good luck for a lifetime of eye safety and health!

REFERENCES

1. Ward, B.-The Eye and Seeing, Franklin Watts, London, 1981, p. 162.
2. http://www.glaucomafoundation.org/education/content.php?i=7
3. http://www.glaucomafoundation.org/info.php?i=20
4. US Eye Injury Registry
5. https://www.WorldEyeInjuryRegistryOnline;EpidemiologyandPrevention
6. Tintinalli, J. et.al.-Tintinalli's Emergency Medicine, McGraw Hill, New York, 1996, p.1063
7. http://www.aging eye.net/visionbasics/uvlightandvision.php
8. http://www.highwaysafety.org/safety_facts/qanda/airbags.html
9. Duma, S.- Biomedical Science Instrumentation, 1997; 33:106-111
10. https://www.highwaysafety.org.
11. ibid. https://www.highwaysafety.org.
12. The American Medical Association Guide to Evaluation of Permanent 1996, p.1063

The Miracle of Hearing

Martin Greenberg, MD

Despite technological advancement, many of our complex bodily functions are still poorly understood. Understandably, we tend to take our senses for granted. Consider our sense of hearing. There are many reasons that hearing is truly a miraculous gift. We can hear the sound of one hydrogen atom moving our ear drum or a rocket launch-a sound over a billion times more intense! Our brain-supercomputer converts the air pressure of a sound wave into complex nerve impulses and somehow effortlessly decodes them into understandable language. More than any other sense, hearing holds the key to our emotional self. Without it, we would probably not be able to complete our law enforcement mission.

The goal of this chapter is to discuss the nature of sound, the anatomy, physiology and pathology of hearing and what we can do to protect this precious gift.

Scenarios
1. "Elaine White, sixty, a professional mediator, was leading a prejudice-reduction workshop (when)…one of the participants uttered a racial slur. "I didn't hear it," White says. The point of the workshop was to encourage people not to ignore racial slurs. Shortly thereafter, White got her first hearing aid. (1)

2. "Medic Up!" We hear the call and leave our cover to enter the rear of the stack. The metallic sound of weapon safeties clicking off in unison in response to a gunshot from the interior of the house raises hairs on the back of our necks. The deafening report of simultaneous flash-bangs disorients us as the team shouts, "Police! Search Warrant!" Occurring in silence, this scenario is unimaginable.

What Is Sound?

Objects that vibrate move particles in their immediate environment. An object's surroundings might be solid, liquid or gaseous. For this discussion, the environment is air. When something vibrates in our atmosphere, it moves the air particles immediately around it. Those air particles similarly move others and create a vibratory "wave" through the air termed *compression*. For example, when a metal object is struck, its sides move in and out. Compression of the surrounding air occurs when the object's side moves out. When it moves in, it pulls the surrounding air particles in, creating a pressure drop called *rarefaction*. A sound wave is created by these alternating compression and rarefaction phases. We hear different sounds partly as a result of the differing speed or frequency of this fluctuation. Increased frequency is heard as a higher pitch. Differing sounds are also created by air pressure driving the fluctuation that determines the sound wave's amplitude or loudness.

The Anatomy of Hearing

While smell, taste, and vision all involve bodily chemical reactions, the sense of hearing is an entirely mechanical process. To hear sound waves traveling through air, the ear must direct the sound waves into the ear canal sensing the fluctuations in air pressure and convert the pressure wave into an electrical signal that the brain can interpret as sound.

The outer part of the ear is called the *pinna*. This visible part of the ear is horn shaped, pointed forward, and has a number of curved ridges. This structure helps determine the direction of a sound as the wave will reflect off the pinna differently depending upon its direction of travel. The brain recognizes these distinctive patterns and determines the direction of the sound's location. The sound is further localized because we have two ears. This bi-aural arrangement allows sound to arrive at the right ear sooner and louder than the left if the sound is coming from your right. In humans, sounds in front of us are heard more clearly than sounds from behind. Some mammals such as dogs and horses have large movable pinnae that can focus on a specific sound. Most of us can't functionally move our ears but we instinctively cup our hands over our ears to improve selective hearing.

Once sound waves have traversed the pinna, they travel into the ear canal and vibrate the *tympanic membrane (ear drum)*. The ear drum is a thin, 10mm wide membrane separating the external ear (ear canal) from the middle ear. The middle ear is connected to the throat through the Eustachian tube. This connection is important since it equilibrates the pressure in the middle ear to equal the pressure in the outer ear. In this way, the tympanic membrane can move freely with equal pressure on both its inner and outer sides. The ear drum is rigid and very sensitive. It is kept taut by the *tensor tympani muscle* that pulls it inward and allows it to vibrate when any part of it is struck by a sound wave. Like a microphone diaphragm, the ear drum moves back and forth with sound wave compressions and rarefactions. High pitched sounds move the drum more rapidly while louder sounds move it a greater distance. An amazing reflex exists to protect the ear against loud, low-pitched noises and also works whenever you speak. The *stapedius muscle* contracts reflexively in these situations, pulling the ear drum in two different directions, making it more rigid and thus less sensitive to low frequencies. This allows you to focus on higher pitched noises by filtering out background noise. It also keeps the sound of one's own voice from drowning out other ambient noises. The ear drum gathers sound while the middle and inner ear process and transfer the information to the brain.

The middle ear serves as an amplifier of sound to allow it to better traverse the liquid medium of the inner ear. Sound wave pressure is magnified by a group of tiny bones in the middle ear called *ossicles*. These are the smallest bones in the body. They are *the malleus (hammer), incus (anvil), and stapes (stirrup)*. The malleus is connected to the inner side of the center of the ear drum. When the ear drum vibrates, it moves the malleus like a lever. The malleus connects to the incus that connects to the stapes. The end of the stapes connects with a broad faceplate to the cochlea of the inner ear. When compression or rarefaction waves push or pull the eardrum, these forces are magnified and transmitted to the *cochlea*. Air waves are thus converted to inner ear fluid waves by the piston-like stapes' action on the cochlea. Sound wave amplification occurs through the differential size of the large ear drum (55 sq. mm) acting upon the smaller stapes (3.2 sq. mm). Concentrating sound wave energy over a smaller area increases local pressure. This is the *principle of hydraulic multiplication*. Amplification also occurs through the anatomy of the bony ossicles themselves. The malleus' lever action is longer than its corresponding tympanic membrane movement. The incus will then move with greater force (Force=Mass X Distance). *This effective amplification system increases the cochlear fluid pressure to about 22X the pressure felt at the ear drum!*

The job of the cochlea is to translate the bony motion caused by the sound wave into an electrical signal sent to the brain. The *cochlea* is a snail shell shaped, trilaminar structure. Its two outer concentric tubes act as one and are termed the *scala vestibuli* and *scala media*. The innermost of these two fluid-filled tubes, the scala media, contains a third structure-the *basilar membrane.* The stapes pushes the oval window in and out of the cochlea. The adjacent, thin round window bulges with increased cochlear pressure. The rigid basilar membrane lies within the length of the cochlea. The stapes push and pull the basilar membrane and develop a fluid wave along the surface of the membrane. This fluid wave travels the length of the cochlea and basilar membrane. The basilar membrane is composed of 20,000-30,000 fibers crossing the width of the cochlea. The fibers are short/stiff near the oval window and long/thin at the other end. All these fibers can be made to vibrate or resonate at different frequencies. Each fluid wave will have a specific resonant frequency causing specific fibers of the basilar membrane to vibrate intensely. Higher frequency waves vibrate closer to the oval window while lower frequencies vibrate at the basilar membrane's "far end." How does the brain get this information and decode it as meaningful sounds? Vibrations in the basilar membrane activate parts of the *Organ of Corti*, a hair-lined structure covering the basilar membrane along the entire length of the cochlea. When the fluid wave reaches a resonant point, it releases its energy to the local basilar membrane and to the Organ of Corti. When local hair cells are moved, they stimulate the cochlear nerve. The cochlear nerve then sends impulses to the brain's cerebral cortex for interpretation. Much like a xylophone, the position of the stimulated Organ of Corti hairs on the basilar membrane determines the pitch of the sound, while the number of stimulated hairs determines the sound's loudness.

    The brain acts like a computer to analyze this complex, raw electrical impulse data into an intelligible form. Exactly how this occurs is not well understood and is truly a miracle of hearing!

More about the Physics of Hearing

We all instinctively know what is meant by the term "sound." Audible sound is defined as the "sensation (as detected by the ear) of very small, rapid changes in the air pressure above and below a static value." (2) The static value is atmospheric pressure that may be measured by a barometer in *pascals*. The standard value is about 100,000 pascals and it may vary with changing weather conditions or altitude. Vibrations causing changes in air pressure are measured in hertz (Hz). 1 vibration/second equals 1 Hz. 1000 vibrations/second equals one kilohertz. Human hearing usually lies between 20-20,000 Hz or equivalently 20Hz-20kHz. Movement of the ear drum as slight as the diameter of one hydrogen atom can potentially be detected. This is certainly another miraculous fact of hearing! The ear is most sensitive to mid-range frequencies of 1-4 kHz. A common example of sound wave creation is a bass stereo speaker. One can see the speaker cone moving back and forth creating a wave of alternating compressions and rarefactions traveling away from the speaker at the speed of sound.

The pressure of a sound wave is measured in decibels (dB). In acoustics, a decibel compares sound pressure in air with a reference pressure. However, decibels are also used to compare pressure in water. The softest sound that can theoretically be heard is 0dB. Continuous exposure to more than 85dB is dangerous. Sounds causing pain, or over 140dB, will cause permanent hearing damage.

The American Academy of Otolaryngology provides some examples of the dB levels of common activities:

0 -The quietest sound you can hear
30 -whisper
60 -normal conversation, sewing machine
90 -lawn mower, shop-tools, truck traffic (Exposure eight hours/day at this level is the maximum unprotected allowable exposure protecting ninety of the population)
100 -chainsaw, pneumatic drill, snowmobile (Exposure two hours/day at this level is the maximum unprotected exposure)
115 -sandblasting, rock concert, auto horn (Exposure fifteen min./day at this level is the maximum unprotected exposure)
140 -firearm muzzle blast, jet engine
180 -rocket launch (3) (Noise causes pain. Even brief exposure to painful noise results in permanent injury!)

The decibel scale is logarithmic rather than linear. 10dB is ten times the loudness of 1dB while 20dB is 100X as loud. This is useful because the ear interprets sound more in a logarithmic than in a linear manner and because the huge range of audible sound is more simply represented logarithmically. In this manner, fourteen-digit dB numbers are avoided. Sound levels can be accurately measured by sound meters that are adjusted or weighted for specific variables such as high or low sound levels. Multiple sound sources are logarithmically added and require a slide rule to compute. As a rule of thumb, the sum of two sound sources cannot be more than 3 dB higher than the louder sound. Sound power level is an industrial term used to describe the total sound energy produced by a machine per second. Appropriate hearing protection for dB levels at varying distances from the machine can then be logarithmically calculated. The speed of sound in air at 0 degrees C. is 331.6 meters/second (m/s). Sound's speed rises slightly with increased ambient temperature. For example, it is 12 m/s faster at twenty degrees C. vs 0 degrees. Interestingly, the speed of sound in water is much faster at 1500 m/s. As previously discussed, loudness is the normal, binaural, human perception of sound intensity. A sound increase of 10 dB will roughly double a sound's intensity except at very low or very high sound levels.

Sound insulation and absorption are important tactical topics to understand as one's sound environment will affect the "stealth" of a covert entry. Sound insulation eliminates the sound path from a source to a receiver. Heavy materials increase sound insulation. Doubling the mass/area of a sound barrier will decrease the transmitted noise by about 6 dB (a sixty percent perceived improvement). Thus, a covert entry into a stone bank building will be initially quieter than an entry into a sheetrock-walled bungalow. Double leaf partitions (two parallel, independent walls) are good sound absorbers with much less mass. Sound absorbers work by converting sound energy to heat or by dissipating sound passing through the absorber (i.e., "silenced" weapons). Improving sound insulation in police agencies/firing ranges would include these principles such as using double paned windows in administrative areas and the use of false plasterboard walls with a large void filled with acoustic quilting. The use of external insulators such as the concrete walls bordering tollways is also common.

Another tactical sound physics question relates to the speed of projectiles creating sound. Most ammunition discharges a bullet at supersonic levels or at least 340 m/s. Exceeding 340 m/s creates a sonic boom as the pressure disturbances, like ripples in a pond, cannot escape the object creating them. They will then coalesce into a *"mach cone"* or *"mach wave"* booming noise named after Ernest Mach who explained the phenomenon in the nineteenth century. For this reason, subsonic ammunition is frequently used with sound suppressed weapons.

Finally, a concept frequently discussed in police academies is the Doppler Effect. The wavelength of an emitted sound (i.e., a siren) will be decreased by the velocity of an emitting source (i.e., a squad car) traveling in the same direction as the sound. So, a car may not hear the siren of an oncoming squad car traveling 60 mph until the squad car is within 100' of the vehicle. A marked drop in the pitch of the siren may be noted as the squad car passes at high speed.

The Pathology of Hearing Loss
One in ten Americans suffer from hearing loss severe enough to limit his/her ability to understand normal speech. Noise can permanently damage your hearing. This type of damage is called sensori-neural or nerve hearing loss. The second major type of hearing loss is termed conduction loss. This is due to ear canal wax deposits (cerumen) or problems with the small bones in the middle ear. Your ears cannot be "toughened."

If you become "used to" a noise level, it has probably permanently damaged your hearing. There is no treatment for this problem once it has occurred. Even hearing aids cannot restore anything near normal hearing.

We previously described the mechanics of hearing and the cochlear nerve that can ideally respond to the movement of even one hydrogen atom. When this incredibly sensitive organ is exposed to over-loud noise, nerve cells begin to irreversibly die. The longer the exposure continues, the more irreversible damage occurs. Generally, hearing damage may occur if you must shout over background noise to be heard, if the noise hurts your ears or makes them "ring" (called *tinnitus*) or if you feel somewhat deaf temporarily after noise exposure. We reviewed the two basic ways sound can be measured. Intensity or loudness is measured in *decibels (dB). Pitch is measured in frequency* (cycles/sec. or Hz/kHz). Young children who have not yet suffered hearing degradation can distinguish sounds from about 20 Hz (the lowest note on a pipe organ) to about 20,000 Hz. (an "ultrasonic" dog whistle). Human speech is in the 3000-4000 Hz range. Our ear is designed to receive these frequencies most effectively. Hearing loss usually begins with the highest frequencies. Problems understanding the high-pitched voices of women and children may be the first sign of hearing loss and may be a mixed blessing. High frequency hearing loss can also distort sound so that "heard" sounds seem unintelligible. Words that contain high frequency consonants such as S, F, SH, CH, H, and soft C sounds will be especially affected (American Academy of Otolaryngology). For law enforcement officers, it is important to know that any close-range firearm discharge may damage unprotected hearing. Louder, large-bore weapons such as a .50BMG caliber sniper rifle will cause more hearing damage than a small-bore weapon such as a .22LR caliber pocket pistol. Very loud noises may also cause an increase in anxiety, blood pressure, and stomach acid.

Disturbingly, significant hearing loss is now affecting children. We live in a much noisier world than in the pre-automotive era. Rock concerts, discotheques, and I-pods are modern phenomena. Many musicians suffer from this problem. About fifty-two percent of classical musicians and thirty percent of rock musicians suffer Music Induced Hearing Loss (MIHL). (4) Almost nine million teenagers in Germany suffered hearing loss per year according to Dr. Henning Wiegels, retired chief of the Ear and Throat clinic in Schwerin. He stated that by the time teenagers reach the age of forty, they will have the equivalently poor hearing of sixty-year-olds. In a German survey, teens with a "several year history of listening to "Walkman" music (the Walkman is the Sony pre-cursor of the iPod) for more than two hours/day and one or more discotheque visit a week recorded an average hearing loss of 10 dB at high frequencies when compared to the other survey respondents." (5) Unlike Switzerland, Germany and the United States do not have legal limits for maximal permitted recreational noise exposure to discos or iPods.

At the other end of the age spectrum, hearing decays with age. Hearing normally begins to decay after age twenty-one. One out of five people has hearing loss by age fifty-five. This type of hearing loss is termed *presbycusis*. It is unclear how much of this loss is due to cumulative environmental factors. Other causes of hearing loss include infections (meningitis, mumps, measles, repeated middle ear infections or otitis media), trauma (ear drum perforations, skull fracture, pressure changes or barotrauma), occupational exposure, wax (cerumen) build up, allergies, foreign bodies in the ear canal, toxic reactions (oto {ear}-toxic medications such as certain antibiotics such as neomycin, diuretics like furosemide, high doses of aspirin and even rare ear tumors.

Laws Regulating Noise Exposure
Repeated exposure to sounds over 85 dB will cause hearing loss. Louder sounds accelerate the damage. For unprotected ears, the allowed exposure time decreases by half for each 5 dB in the average noise level. Exposure is limited to 8 hrs./90dB; 4 hrs./95dB and 2 hrs./100dB. The highest exposure for unprotected ears is 115dB for 15 min./day. No noise above 140dB is permitted. This means that hearing protection must always be worn when using firearms in any situation. OSHA, the Occupational Safety and Health Administration, requires that a hearing conservation program be established for workers exposed to an average of at least 85dB noise during an eight-hour day including a yearly hearing test (Hearing Conservation Amendment of 1983). Hearing protectors are required when the average eight-hour daily noise level is greater than 90dB. Here, employers must offer a free ear plug and earmuff set to all employees. If high pitched hearing loss occurs greater than 10dB, the worker must be informed and wear hearing protectors for noise greater than 85dB/day. Larger losses require referral to an ear, nose, and throat (ENT) specialist physician. Since truck traffic averages 90dB, a legal question arises regarding mandatory hearing protection for all traffic officers.

Testing Hearing Loss

If you are concerned about possible hearing loss or wish to simply have a baseline hearing study performed (a very good idea) a medical history, physical exam, and hearing studies will need to be performed. The medical history may include whether hearing loss seems to be in one or both ears; whether the loss is mild or severe; whether decreased ability to understand speech or to locate the source of a sound is present; whether the loss began before age thirty or how long it has been present and whether other symptoms such as tinnitus or ear pain is present. The physical exam will include an exam of the ear canal and ear drum with a device called an otoscope inserted into the ear canal to look for various types of abnormalities. Hearing tests measure different aspects of our hearing ability. We recall that the normal range of human hearing is from about 16-16,000 Hz while animals can hear up to about 50,000 Hz. General screening tests include blocking one ear at a time and checking the ability to hear different sounds such a whisper or a ticking watch. Tuning fork testing of air hearing conduction involves holding a vibrating tuning fork at the side of the head and hearing the sound. Bone conduction testing involves touching the vibrating tuning fork against the mastoid bone behind each ear. Communications headsets may utilize either air or bone conduction. Audiography delivers pure tones to each separate ear at controlled intensities while the minimum intensity to hear each tone is graphed. Screening studies usually deliver two tones at 256 Hz and 4,096 Hz at 5 and 10dB (the normal speech range). Detailed studies include low tones (64 Hz) at 1 or 2 dB, intermediate tones at less than 10dB and high tones (11,584 Hz) at 10dB. Hearing loss can be graphed by the threshold dB level needed to hear a given tone.

Preventing Hearing Loss

Hearing protection devices decrease the sounds that reach the eardrum. They may be ear plugs or earmuffs. Ear plugs are inserts that effectively provide an airtight block to the ear canal. We are all familiar with them. An improperly fitted or dirty plug may irritate the ear canal and even cause an outer ear infection (otitis externa or swimmer's ear). Earmuffs fit over the entire ear and seal the pinna and entire ear canal against ambient noise. They are connected by an adjustable band. Earmuffs will not seal over eyeglasses or long hair. They must be adequately adjustable to fit properly. Properly fitted earmuffs or ear plugs reduce sound by 15-30dB. (6) Ear plugs are better for low frequency noise while earmuffs are better for high frequency noise. Wearing both plugs and muffs adds another 10-15dB protection. Both should be worn when noise levels exceed 105dB. Cotton wadding only reduces noise levels by about 7 dB and is not recommended for hearing protection. Unfortunately, only half of the potential benefit of hearing protection is generally accrued because of intermittent use and/or poor fit. If hearing protection fits well, one's own voice should sound louder and deeper. Because noise is measured logarithmically, if a hearing protector gives 30dB noise reduction when worn constantly during an eight-hour day, it will give only 9dB protection if removed for only one hour during that time! Remember that there is a ten time increase in noise energy for each 10dB sound increment. (7) Like experiencing a sunburn, noise exposure and the damage it causes is cumulative. Total daily dB exposure calculations should include work, home, and play settings. You should check the protection rating of your earmuffs and plugs. Together, they should reduce average noise levels to below 90dB in your particular setting.

Summary
While the anatomy and physiology of sound and hearing is fascinating, we need to use these insights to protect our gift. Do not become complacent or embarrassed about using hearing protection in noisy surroundings. Be aware of noise

hazards at home, at play and at work. If indicated, use hearing protection constantly for your full shift. Make sure you've got adequate hearing protection for your surroundings. Remember that sound related hearing damage is cumulative and you may have only one opportunity to avoid permanent hearing loss. Treat your gift with respect and it will serve you well in return.

REFERENCES

1. 3/26/2001; Time; Megan Rutherford
2. http://www.ear.berkeley.edu/acoustics.html
3. http://www.ci.vancouver.wa.us/health/hearing1.html
4. http://www.hear-it.org.
5. Ibid. http://www.hear-it.org.
6. Op. Cit. http://www.ci.vancouver.wa.us/health/hearing1.html
7. ibid. http://www.ci.vancouver.wa.us/health/hearing1.html

Decisions, Decisions, Decisions... Improving Critical Incident Survival

A Unified Theory of Stressful Decision Making

Martin Greenberg, MD

INTRODUCTION

The purpose of law enforcement training has been to equip law enforcement officers with the knowledge and training they need to perform their duties in as safe and effective a manner as possible. We have not always provided them with these tools. Classic law enforcement training has been rooted in learning theory that promoted rapid knowledge and technical skill loss in a short period of time rather than learning for a lifetime. As trainers and practitioners, we can do better. What modern learning theory principles can we apply; what scientific understandings of how we perceive our world and mentally process that information under stress, will give our brothers and sisters a better chance at successfully managing their incredibly stressful and dangerous calling? Stated differently, it is "giving them everything they need to (safely) go through the door." These days, however, the door might be in a search warrant service or in a courtroom afterwards. We need to train officers to go through both doors. In this chapter, we hope to present an understandable perspective explaining current medical knowledge about how we perceive our environment. We will explain the human physiological reaction to stress, and an accepted theory regarding decision making under stress. Finally, we hope to relate this information to managing the environments in which we find ourselves to successfully resolve our calls for service while limiting the risk to ourselves and our community.

What is the goal of understanding the process of making a stressful decision from many, seemingly diverse perspectives? The primal need to understand important topics is almost ageless. Consider *the parable of the blind men and the elephant.* It is traced back even to Buddhist and Hindu texts. Loosely paraphrased, it describes a group of blind men who discover an elephant but who are not aware of its form. Each man grasps a different part of the animal and separately comes to the conclusion it is a snake, a pillar, a fan, a rope, a wall, or a spear. Had each man been exposed to more parts of the animal, they would have had a more complete understanding of it. Of course, the elephant was dependent upon *all* of its parts to survive. Fully understanding the elephant required an understanding of how all its parts worked together, and this understanding could only be approximated. So, too, it is with stressful decision making. Its seemingly diverse elements are both interdependent and interactive. Psychological elements, for example, both guide and are guided by their anatomic, neural, and hormonal counterparts that together interact towards a behavioral outcome. As in the parable, each element of the stressful decision making process has previously been explored independently; but also as in the parable, their *unified* function must be considered to finally "see the elephant."

To begin, the Federal Law Enforcement Training Center (FLETC) OODA Loop Model is used as a basis to understand the officers' relationship to their environments and their decision-making process. In their Environmental Influence on De-Escalation and Decision Making (Homeland Security 10/22 #5058), they state: "Being able to explain both *how* and *why* officers make decisions is the result of understanding the interplay between the conscious and the subconscious mind for our purposes, the OODA Loop will prove to be an excellent way of framing and conceptualizing the decision-making process in the context of law enforcement use of force encounters."

The OODA Loop

Understanding How We Decide Under Fire. As both a police officer and trauma surgeon, I've seen how critical understanding and optimizing the OODA Loop is to success. This chapter opens with a breakdown of this process: Observe, Orient, Decide, and Act. It mirrors how we naturally process quick decisions. In high-risk scenarios, our ability to move quickly and expertly through this loop often determines its outcome. My goal is to help you understand how stress impacts each step, and how we can train ourselves to loop faster and more effectively under pressure.

The OODA Loop is a decision-making theory formulated by Air Force Colonel John Boyd (ret.). Most simply, it is a four-step mental process we all go through when carrying out any action. The four steps are Observe, Orient, Decide, and Act. Unfortunately, they are frequently quoted in a superficial, linear manner or as a catch phrase such as "getting into someone's OODA Loop." In either case, their true strategic meaning is misunderstood. Colonel Boyd was not a prolific author but presented his theory during long Air Force briefings. [1] He was known as "forty second Boyd" and reportedly had a standing bet he could maneuver his plane from a position of disadvantage into a winning dogfighting position in forty seconds using his theory. He reportedly never lost a bet. It will become clear that he described simply a learning system all humans are neurologically hard wired to use in any rapidly changing environment. Boyd understood that we live in an ambiguous world that we can only incompletely understand. We all have what Boyd termed mental concepts or schema we adjust to the current situation as in a play we hope will have a successful ending. We have seen that experts have successful goal-oriented schema while novices do not. Even the best schema must be constantly changed by outward events to remain effective. Boyd points out that Godel's Incompleteness Theorem states that any model or schema must be constantly updated to remain current. Heisenberg's Uncertainty Principle states that we can never precisely understand reality because we can never simultaneously measure all aspects of an object. Lastly, the Second Law of Thermodynamics states that systems evolve spontaneously towards increased states of entropy (disorder). Boyd interpreted this to mean that to the extent schema are treated as closed or fixed systems they will be incapable of updating to a constantly changing reality. To avoid this, the four step process must constantly be repeated and modified. He understood that observations were based upon outside information and events. Orientation was based upon existing schema, "naturalistic decision making" and new information. Resulting decisions might blend directly into actions. Feedback loops from decision/action to observation continue the loop. There is disagreement about which loop step is most important. Each step, however, must be successfully mastered to "win." Here, losing means dying. Msg. Paul Howe realized that compressing the loop faster than one's opponent generally means winning. He quotes Boyd as stating, "The speed must come from a deep intuitive understanding of one's relationship to the rapidly changing environment." [2] Therefore, one must understand what to look at and when to do it. How then does one bring chaos to an enemy's mind and disrupt their OODA Loop? Look at each step of the process.

To **Observe** is to be aware of one's surroundings. Having one's "head on a swivel" is a familiar term for this. Col. Jeff Cooper's Condition Yellow or relaxed awareness is another similar explanation. Attention to one's surroundings is necessary but not sufficient. Purposeful and appropriate directed attention may be sufficient. A keen observer (an expert) must discern relevant environmental information. A novice will be overwhelmed with unnecessary information scanning an entire area while relevant information, for example, might include an opponent's hands or windows from where one might be shot.

To **Orient**, according to Howe, is to then place oneself in a tactically superior offensive position using motion, cover and concealment. [3] Movement, or "getting off the X," may improve your offensive posture and simultaneously disrupt your opponent's OODA Loop. For example, in the movie Top Gun Maverick, Tom Cruise flies his jet between his two pursuing students, disrupting their OODA loops and gaining tactical superiority. Boyd felt that this was the most important step in the process and termed it *schwerpunkt* or focal point. [4] He felt that our schema or mental concepts mostly exist here and shape our overall response. Can "expert" pre-existing schema (the OODA loop Orientation stage) cause relevant (expert) observations or vise-versa? Is it the chicken or the egg? In any case, being willing to modify one's schema constantly based upon new information is mandatory. Boyd used the term destructive deduction and creative induction to describe this process. [5]

The **Decision** process based upon the last two steps should be clear and straightforward. Howe feels that understanding simple rules of engagement (ROE) here is crucial for the military, law enforcement and the citizen. [6] A famous Chicago Police Department Inspector often taught that "you need to know the law, what you can do and be able to do it immediately." While hesitation may be personally fatal, Realistic De-Escalation© [7] or disengagement may be most appropriate in situations where your "reaction" cannot possibly beat their "action." Keep this in mind when deciding how to Act.

To *Act* per Boyd is to test your plan. Its result will feed back and modify the next loop. Howe feels that this is the most important step in the loop. Knowing how to automatically and reproducibly perform this technical step (i.e., making a precision shot) is mandatory. In a literature review, Force Science has determined that many hours of training are a prerequisite for experts in different sporting fields to achieve their expert status. It is hypothesized that achieving automaticity frees the mind to concentrate on relevant external stimuli. It is an expert characteristic that combined with intense, appropriate external focus allows improved emotional control that suppresses deleterious cognitive stress related cortical (brain) input. [8]

The Quiet Eye

What Experts See That Others Miss. One thing that separates elite performers from the rest is how they "see" under stress. I introduce the concept of "The Quiet Eye" to explain why focused, appropriate visual attention is so important. In both tactical medicine and law enforcement, what you see—and when you see it—can mean the difference between success and failure. This section draws a direct connection between expert visual fixation, timing, and performance in real-world encounters.

Have you ever had the rare experience of effortlessly performing a sport at dramatically higher levels than you expected? Elite athletes in multiple sports do this regularly and have in common the ability to visually focus on important environmental cues at appropriate times longer than their non-elite counterparts. Sports psychologist Dr. Joan Vickers discovered this phenomenon and termed it "The Quiet Eye." [9] This momentous discovery linked visuomotor performance under stress with the young and burgeoning field of eye and brain neuroanatomy. In order to understand this important phenomenon and its implications, we need to understand the complex anatomy of the visuomotor system.

The Eye: A Human Camera/Computer

Think of the eye as an extremely adaptable computer. Like a camera, light enters the eye through its front and passes through a lens called the cornea. Like a camera, the light reaching the lens passes through a diaphragm called the iris that may enlarge or constrict to control the amount of entering light. Also like a camera capturing an image on photographic film, light passing through the lens is bent so that an inverted, reversed image is produced upon the retina in the back of the eye. Instead of film or a digital copy, the retinal image is transformed into electrical signals transferred through the optic nerve to the brain's occipital lobe. Unlike a camera that focuses light by moving its lens, the eye focuses light by changing the shape of its lens. Rays of light entering the front of the eye are bent towards the center of the retina as they pass through the convex transparent lens that is thicker in its middle. This bending of light rays causes them to cross, invert and reverse the image cast upon the retina. In a complex way, the brain adjusts this image producing an accurate mental picture.

When viewing a distant object through a normal eye, parallel light rays pass through a flat lens with relaxed surrounding ciliary muscles and focus precisely upon the retina. With closer objects, light passing through the lens must be bent more to create the same precise retinal focus. The ciliary muscles then constrict causing the lens to thicken (become more convex) and restore focus. The process of clear viewing of both near and far objects is called accommodation. As we reach forty to fifty years of age, the lens becomes less pliable and our ability to accommodate dramatically diminishes. As lengthening our arms are an impractical solution to this problem, reading glasses may be needed.

When viewing an object, our eyes move together so they will point directly at the "target." With a distant object, parallel rays of light pass from the object to the fovea, the point on the retina producing the sharpest image. The *fovea* is defined as the center of the retina within 3 degrees of visual angle. The visual angle is the size of the image cast upon the retina by a viewed object. It is measured as an angle in degrees with the formula visual angle in degrees = two arctan {size/2 x distance}. The fovea comprises less than one percent of retinal surface but uses greater than fifty percent of the occipital visual cortex. As part of the central vision system, the enlarging circular area of the macula lutea includes 4-10 degrees of visual angle while the remaining central area is up to thirty degrees. Our eyes are spaced about two and a half inches (6 cm) apart. Outside this retinal area lies the ambient or peripheral vision system. This system responds to movement and related information especially in low light situations. Our eyes are in constant motion. *Fixations*, or focusing on a resting object, last at least 100ms. *Saccades* are quick eye movements from one object to another. Saccades last from 60-100ms and we average about three saccades/second in normal viewing.[10] The brain suppresses visual information during saccades to prevent a blurred visual image from being processed and "fills in" the blank spots with most recent images. Following a moving object for greater than 100ms is termed *pursuit tracking*. Our visual system is always attempting to obtain the clearest foveal view of observed objects. This constant, smooth centering action allows for 15 degrees of eye motion prior to head motion. Therefore, *what we experience as a stable visual image really is an amalgamation of fixations, pursuit tracking, saccades, memory, and eye/head motion*. Think of the central and ambient visual systems as distinct but working in unison. While viewing a close object, our eyes must "turn in" to allow light to strike the fovea. This process occurs automatically and is called *convergence*. While children can converge (focus) on objects only three inches (7.5 cm) away, adults can focus clearly from only about five and a half inches (14 cm). Another benefit of our widely spaced eyes is stereoscopic or binocular vision. Each eye sees slightly different pictures overlapping in the brain's visual centers. Determining differences between the images allows a distance determination. Since each eye's "picture" overlaps, the brain receives an image in which the central part is made from both eyes and is therefore very clear and stereoscopic. The left half of the retinal visual field of both the left and right eye is directed to the brain's left cortical hemisphere. The right half of both left and right retinal visual fields travel to the right hemisphere. The entire image is called the visual field. Interestingly, the nose actually blocks a large part of each eye's visual field. [11]

More Eye Anatomy

The retina is the lining of the back of the eye. It detects the upside-down, inverted image cast upon it and converts it into electrical signals transmitted through the optic nerve to the brain. The retina contains special photoreceptor (light sensitive) cells called *rods and cones*. There are about 125 million rods and seven million cones oriented differentially with most of the cones packed into the centrally located fovea. Each cone or two connects to a nerve fiber in the fovea as compared to a nerve fiber per 300 rods in the rest of the retina. For this reason, the projected foveal retinal image is seen most clearly. Rods and some cones are otherwise dispersed over the remaining retina. Light hitting the retina must first pass through a plexus of only about 800,000 nerve fibers called *ganglion cells*. These nerves link the photo-processing cells in a poorly understood manner. Nerve fibers coalesce into the optic disc and leave the eye as the optic tract. The optic tracts combine to form the optic nerve. Since there are no rods or cones in the optic disc, it is called the *blind spot*. Blood vessels branch from the blind spot in an arborizing manner. Viewing these blood vessels with an instrument called an ophthalmoscope gives important information about many medical problems. Rods, as their name suggests, are long, thin cells containing a purple-colored chemical appropriately called visual purple or *rhodopsin*. When visual purple is exposed to light, it is "bleached" and loses its color. An electrical signal is then produced and passed to a connecting nerve fiber. Rods respond best to white light and "see" in black, white, and gray.

This is the anatomic basis for night vision. Rods are inactive in bright light. It takes twenty to sixty minutes for rhodopsin (and night vision) to regenerate. Cones are responsible for color vision. They contain chemicals responsive to red, yellow-green, or blue-violet. All other colors are variations of these primary colors. Cones outside of the fovea are not evenly spaced so color vision is not accurate when we are not looking directly at an object. To avoid bleaching a particular group of rods or cones, our eyes are always moving. Different sets of photoreceptors are being continually stimulated. Their shifting messages are translated by the retinal neuronal network and by the brain into a clear picture. Another benefit of this visual tremor is that we are kept from becoming aware of our blind spot that would appear as an empty hole in our visual field. The edges of the retina contain mostly rods that are stimulated by even small movements. Peripheral vision detects motion. As previously discussed, the eyes reflexively swivel toward the moving object to center it onto the fovea for a clear picture. Visual information is transferred from the retina to an area of the outside back of the brain called the *occipital cortex* via the two optic nerves and tracts. Light from our right side is viewed by the right side of each retina and vice versa. Data from the left-hand side of each retina is transferred to the left side of the brain. Correspondingly, data from the right side of each retina is transferred to the brain's right side. To accomplish this, the inner or nasal optic tracts (half of each optic nerve) must cross. The crossover point, centrally located near the hypothalamus in the brain, is called the *optic chiasm*. After this decussation, they continue as optic tracts. The result of this arrangement is that both halves of the brain receive information from both eyes. Both retinas are now seeing the same thing, enabling stereoscopic vision. Eye motion is controlled by 6 extra-ocular muscles. Through the action of these muscles, the eye may be moved 50 degrees up, 35 degrees down, 45 degrees externally, and 50 degrees internally. In a complex and poorly understood way, the brain allows both eyes to move synchronously by precisely contracting different extra-ocular muscles and calculating the speed of the tracked object. This complex feat is in itself a miracle of sight!

The brain allows both eyes to move synchronously by precisely contracting different extra-ocular muscles and calculating the speed of the tracked object. Tear glands above and lateral to each eye produce 0.5ml of tears each day. Tears are spread over the cornea by the eyelids every two to ten seconds through reflex blinking. They contain the agent lysozyme that destroys harmful organisms. Tears are drained into a small tear sac at the inner edge of each eye squeezed empty with each blink. They drain into the nasopharynx (the back of the throat) and are swallowed.

The complex neuroanatomic pathways visual information traverse within the brain have only been mapped over about the last forty years and this evolving field of knowledge is certainly still in its infancy.

What Is Stress?

What Your Body Is Doing When Seconds Count. Stress doesn't just affect your mind—it hijacks your body. In this section, I walk you through how stress hormones impact your ability to think, act, and survive. Understanding your own stress response is the first step to gaining control in a chaotic environment.

Police work is constantly referred to as a high stress profession. *Stress* may be defined as outside forces affecting the individual. Although we think of stress as a negative factor, it is the force driving natural selection and has created the plant and animal kingdoms as we know them. Man is the most adaptable creature on the planet as a result of the stresses he has successfully faced.

Historically, the French physiologist Claude Bernard described the concept of maintaining the internal environment of the body, or *"milieu interieur."* Equilibrium exists in the body that is threatened by external stressors such as temperature changes, predators, or diseases that must be reacted to and successfully managed. The neurologist Walter Cannon used the term *"homeostasis"* to describe this relationship and to recognize that emotional stressors existed. He described the *"fight or flight" response* and traced it to the release of norepinephrine (nor-adrenaline) from the "medullary" section of the adrenal gland. This is the hormone responsible for the critical incident stress responses of tunnel vision, auditory exclusion, and slowed time perception that the tactical community has heard so much about. Hans Selye described the pituitary gland (the master gland) and its control of the hormone *cortisol* secreted by the "cortical" section of the adrenal gland. He coined the term "stress" and performed experiments exposing rats to constant adverse stimulation. In this environment, rats displayed enlarged adrenal glands, gastrointestinal ulcers and a degradation of the immune system. He called this negative state *"The Stress Syndrome."* It became clear that over-stimulation of these bodily reactions could act like a disease and damage the body faced with too much external stress.

Normally, the stress response involves the brain that signals the adrenal medulla to release nor- epinephrine. The hypothalamus and the pituitary gland mediate the intermediate, maintenance stress response including the release of cortisol and other hormones. The resulting behavioral response includes increased arousal, focused attention, a diminished pain response, and shutting down of the gut. How does the stress response actually happen? The *"hardware" mediating the stress response includes the interaction of two systems: the hypothalamus-pituitary-adrenal (HPA) axis and the sympathetic nervous system (SNS).* The SNS releases norepinephrine when triggered by an area of the brain called the locus coeruleus. A feedback loop exists between the systems that are both interactive and affected by an individual's genetics. No two people respond to stress identically.

Within the HPA axis, the hypothalamus releases a hormone called Corticotrophin Releasing Factor (CRF). CRF travels through the bloodstream to the pituitary where it causes the release of another hormone, Adreno-Cortico-Trophic Hormone or ACTH. ACTH travels similarly to the adrenal cortex to release stress hormones including *cortisol*. Cortisol is a steroid that in continued high blood levels causes the stress response. A feedback loop normally exists in the presence of high cortisol levels to cause the pituitary to shut down ACTH production and moderate the blood cortisol level. The locus coeruleus activates the sympathetic nervous system (SNS) that releases nor-epinephrine and controls "automatic" bodily functions such as heart and breathing (respiratory) rate, blood pressure and preferential large muscle blood supply. The link between the HPA axis and the locus coeruleus (SNS) is an area of the brain called the limbic system. This is the brain's emotion and memory area. An activated SNS can be moderated by reassuring memories or the emotional relief of realizing a situation is actually non-threatening. The limbic system is like a computer that in milliseconds performs a stress analysis based upon current information to decide if a stressor is truly dangerous. Prolonged experimental stress in lab animals causes dysfunction in this system and causes the stress syndrome including high blood pressure, muscle wasting, decreased appetite, sexual dysfunction, ulcers, immune system suppression and depression. The Stress Syndrome seems to duplicate many officers' depression and medical problems. Drugs like cocaine and amphetamine hyper-sensitize the stress response. Chronic maternal stress can even affect her fetus with resulting life-long dysfunctional stress responses. Unpredictable/uncontrollable stress maximizes the stress syndrome.

In summary, uncontrollable, unpredictable, constant stress may cause profoundly negative effects including all aspects of the stress syndrome. The stress syndrome may be a cause of depression and health problems in law enforcement officers. A final bad consequence of experiencing prolonged, uncontrollable, negative situations is a learned helplessness and hopelessness leading to anxiety and clinical depression.

Autonomic and Hormonal Controls of the Stress Response

Behind the Scenes of Survival. Let's delve deeper into the physiology behind the stress response, especially how the autonomic nervous system and hormonal surges influence performance. As a surgeon and operator, I believe it's not enough to just "react"—we need to know why our bodies react the way they do. Preparing for success or failure, this knowledge gives you a survival edge.

How does the cardiovascular system respond to stress? The heart is a muscular pump moving blood throughout the body. It has four chambers. The right atrium receives oxygen poor venous blood and transports it through the tricuspid valve to the right ventricle where it is pumped through the semilunar valves and through the pulmonary arteries to the lungs. There, it receives oxygen and returns to the left atrium via the pulmonary veins. Blood then crosses the mitral valve into the left ventricle and is pumped through the aorta to the body. It must pump continuously to achieve this goal and has an intrinsic neural (nerve) conduction system generating the electrical impulses facilitating its contractions. These impulses are recorded on the electrocardiogram (ECG). The ECG's "P" wave reflects atrial depolarization causing atrial contraction. The "QRS" wave indicates ventricular depolarization and contraction. The "T" wave reflects ventricular repolarization and relaxation allowing the cycle to repeat. See Fig. 1.

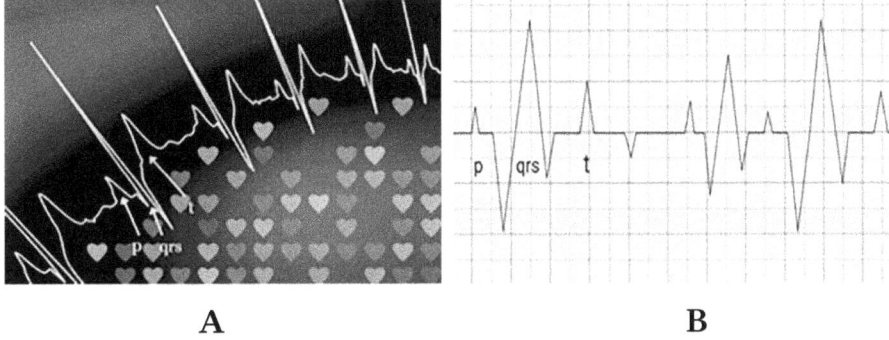

Fig. 1 (A&B): "p"/ "qrs"/ and "t" waves

Electrical conduction begins within the *sinoatrial (SA) node*, a nerve bundle at the start of the intrinsic electric pathway in the right atrium. It proceeds along this path through the *internodal pathway* and then through the *atrioventricular (AV) node*, located in the left lower corner of the right atrium between the right atrium and left ventricle where conduction may be delayed by neural and hormonal input.

Finally, the electric impulse continues on its pathway through the AV bundle, the neural "bundle of His" and then through the *Purkinge nerve fibers* in the ventricles. Without regulation, the SA node would beat at about one hundred times/minute. See Fig. 2.

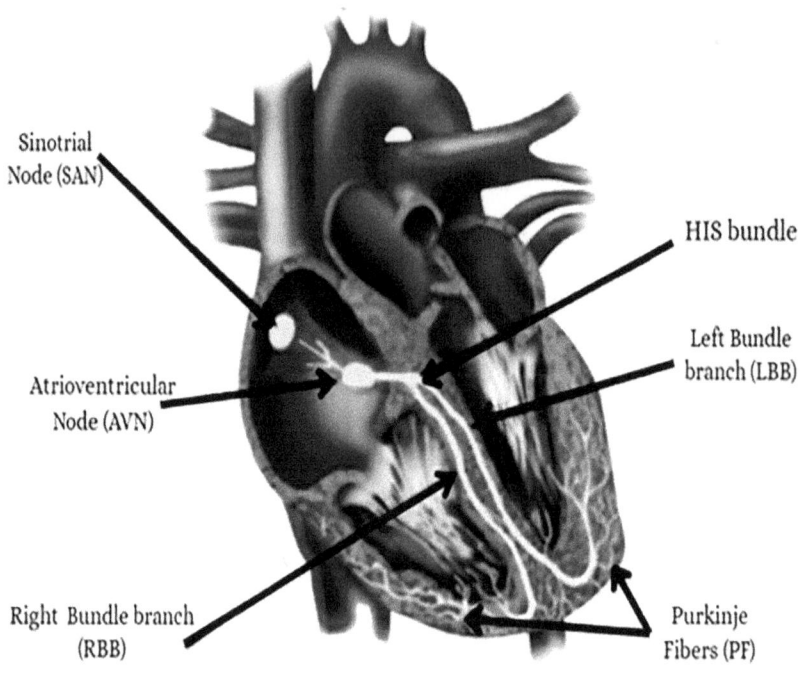

Fig. 2

However, it must respond to the changing demands placed upon it through neural, endocrine and other controls. (12) The *autonomic nervous system* is a component of the peripheral nervous system and includes its *Sympathetic Nervous System (SNS) and Parasympathetic Nervous System (PNS)* components. At this point, we will refer to the sympathetic nervous system as the SNS and parasympathetic nervous system as the PNS. The SNS prepares the body for stress while the PNS restores the body to its resting state. The SNS releases the neurotransmitter and hormone *norepinephrine* (NE) while the PNS similarly releases the neurotransmitter *acetylcholine* (ACh). We will refer to norepinephrine as NE and acetylcholine as ACh in our discussion. The cardiac effects of NE release increase heart rate and contractility. ACh release has the opposite effects, lowering both heart rate and heart muscle contractility. Interestingly, blood vessels lack PNS innervation and their "tone" or tension is maintained by constant baseline sympathetic stimulation. The medical term "shock" refers to the loss of vascular sympathetic tone and resultant low blood pressure for a variety of reasons. The *net* neurologic effect on the heart is therefore a balance between the SNS and PNS. [13] Both the SNS and PNS are each arranged using a two neuron (nerve) system linked by a neural hub called a *ganglion*. The nerve leading to the hub is termed a *pre-ganglionic neuron*. The nerve exiting the hub is called a *post-ganglionic neuron*.

Electrical messages for both the SNS and PNS are sent through them stimulating ACh release at their junction in the hub (aka ganglion) connecting them. See Fig. 3.

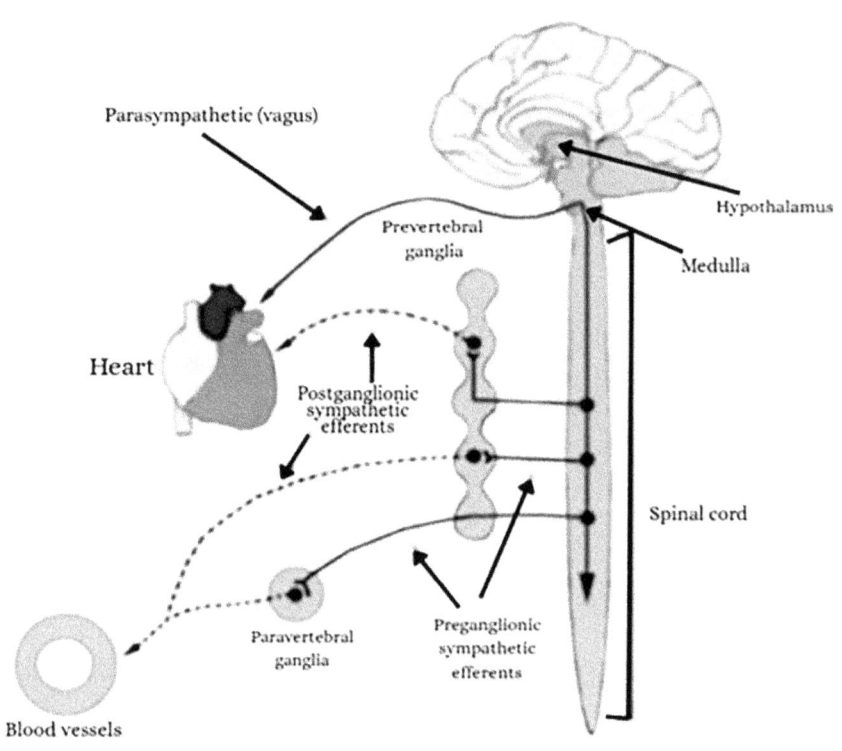

Fig.3

The Sympathetic Nervous System- The cardiac nerves of the SNS originate from the thoracic spinal cord segments T(Thoracic)1-T(Thoracic)4. PNS nerves originate within the midbrain, pons and medulla oblongata. *SNS preganglionic neurons are short* while their postganglionic neurons are longer. On the other hand, *PNS preganglionic neurons are relatively longer* while their post ganglionic neurons are short. The neurotransmitter in the connecting ganglion of the two linked, pre and post ganglionic nerves in *both* the SNS and PNS is acetylcholine (ACh). This transmission is called *cholinergic*. The sympathetic (SNS) *end organ* neurotransmitter (located at the end of the sympathetic postganglionic neuron) to the heart and blood vessels is NE (norepinephrine). Anatomic structural sympathetic stimulation of muscles and nerves by norepinephrine is then called *adrenergic*.

Sympathetic Nervous System Receptor Sites- The Greek symbols alpha1, alpha 2, beta1 and beta2 represent the 4 adrenergic receptor sites in the heart's sympathetic nervous system. *Beta1 receptors* are located in the sino-atrial (SA) and atrio-ventricular (AV) nodes. Beta1 receptors are also located in atrial and ventricular cardiac muscle. Their stimulation of the sino-atrial (SA node) increases heart rate through increased atrio-ventricular (AV) node conduction velocity and heart muscle contractility. *Renin* (a kidney hormone) is also stimulated maintaining blood pressure/volume and sodium levels. [14] *Beta2 receptors* are present in the smooth muscle of blood vessels including the heart. Their effect is to dilate these vessels increasing circulation especially to the heart, kidney and skeletal muscles. *Alpha1 and 2 adrenergic receptors* are also present and may, confusingly, cause mild vascular constriction.

The Parasympathetic Nervous System - The *vagus* nerve is the 10th cranial nerve and carries 75% of the PNS innervation to the heart, lungs and many other visceral organs. (See fig. 3) Unlike the SNS where autonomic ganglia are connected to long postganglionic neurons reaching their target organs, PNS autonomic ganglia reside within their target organ's walls including the heart and kidney. Remember that PNS preganglionic neurons are relatively long and that ACh is the sole neurotransmitter of the PNS.

Parasympathetic Nervous System Receptor Sites- PNS receptor sites are termed *"cholinergic."* ACh is formed by combining choline and acetyl-COA molecules in the synaptic vesicles located in the ganglion (hub) connecting the pre and post ganglionic parasympathetic neurons. Calcium then binds to these vesicles. ACh is released and diffuses across the space within the ganglion to stimulate electrical impulses to traverse the short post ganglionic neurons. Cholinergic end organ receptors in its target organs are then stimulated. The ACh is then hydrolyzed back into its component molecules, choline and acetyl CoA, by the enzyme *acetylcholinesterase* that is present in the synaptic gap within the ganglion. It is then ready to resume another neuro-transmission cycle. Like adrenergic receptors, there are two PNS cholinergic end organ receptors. *Muscarinic receptors* are in the target organs of the short, postganglionic PNS neurons. Like alpha and beta- adrenergic receptors, there are also two types of cholinergic muscarinic receptors. *Muscarinic2* receptors are located mostly in the heart muscle atria and its nodal tissue. When bound to *Muscarinic2* receptors, ACh slows the heart's rate. This results in a lowered cardiac output by also lowering stroke volume. *Cardiac output (CO) is determined by heart rate (HR) x stroke volume (SV)* and is thus under atrial control. Muscarinic3 receptors reside in blood vessels and dilate them through the production of nitric oxide. It is questionable whether decreased cardiac muscle contractility occurs due to muscarinic stimulation.

Vasodilation Occurs with Sympathetic Nervous System (SNS) Stimulation- In light of the vasoconstrictive effect of norepinephrine's adrenergic receptors, it may seem unclear how an overall vasodilation occurs with SNS stimulation. We remember that blood vessels receive only sympathetic innervation and capillaries receive no innervation. The SNS continually releases NE stimulating alpha1 (constricting) and beta2 (relaxing) receptors resulting in a net constricting effect with more alpha1 than beta2 effect. However, the *adrenal medulla also releases epinephrine with SNS stimulation that activates these receptor sites but with more affinity to beta2 receptors causing vasodilation.* This results in a *net* vasodilation effect. When a severe low blood pressure/volume problem is detected, the resulting high epinephrine blood levels may then cause a vasoconstrictive effect.

Autonomic Reflex Arcs-Autonomic reflex arcs also modulate the SNS. *Baroreceptors* (pressure receptors) in the distended aortic arch sense hypertension (high blood pressure) and send messages to the rostral ventrolateral medulla in the medulla oblongata of the brain stem. Sympathetic inhibition and parasympathetic activation then occur to lower the heart rate and cardiac contractility. Other baroreceptors in the vena cava and pulmonary veins respond to hypotension (low blood pressure) causing release of antidiuretic hormone from the hypothalamus and renin from the kidney to maintain blood volume and pressure. Most interestingly, distended *atrial baroreceptors* increase heart rate through SNS activation of both the medulla and the sino-atrial (SA) node that increase cardiac output and decrease atrial distension. CNS and peripheral vascular *chemoreceptors* monitor low pH and CO_2 levels and may send signals to the medulla to decrease PNS and increase SNS activity to normalize these values. *In summary, multiple baroreceptor and chemoreceptor reflex arcs exist* to modulate the cardiovascular system under stress. *The unique atrial baroreceptor reflex arc is of special interest.*

Finally, it's important to appreciate that SNS mediated vascular resistance controls blood pressure. Changes in vascular resistance are inversely proportional to a vessel's diameter to the fourth power. A small increase in vessel diameter will therefore cause a large drop in vascular resistance and blood pressure.

Neuroanatomy

Your Brain on the Battlefield. Decisions under pressure are made in specific areas of the brain. This section links what we do in critical moments to how our brains process visual, emotional, and motor input. From perception to movement, tactical decisions are built neurologically. This understanding can sharpen both training and field performance.

After information traverses the optic nerves, it enters the lateral geniculate nucleus (LGN). The LGN is an area deep within a sensory filtering organ, the *thalamus,* between the brain's parietal and temporal lobes. From there, it is sent through the optic radiations to the occipital lobes in the back of the brain. The occipital lobe is subdivided into five general areas (V1-V5) that sequentially filter visual data. Ninety percent of the information from the LGN passes to V1 that is responsible for direction, color, contrast, form and ocular dominance.[15] [12] Areas V2-5 all have unique filtering and dissemination functions. Notably, areas V3a and V5 direct data to the dorsal parietal and frontal lobes called the dorsal stream or attention network (DAN). Information sent from areas V3 and V4 are directed ventrally through the temporal lobes to the frontal lobe areas through the ventral stream or attention network (VAN).[16] These are actually two distinct forms of visuomotor information processing. The dorsal stream is responsible for orientation of gaze and attention. It is also known as the "where" pathway. It also updates the location of objects upon which we concentrate. It is a kind of master map of our immediate vicinity. The ventral stream handles sudden anticipation and planning and involves emotional responses regulated by the amygdala. It is also termed the "what" pathway. The dorsal system can act quickly; the ventral system cannot. Data then travels through the somatosensory cortex in the parietal lobes where touch related sensations are processed and then into the frontal lobes. This is where decisions are made. The pre-frontal cortex plans movements. Finally, data advances to the premotor cortex to organize motion and then to the motor cortex to initiate movement. *Interestingly, the anatomic pathway we have just described closely mirrors Col. Boyd's OODA loop.* What he described functionally has now been mapped out neuro-anatomically.

How do these anatomic pathways contribute to the sustained appropriate attention experts in sport (or during law enforcement critical incidents) demonstrate? The dorsal and ventral streams or attention networks may provide an answer.[17] Through medical imaging including Positron Emission Tomography (PET scan) and functional magnetic resonance imaging (fmri) used during attention studies, the Dorsal Attention Network (DAN) was found to be active in maintaining goal directed attention and spatial focus while the Ventral Attention Network (VAN) was active in switching attention from one location to another.[18] The DAN may inhibit potentially harmful VAN distractions and negative emotions. Goal directed attention through the DAN is termed top-down control and the brain's anatomic structures involved in this pathway include the intraparietal sulcus (IPS), frontal eye fields (FEF), anterior insula and anterior cingulate gyrus with deactivation of the VAN's superior temporal gyrus. [19] The medial frontal cortex and cingulate gyrus were also identified as being active in tasks requiring high cognitive control. [20]

Vickers formally defines The Quiet Eye phenomenon "as the final fixation or tracking gaze that is located on a specific location or object in the task space within three degrees of visual angle for a minimum of 100ms." [21] Experts will have a longer QE onset and duration than non-experts. The QE offset may be after the action is completed and may be variable depending upon the specific task. More relevant information may be garnered by experts in this way. Of course, the dorsal and ventral systems both have important information processing roles to play but in times of expert focused attention, the dorsal system seems to be dominant. There exists a "QE paradox" stating that although it is postulated that faster neural processing is generally better (the neural efficiency theory), longer or slower QE intervals are foundational expert traits. [22] Although this dichotomy remains unresolved, suggestions are that more complex situations may require more complex or slower processing and/or that the Bereitschafts Potential may play a role in unloading processing demands in expert schema. You may have had a sports experience of "being in the zone" when you performed at your best without considering the sport's technical elements. At those times, pressure to succeed seemed irrelevant. On the other hand, you may have felt overwhelmed and then you may not have performed well. In the sports world, poor performance due to anxiety is termed choking. What role does anxiety play in affecting poor performance? Psychologists describe two types of anxiety. Cognitive anxiety is the feeling that one cannot meet the current challenge and is an emotional state. Somatic anxiety is the physical perception of the anxiety state, possibly including sweating, nervousness, and increased heart rate. Although both types of anxiety are detrimental, cognitive anxiety is worse. [23] Different theories abound to explain the detrimental reaction of poor performance under stress. The *BioPsychoSocial Model of Challenge and Threat (BPM)* and the *Attentional Control Theory (ACT)* **both** hypothesize that the "top down" DAN network driven attentional control is limited by anxiety with "bottom up" VAN network emotional intrusions and distractions.

The BioPsychoSocial Model of Challenge and Threat (BPM)

The Power of Perception. Do you see a scenario challenge—or a threat? Your answer influences your performance. Here, I explore how this model helps explain behavior in high-stress moments. I've seen firsthand how the perception of control, confidence, and resources transforms performance. My aim is to give you the tools to tip that balance toward a challenge state and away from the dysfunction or paralysis of a threat.

The *BioPsychoSocial Model of Challenge and Threat (BPM)* distinguishes between perceived challenge and threat states. In this model, just prior to a stressful event the individual evaluates their chance of success. If success is perceived as likely, a challenge state exists allowing "top down" focused performance. If not, then a threat state exists causing "bottom up" distracted, emotional, poorer performance. [24] How, then, does one decide what is a "challenge" or a "threat?" Stress may occur when external demands are perceived as exceeding one's ability to cope with them. [25] Coping with stress is a vital survival mechanism. The *Stress and Coping Theory (SCT)* posits that an individual makes a cognitive appraisal of the relationship of an event to their personal welfare in a both a primary and secondary manner. The primary appraisal determines if harm may result. Secondarily, it is determined whether the harm can be avoided or used to one's benefit. Should one seek more information or avoid acting? Is the stressor relevant personally and can one prevail in the encounter? At this point, the encounter is determined to be challenging (a positive outcome) or threatening (a negative outcome).[26]

Negative emotions accompany the cognitive appraisal of threat per the Stress and Coping Theory (SCT) of Lazarus and Folkman. [27] The Biopsychosocial Model of Challenge and Threat (BPM) develops from this theory by assuming that the two reactions to stress are either challenge or threat. [28] Challenge is cognitively good while threat is emotionally bad. Here, challenge or threat states are the end result of the cognitive evaluation rather than part of the evaluation process. The SCT theory focuses on behavioral results. The BPM theory focuses on physiological ones. [29] In the BPM, when an individual is in an engaged, self-relevant, motivated performance situation, a psychological evaluation of the actual and/or perceived personal and environmental resources and demands occurs. Two potential pathways are then possible. If high resources and low demands are deemed present, the challenge pathway exists and results in the physiologically measurable activation of the SNS we have previously discussed. If, on the other hand, low resources and high demands are deemed present, the threat pathway exists resulting in PNS and HPA activation. SNS activation physiologically results in increased heart rate, increased cardiac output and lowered total peripheral vascular resistance (TPR). Lowered TPR or vasodilation (vascular dilation) increases blood flow and nutrient supply to target organs. Conversely, in the threat state, lowered cardiac output (CO) and higher total peripheral resistance (TPR) result in vasoconstriction (vascular constriction) and decreased blood and nutrient supply to critical target organs needed during the stress response. [30] Both self-relevance and task engagement are important elements of the BPS. An individual's resources may be both internal and external including their internal "expert" qualities, knowledge and technical abilities and/or their external positive peer support, intel, gear, etc. [31] *Challenge and threat assessments are viewed as the opposite ends of a continuum* that an individual's unique response falls within. In other words, we are always *both* challenged and threatened in any stressful situation. Situational perceived demands versus total perceived/actual resources will determine where on the continuum we fall. Top down cognitively engaged behavior may lead to a challenge state with better mental, cardiovascular and other physiologic tools to obtain a successful outcome. *The threat state, on the other hand, prepares the body for action but also for its inhibition should goal abandonment and escape be necessary.* Physiologic markers here include a relative decrement in CO, an increase in TPR and large shifts in blood pressure (that would otherwise be maintained in the challenge state) due to SNS response dampening by the PNS including the "emotional" HPA axis. Actual physiologic data can then be used to measure changing challenge and threat states rather than purely subjective, potentially inaccurate self-reporting.

We can see then how psychological states can affect physiologic responses but how does the social element fit into the model? In 2002, Mendes, Blascovich et. al. studied interactions between white and black men rated as advantaged or disadvantaged. Of all the possible combinations, study partners were challenged and did best when paired with white, advantaged men. [32] Our expectations or biases may play a role in determining the degree of presenting threat that research psychologist Daniel Kahneman would call our "always on" mental System 1. When an experimental expectation was "framed" as financially beneficial, BPM physiologic data revealed a relative challenge state as compared to one with a losing financial scenario. [33] Even increased "safe" interactions with minority or what Blaskovich terms "stigmatized" groups can result in later, challenge-like physiologic responses. [34]

Electroencephalography (EEG) studies have shed light on the anatomic neural areas involved in stressful decision making. The four neural frequencies studied are theta (4-7Hz) that are activated in focused attention, low alpha (8-10 Hz) activated in inhibitory activity, high alpha (11-13 Hz) and low beta (14-22 Hz). [35] Simultaneous activation of different anatomic areas indicates coordinated neural activity.

Cavanagh and Frank have demonstrated a correlation of activation of the prefrontal cortex, anterior cingulate gyrus and theta wave production in situations requiring increased motor control through concurrent PET scan and EEG monitoring. [36] This suggests that in times of an increased need for cortical control the mid frontal cortex and anterior cingulate gyrus produce theta waves that activate other DAN components and help to organize a successful motor response. EEG studies in competitive elite level shooting and golf putting have showed reduced activity in the temporal lobes that are in the VAN pathway. Concurrently, increased activity in the prefrontal and mid cingulate gyrus areas was demonstrated. [37] Vickers and Williams document studies showing expert shooters strongly activating mid-frontal and anterior cingulate regions at the time of trigger pull compared with novices and also correlate the expert QE interval at those times as compared to novices. [38]

In summary, it appears that experts under stress utilize a longer, appropriately focused QE interval at the correct time that is accompanied by an activation of the DAN with concurrent VAN suppression. DAN activation stimulates theta wave production by the mid frontal cortex and anterior cingulate gyrus. Theta waves then have wide ranging effects throughout the brain to further coordinate the most appropriate motor response. Cavanagh and Frank stress that theta wave central hub-like origin in the center of the brain facilitates this effect. [39] Is there really an ongoing battle in the brain between the DAN and VAN in times of stressful performance? In the Disney movie Fantasia (Disney studios, 1940), the sorcerer's magical hat is used by his apprentice in an unsuccessful attempt to control his magical broom. Panic then ensues until the sorcerer returns and restores harmony to the previously discordant scene. Are theta waves similarly the conductor of our neural orchestra? Is the expert QE interval activating the DAN? Is an expert schema responsible for a long QE interval? Certainly, these are all elements of expert performance. We are at the beginning of these discoveries that will surely continue to grow in time. But even now, we know that expert QE and scenario "expert schema" training will advance our ability to survive use of force critical incidents.

The Attentional Control Theory (ACT)

The Battle Between Focus and Fear. In this section, I explore how stress and anxiety disrupt our ability to stay on task. Whether in the operating room or during a critical incident, we need to filter out distractions and stay focused on the mission. I break down how anxiety compromises executive function and what elite performers do to stay locked in when it matters most.

Corbetta and Shulman reinforce the concept of two attentional systems normally working in unison but at cross purposes when under stress. One, influenced by goals, knowledge and training is termed the top-down, faster, Dorsal Attention Network (DAN) we have described, while the other, slower, stimulus and emotionally driven system is termed the bottom-up Ventral Attention Network (VAN). As previously discussed, the DAN is generally centered in the brain's pre-frontal cortex while the VAN traverses the temporo-parietal and ventral frontal cortex. [40] It has been shown that humans have a limited amount of attention to direct towards any problem. Our short term, or *working memory*, is composed of a *central executive* that fulfills the functions of switching attention between tasks, selective attention, attention inhibition, and updating working memory. [41] Cognitive anxiety, the result of demands exceeding perceived and/or actual resources, disrupts the normal DAN/VAN balance and results in VAN dominance, increased distractibility, and poorer cognitive, goal oriented performance. [42] For example, more anxious individuals were shown to have poorer performance on the psychological *Stroop Test* where participants must name the colors of neutral and threatening objects as quickly as possible. [43] Also, anxious individuals did less well on anti-saccade testing where they had to avoid looking at an irrelevant object. Fewer saccades indicate greater task focal attention and are a measure of distractibility. Greater saccade numbers indicate increased task distraction and a relative loss of the central executive's inhibition function or inability to ignore irrelevant stimuli. [44] Please note that this is not the "deer in the headlights" problem "novices" face when ignorant of important environmental cues. This represents an *active inability* to maintain task focus. In summary, cognitive anxiety affects the executive function of working memory by causing increased distractions through a decrement of its inhibition function. This results in a relative loss of task focus and poorer goal related performance.

"Naturalistic" or Recognition Primed Decision Making and Training Options

Training the Mind to React Like an Expert. We don't rise to the occasion—we fall to our training. I introduce Naturalistic (Recognition Primed) Decision Making as a model for how real-world decisions are made: fast, intuitive, and experience-driven. This approach mirrors how we all succeed in time-compressed environments. I also explore how building strong "schema" through experience can make the right response feel automatic.

Making decisions in a critical time compressed incident is not an Aristotelian or stepwise, logical process. Rather, it is a process of matching environmental cues with similar prior personal experiences.⁽⁴⁵⁾ An action plan based upon these successful experiences is initiated in an OODA Loop manner. Dr. Gary Klein has spent his career as a research psychologist studying this learning paradigm which he termed *"Recognition Primed or Naturalistic Decision Making"* in 1985. ⁽⁴⁶⁾ Our prior experiences "set the stage" for, or model, our current decisions. These experiences are termed schema. We all have schema but the more experienced or expert we are, the more successful our plan or schema will then be. "To understand why you want (the) skill sets built into your long-term unconscious memory, you should be familiar with the Theory of Schema, which states that "The conscious mind is slow, but the unconscious mind is fast." ⁽⁴⁷⁾ The result of a time compressed decision will not be as optimal as one made in a leisurely, logical manner. They ideally are then a best compromise that Dr. Bill Lewinski and others term *"satisficing"* (satisfying and sacrificing). ⁽⁴⁸⁾ Most successful schema then rely upon expert prior knowledge and planning and the ability to appreciate and use important environmental cues.

Being goal rather than process oriented implies being outwardly rather than inwardly focused. Having the ability to understand how others will react during a critical incident and using that knowledge to one's benefit is the basis of *Game Theory*. ⁽⁴⁹⁾ For example, the great hockey player Wayne Gretzky was not the largest, fastest, or strongest player among his peers but was able to "read" a play in order to be in the right place at the right time to win. Being outwardly focused generally and specifically implies *automaticity* in the technical aspects of the game. If the game is a critical incident, internal technical shooting concerns such as the correct grip, breathing, stance or trigger squeeze must be reduced to automaticity or eliminated from conscious thought by many repetitions of correct training. Recall Paul Howe's discussion of the "Act" portion of the OODA Loop discussed above. In fact, expert technical performance may actually "free" one's mind to better focus on critical external cues. Research psychologists have termed this preparatory mental pathway the *Bereitschaftspotential.* (50) Once automaticity is achieved, our mental puzzle can be completed by learning "winning" schema in common tactical situations. This is accomplished through realistic, aka "high fidelity" scenario training. Long term retention of life saving schema is best obtained this way rather than in a classroom setting. In fact, even *thinking* about winning schema may have a beneficial training effect. While classroom (also called block and silo) training rapidly degrades, realistic scenario training persists. The U.S. Marshals Service has adopted this approach developed by Force Science Institute© with great success.

The Force Science© training approach has 10 basic tenets:

1. The law enforcement profession requires the integration of a variety of sophisticated interdisciplinary skills.

2. Context and scenario-based training should begin early in training and then escalate in difficulty and realism as necessary to develop insight, motivation for learning, integrated skill development, maximum learning, retention, and skill transferability.

3. "Block and silo" instruction produces rapid gains in skill-building and the illusion of learning, but also ensures the fastest deterioration of those skills and should be abandoned as a form of long-term skill-building.

4. When spread throughout the learning process, short burst, frequent, and integrated skills training and practice improve performance and retention.

5. The blending of skills (interleaving), in both instruction and practice, is critical for effective transference and real-world application.

6. Building skills to an automatic level (automaticity) facilitates real-world performance and decision-making and is often the product of "mindful practice."

7. Significant improvement in skill development can result from proper instructional feedback and video modeling.

8. When properly arranged, pre-service training provides opportunities to develop social and emotional intelligence within current training timelines.

9. Utilizing specialized "workgroups," journaling, group training, and interaction throughout a training cycle promote motivation, competition, interpersonal insight, and change. It facilitates the development of social and emotional functioning.

10. Law enforcement is a profession that is characterized by time-compressed, high-risk decision- making, often involving encounters with very difficult people. Training for expert decision-making in real-world (clinical) settings should occupy at least one-third of the pre-service curriculum and a regular portion of the in-service curriculum. [51]

Applications of Theory to Police Training

From Theory to the Street. Everything leads to this point: how do we turn insight into action? I review the evolution of police training and advocate for scenario-based, high-fidelity approaches that mirror the realities we actually face in life. I offer strategies to help ensure that critical decision-making becomes second nature—because that's what survival demands.

Most of the advances in neurobiology and modern psychological learning theory we have discussed have occurred in the last thirty-five years. Dr. Bill Lewinski summarized similar advances in law enforcement education by stating, "In the 70's, the police community started to focus on the implications of fight, flight, and freeze on officer performance. In the 80's, we started identifying the factors connected to police performance and stress, such as elevated heart rate, tunnel vision, shaking and trembling reactions, and diminished judgment. The focus was on the negative elements of stress arousal. That led some researchers to focus on how to get officers' pulses down during critical incidents to perform better...In the 90's, we saw the exercise community move away from the negative aspects of stress and focus on how arousal could benefit performance. The police community focused on positive self-talk, breath regulation, mental rehearsals, and "when/then thinking to avoid emotional recoiling in the face of unexpected challenges. From the 2000's through today, we've highlighted the benefits of arousal on focus and performance." [52] In 2008, Force Science enlisted Dr. Joan Vickers to study gaze patterns in "elite" vs. "ordinary" police officers. Dr. Vickers, as we have previously noted, is a pre-eminent sports neuropsychologist who was the Director of the Neuro-Motor Psychology Laboratory in the Kinesiology Research Center, University of Calgary in Canada. Using eye tracker eyeglasses, the exact location of the wearer's gaze was pinpointed every 33.33 milliseconds. In a dynamic, realistic, live action scenario, officer response requiring deadly force was recorded via specialized computer software. Elite officers demonstrated the "quiet eye" gaze pattern and had significantly better results. [53] The effect of increased heart rate negatively affecting performance was increasingly questioned. In a 2019 study, Arble et al., found that increased physiological arousal as documented by increased heart rate, cortisol (a stress hormone) and anti-thrombin (a blood thinner physiologically released when under stress) levels, correlated with diminished verbal communication ability but *not with non-verbal ability or tactical performance.* [54] This suggested that increased heart rate was *not* a decrement to elite level performance. [55] This again raised the issue of "good" stress (eustress) vs. "bad" stress (distress).

Building on Dr. Joan Vickers' "quiet eye" research, it showed that "elite" officers displayed superior "game theory" as compared to their "regular" counterparts by exhibiting longer concentration focus at the right place and time. This resulted in their superior performance. To try to determine the effect of experience (relevant training) on superior gaze patterns, Force Science performed what has become known as "The Mesa Study," as it was conducted with the Mesa, AZ and Hillsboro, OR police. This was a combined effort by Drs. Bill Lewinski, Nick Murray and Robert Horn. Here, officers were fitted with heart rate monitors, body cameras, and eye-scanning glasses. This allowed measurement of their scanning patterns including duration and relevance to success in the 5-minute scenario involving a car crash and subsequent critical incident involving the responding officers. The data fell into 2 groups. In the "low relevant scan rate" group, meaning those with a longer "quiet eye" on relevant scenario cues, performance greatly exceeded the high scan group. Both groups had similarly high heart rates of 170-180 bpm. The low scan group, exhibited *eustress* and 85% returned gunfire from a superior tactical position while the high scan group exhibited a distracted, threat behavior state, *distress*, and returned gunfire only 50% of the time. The low scan group had prior tactical or military training while the high scan group did not as their only demographic difference. Interestingly, years of police service were *not* a defining factor. This study demonstrated that high heart rates were not related to poorer performance (although also present in *distress*), but that *expertise* was related to superior "game theory," superior performance, a challenge state, and *eustress*. [56][57] Of course, scenario *training must have both psychological and physical fidelity*. Lon Bartel, VirTra's® Director of Training, explained that "psychological fidelity (emotional fidelity) is the level at which a simulated task or event can evoke a feeling of realism in the student," while "physical fidelity is the degree to which the simulated event duplicates the appearance and requires performance and actions consistent with real world task constraints." [58] Experience, therefore, may allow officers to view a high eustress incident as a "top down" challenge rather than as a "bottom up" distressing threat. In that vein, might we consider the similarities between police and athletic training? Could the same factors that boost athletic training also apply to law enforcement? Dr. Lewinski points out that the average police recruit receives about 70 hours of firearms training while standing on a range with no return fire. This training situation lacks decision-making requirements. Furthermore, he states that this is the equivalent of half a semester of high school level team sport training. Even high schoolers practice and compete to gain "game theory" unlike the police recruit. Rather than high heart rates, could inexperience and "test condition novelty" be responsible for novice officers' bottom-up thinking? Are we putting the equivalent of a one semester high school athlete into a pro game where the stakes are life and death? [59]

The Importance of De-Escalation Training

Dr. Greenberg's Sidebar

When I became a police officer in 2002, my agency's firearm instructor counseled me that I needed to become "a professional gunfighter" when I was out on the street. While developing expert technical firearms training or automaticity was stressed, it was basically left up to me to figure out the rest of the survival equation. Verbal Judo© by George Thompson was required reading in the police academy but his basic principles of empathy and active listening were never discussed or trained. Empathy is putting oneself in someone else's shoes. Sympathy is feeling sorry for them. You can't make someone feel understood if you don't look at things from their perspective. Empathy is mandatory while sympathy is optional. It took some time for me to understand the importance of garnering verbal compliance using these tools. However, when I put them in my communications tool belt my job as a law enforcement professional and as a practicing orthopedic surgeon dramatically improved. As a personal example, I was employed on a part time basis as an orthopedic surgeon in an HMO. Patients were scheduled for me to see every six to ten minutes. I evaluated about thirty patients each session. The patients rated their doctors every three months. Doctors needed at least a ninety percent rating to maintain employment. I read Verbal Judo after my first three months at that job. I thought I was doing great and had excellent surgical results during that time, but my patient evaluation score was only seventy-five percent. In fear of losing my job, I decided to put verbal judo principles to work. I welcomed patients to the practice. I maintained eye contact. I asked them what they expected and how I could help. I used non-medical language to explain everything. I tried to make them feel like the most important person in the room and that I was there for them. In spite of having only six minutes to do this, my ratings went up to ninety-four percent at the next evaluation. Technically, I was the same (hopefully expert) surgeon from one three- month interval to the next so what changed? My patients felt empowered by being viewed as important people. They were then willing to follow helpful health recommendations that they viewed as being in their interest.

Verbal Judo© with its emphasis on empathy and encouraging people to act in their self-interest was one precursor to the Realistic De-Escalation© course currently offered by Force Science Institute©. Learning "expert" de-escalation or disengagement schemata in the appropriate settings are as important as being "a professional gunfighter."

The International Association of Chiefs of Police (IACP) defines *de-escalation* as: "Taking such action or communication verbally or non-verbally during a potential force encounter in an attempt to stabilize the situation and reduce the immediacy of the threat so that more time, options, and resources can be called upon to resolve the situation without the use of force or with a reduction in the force necessary." (IACP, n.d., 2019). They suggest that a more complete understanding of all aspects of a situation an officer may find him or herself managing may more likely lead to a less or nonviolent outcome than simply considering the "Graham" factors at play. This will include information learned prior to encountering a "subject," management of the actual encounter, and the official description of the encounter afterwards. Protecting oneself going through the door of a courtroom will prove to be as important as going through the door in the service of a search warrant.

In the Jamie Ceballos v. Husk (2019) case, the federal 10th Circuit Court found that the officers *failed* to obtain Crisis Intervention Training (CIT), and that their failure to use de-escalation techniques, their quick approach, the subject's diminished capacity to reason, and their failure to contain the subject created the *jeopardy* that necessitated their use of force by poor pre-force decisions. *Objectively reasonable decisions became reckless decisions when viewed in this light and qualified immunity was denied.* Signed on the second anniversary of George Floyd's death, May 25, 2022, President Biden issued Executive Order 14074. This executive order encouraged de-escalation training via federal grants, placed a federal ban on chokeholds and created a national registry of officer misconduct. The message it delivered was that de-escalation measures (that we will refer to as Force Science© *pre*-suasion and *per*- suasion considerations) will be taken into account in the same way as Graham v. Connor elements when deciding the "objective reasonableness" of use of force encounters.

Of course, the concept of de-escalation is not new. Foundational police tactics have always included the use of cover, concealment, and barriers. Officers have routinely waited for additional resources (CIT, EMS, K-9, etc.) and backup to arrive on scene. Maintaining scene safety and creating discretionary time to mitigate risk are fundamental principles. Other time-tested approaches include having a "measured" approach to critical incidents; gathering maximum intelligence; calm, single officer communications and subject physical geographic containment. Equally important was the appraisal of exigency and when de- escalation was not indicated.

In today's world, officers will be judged *retrospectively* whether their decisions regarding their physical environment (that the Federal Law Enforcement and Training Center {FLETC} terms E-2) and the subject's (that FLETC terms E-3) may have been reckless resulting in the denial of qualified immunity. *Documenting* clearly why you did what you did, including de-escalation and Graham factors (that we will refer to as Force Science© *post*-suasion considerations), now becomes critical. FLETC summarizes the Graham Factors with the abbreviation *SIRF*. This stands for the *Severity* of the crime, the *Immediacy* of the threat, the *Resistance* of the subject, and their potential *Flight* risk. FLETC views a use of force encounter as an interaction of 3 environments, or *ecosystems.*

***Ecosystem** 1* represents the officer him (her) self, including the totality of their physical/mental fitness, mindset, training and abilities.

***Ecosystem** 2* represents the complete environment in which the encounter occurs including but not limited to an urban, suburban, rural setting, traffic density, ingress, egress roadways, pedestrians or other civilians in the immediate area, available potential weapons to the subject, backup and miscellaneous law enforcement resources and other relevant factors.

***Ecosystem** 3* represents the subject(s) themselves again including but not limited to *SIRF* Factors, potential exigency of the circumstances, possibly a brief TEB psychological evaluation (to be discussed) and other relevant factors.

In the Ceballos decision, the 10th Circuit described problems with the officers (E-1), the scene control (E- 2) and the subject's evaluation (E-3). Problems with the officer's environment (E-1), the physical environment (E-2) and the subject's environment (E-3) were all specifically cited. Approaching a use of force incident as a *philosophy rather than a checklist* to be completed is recommended. The officer, their physical surroundings and the subject are all constantly interacting and possibly changing. Understanding each environment separately will help to improve their interactions and hopefully the event's outcome.

FLETC defines E-1 as "The dynamic and continually changing conditions of the officer." This includes their "internal" conditions such as their conscious mind, subconscious mind and emotional states, and their "external" conditions or, in other words, their behaviors. A good question to ask at this point is "How do your 'internal conditions' affect your behavior and influence everyone else's (other officers, the public and the suspect)?" Officer wellness and fitness is synonymous with mind and body wellness and fitness. Pillars of mental fitness might include the psychological, spiritual, and legal behavioral and social realms. Pillars of "body" wellness and fitness might include the physical, nutritional and tactical realms. When all these realms are well developed, the officer may be more likely to perform at their peak level in times of stress. Think of yourself potentially as an elite athlete whose mind and body are disciplined and ready to perform at an extraordinary level.

E-2 is the scene including cover, concealment, barriers, and distance from the subject. The officer has the ability to manipulate the scene to their advantage by maximizing and leveraging all of these factors. Force Science uses the term the "Respons-ability Zone" to emphasize this point.

We have seen how Col. Boyd and his OODA Loop have presented a prism through which our decision- making process becomes understandable. As we previously said, Col. Boyd felt that our schema or mental concepts mostly exist in the Orientation step and shape our overall response. We have also discussed Dr. Gary Klein and his *Naturalistic or Recognition Primed Decision-Making Theory of Schema*. Through expert Recognition Primed or Naturalistic Decision making, one's subconscious mind will recognize important threat cues allowing them to immediately respond rather than being overwhelmed by irrelevant stimuli. Understanding your training and abilities (E-1) will allow you to optimize the scene (E-2) and improve outcomes regarding the subject (E-3). Can "expert" pre-existing schema (the OODA loop Orientation stage) cause relevant (expert) observations or vise-versa? Is it the chicken or the egg? In any case, being willing to modify one's schema constantly based upon new information is mandatory (if you get the chance). Boyd used the term *destructive deduction and creative induction* to describe this process. According to Boyd, *Orientation* was the most important OODA Loop step. This means that officers must be able to understand (orient) their abilities (E-1) related to the environment (E-2) and the suspect (E-3). Boyd wrote, "Orientation shaped observation… Without the context of Orientation, most Observations would be meaningless." (Osinga, 2007) Boyd agreed with Msg. Paul Howe in stating that a deep, or *expert,* understanding of yourself, your environment, and your adversary was crucial in a successful orientation stage.

Boyd quoting Sun Tzu: "Know your enemy and yourself; in one hundred battles you will never be in peril." and "…seize that which your adversary holds dear or values most highly; then he will conform to your desires." How then can Sun Tzu help us to understand de- escalation? We assume that people "hold dear and value most highly" their sense of dignity and self-respect. Taking reasonable measures to preserve the subject's self-worth can encourage the appropriate subject TEB matrix group to comply with your requests. E-3 is the "dynamic and continually changing conditions" of the subject. This includes the subject's *TEB (Thoughts, Emotions, and Behavior) Matrix* and actions before and during the encounter. Another good question to ask here is "How will the subject's TEB Matrix (E-3) affect your evaluation and decision making (E-1)?" The TEB Matrix© was developed by Dr. John Azar-Dickens of Force Science.[61] The San Francisco PD Crisis Intervention Team (CIT) credits this model with their nationally recognized leadership strategies in de-escalation *and* knowing when these strategies would not be feasible (San Francisco Police, 2020). Briefly, *Thoughts* may be clear or clouded; *Emotion* may be high or low; and *Behavior* may be compliant or non-compliant.

Each of these potential 8 *TEB* combinations can be evaluated from the perspective of Approach Style, Psychological Status, Volatility Risk, Volatility Type, and other factors. This sounds confusing but it is very nicely displayed in a table for quick reference if needed. See Fig. 4.

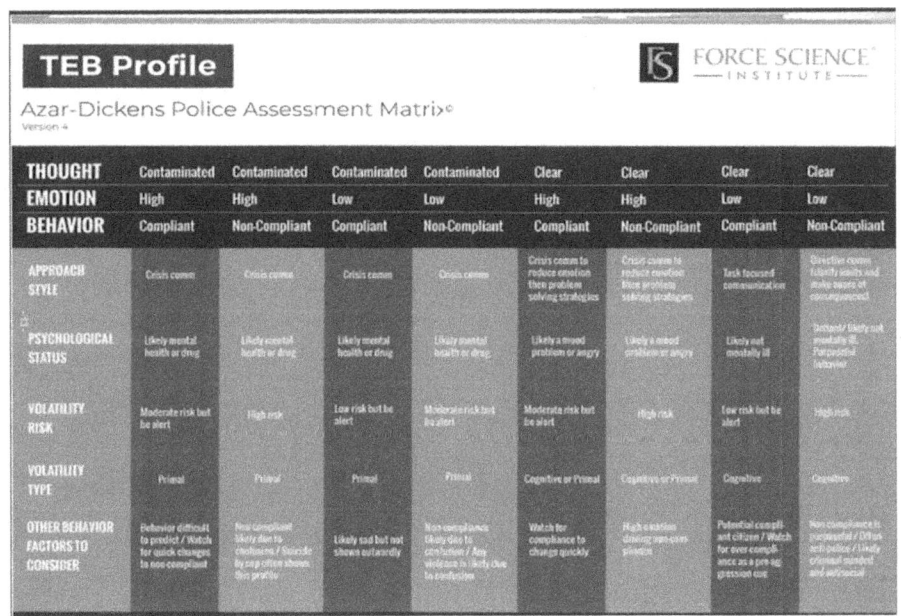

Fig. 4 : Azar- Dickens Assessment Matrix version 4 [62, 63]

The San Francisco Police Department is recognized as having the nation's premier Crisis Intervention Team (CIT). In 2020, they reportedly peacefully resolved 99.9% of their calls for service. (San Francisco Police Department, 2020) They credit the training in the Thought, Emotion, and Behavior (TEB) model provided by Force Science as instrumental in their success. Furthermore, they felt that "… the perceived Thoughts, Emotions, and Behaviors of a subject in crisis directly impacts and informs the officer's abilities to de-escalate the situation and peacefully resolve the incident." (San Francisco Police Department, 2021) Let's explore each component of the TEB matrix:

Perceived Thinking: Clear or Contaminated

Clear Thinking: The subject may be capable of logical/rational thought. They may be more likely to be persuaded or comply with directions.

Contaminated Thinking: The subject has lost the ability (temporarily or permanently) to rationally understand their situation. There are many problems that may contribute to contaminated thought including mental illness, medical illnesses including diabetic hypoglycemia (low blood sugar), environmental toxins, substance abuse, brain damage (head injury), excited delirium, or developmental disabilities including autism or intellectual delayed development to name just a few.

Emotion: Perceived emotion may be termed low or high.

High Emotion: May leave the subject in a *"cognitive"* or *"primal"* state. Subjects may be reasoned with more easily if their thinking is cognitive, meaning that they can possibly listen and reason.

Low emotion: This could be caused by many things such as depression, ambivalence, etc. Or, very importantly, it may represent an inability or *unwillingness* to participate in deescalation discussions

A Cautionary Note: High emotion may presage subject volatility. Low emotion may presage danger in a "suicide by cop" or in a psychopathic manipulation scenario.

Behavior: Behavior may be termed compliant or non-compliant.

Compliant behavior may allow the officer to attempt deescalation techniques.

Non-compliant behavior may signal that objectively reasonable force may be necessary.

The SFPD CIT's experience suggest that when the *trifecta including: Contaminated thought; High emotion; and Non-compliance* (including the totality of the circumstances and SIRF factors) are present, "they point to a greater likelihood of volatility and exponentially diminish an officer's ability to successfully engage in de-escalation strategies." (SFPD, 2020/2021) They suggest that officers *look for the trifecta first.* De-escalation techniques may still be attempted here, but barring exigent circumstances extra care should be considered because rushing into the scene may unnecessarily escalate the situation. FLETC research shows that high emotion suspects were 3X as likely to resist, suspects were 1.5X as likely to resist with evidence of wrongdoing, and contaminated thinking suspects were 9X as likely to display some level of resistance. Prior to "setting the stage" for an encounter consider the *Force Science Pre-suasion Tool©* (Force Science Realistic De-Escalation Instructor Course, 2021) if possible. Its nine categories are as follows:

1. Authorities- What is the lawful and articulable framework for your actions?

2. Exigency- Is there a public safety threat present that requires immediate action, or can critical discretionary time, space and containment issues be addressed?

3. Approach Style- Based upon current information, would a lower profile approach be wise? Are you concerned with a possible suicide by cop or ambush?

4. Mission- What is your goal and how does that affect the urgency of your plan?

5. Information v. Intelligence- Information is what you may have heard about the situation. Intelligence is vetted information that is known to be accurate. What important intelligence may be needed to clarify the action plan?

6. Anticipation of Actions- How might the subject behave? Engage in an "if-then" mental scenario of possible reactions.

7. ICEN- Isolate, Contain, Evacuate, Negotiate- This critical series of steps should be considered to stabilize the situation and to allow negotiations to possibly begin.

8. Needed Resources- Do you have the resources and training to most successfully complete your mission? Here is where possibly needed resources such as EMS, CIT, backup, rescue teams, appropriate tools, etc. be considered and requested even on-route to the call.

9. Maneuver or Disengagement- How will exigency affect appropriate distance and cover considerations? Are all the above-mentioned issues still in flux?

Special emphasis should be placed on this issue in light of the Ceballos case and Executive Order 14074. FLETC states that "officers should avoid intentionally and unreasonably placing themselves in positions in which they have no alternative to using deadly force."

Three preliminary conditions "set the stage" for de-escalation. They are, *Discretionary Time, Space* including distance, barriers and cover, and *Containment*. What are the benefits of each one?

Time: *Increasing time* allows proactive rather than reactive decisions.

Good communication/rapport building is a function of adequate time, suspect reciprocity and a safe environment for the officer (E-1), the public (E-2), and the suspect (E-3). (Allison et. al. (2014) Increasing time (slowing things down), absent exigent circumstances, allows for *ICEN: Isolate, Contain, Evacuate, and Negotiate* (an important element of the *pre-suasion checklist*).

Space: Remember the Ceballos case: recklessly diminishing space may inadvertently increase the likelihood of the use of force and result in the retrospective denial (by the court) of qualified immunity. Again, we consider *The Force Science© Respons-ability Zone*. Every effort should be made to maintain space and utilize cover, concealment and physical barriers.

Distance: The goal of obtaining reasonable *Distance* and a *Containment Zone* is to limit the subject to a specific area. In establishing the zone, we wish to remove the public and weapons of opportunity from the containment area and attempt to bring the subject "back to the officer(s)" rather than enter the subject's area of familiarity if possible. The goal is to maximize discretionary time and increase the distance it would take for a suspect to attack the officer(s) or the public.

This may also allow time to understand why the subject may be non-compliant in the first place.

Of course, basic organization of an officer's "team" response may be necessary. Some simple roles would include assigning *contact and cover officers* where the contact officer does the communicating. More elaborate roles might include an arrest team, k-9 unit, medical team, less lethal equipment, etc. Understanding *when* de-escalation is an appropriate tactic is important. In exigency, discretionary time may be limited or absent. SFPD CIT (2020) reported that 43/51 (84%) of critical incidents had little or no discretionary time. 35% were classified "suicide by cop" significantly compressing time frames. The following year, SFPD (2021) reported that 50% of force incidents had no discretionary time. The other 50% of mental health related calls had only limited discretionary time. This adds up to *100% of mental health related calls for service in 2021 having limited or no discretionary time.* The takeaway message from this data is that Graham (SIRF) Factors, including the immediacy of the threat become more important and considering/*preparing for as many Presuasion Elements as possible before you arrive* at the scene can only help as you may not have time to prepare for them when you arrive. If you decide that de-escalation techniques are appropriate, how can this be effectively communicated? Of course, books have been written and courses have been developed to address this critically important and difficult topic. Verbal Judo© written by George Thompson and the concepts of empathy, sympathy and active listening have been discussed.

Vecchi outlined a sequential communication strategy he named *The Behavioral Influence Stairway Model (fig.5).* (60) (61)

This 5 step communication strategy designed to "effect behavioral change in other people" includes:

1. *Contacting the suspect;* a single officer should handle direct communications with the suspect.

2. *Demonstrating empathy; body language should match verbal language.* Remember the adage, "verbal communication is only 6% words."

3. *Developing rapport;* Are there "vanilla" topics about which you might find common ground?

4. *Using directive communication*; including logical, emotional, or characterological persuasions to bolster self-worth or avoid shame.

5. *Influencing behavioral change.*

Discretionary Time is necessary to successfully ascend the stairway. Please don't skip any steps climbing the stairway. Spending more, rather than less time in each step and/or repeating steps is recommended if there is any question about making an *active listening* connection. Getting training in all these persuasion techniques in a recommended course is highly recommended if it is available to you. See Fig. 5.

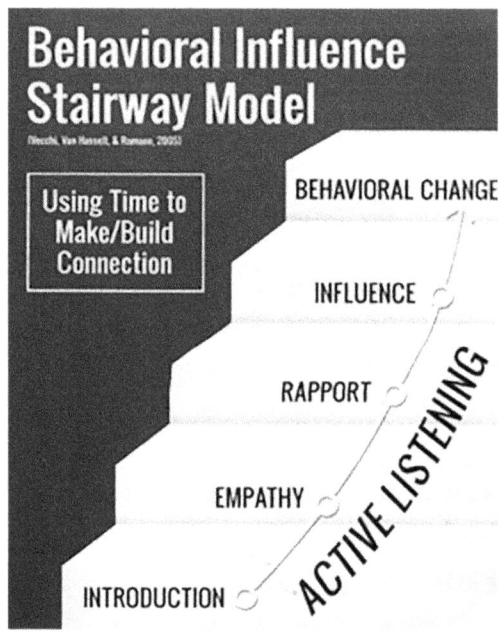

Fig. 5: The Behavioral Influence Stairway Model [60][61]

Finally, how do you incorporate de-escalation principles into written and oral reporting that Force Science calls *Post-suasion Principles?* To simply summarize their essence, try to *incorporate all the Force Science Pre-suasion and FLETC SIRF (Graham) factors* in the officer's written and verbal reporting. Consider obtaining 2 sleep cycles prior to submitting these reports if possible. You're painting a picture; make it a masterpiece!

Summary

In a stressful decision making situation one asks oneself if winning is possible. To do this, we weigh the pluses and minuses. The Biopsychosocial Theory of Challenge and Threat dictates to what degree we are challenged or threatened. What similar situations have we encountered in the past that have been successful? Our neural pathways will then be a mixture of cognitive top down or emotional bottom up thinking with the hormonal and physiological changes accompanying each decision path. The advance preparations we have made and the "expert" training we have received will provide added resources to the mix. Automaticity of actions will help free our appropriate attention towards appreciating important external cues. We hopefully will then act most efficiently and appropriately to resolve the problem.

Finally, always remember that the decision to think rationally is a conscious one. For example, I was alone in the operating room late one night with a patient who had traumatically dislocated all the small bones of his hand: a bag of marbles. Like a puzzle, they needed to be reassembled in their proper position and alignment. I had never seen or done that before. I became terrified I might fail. There was no back up. I felt my heart start to pound and my brow start to sweat. If I couldn't reconstruct the anatomy, the patient would lose his hand. I consciously told myself I couldn't allow that to happen. How to proceed? Possibly, realigning several bones at a time and then joining the groups together? That was working! I felt myself gaining emotional control and thinking more clearly. Cognitive thought was dominating and the hand was saved. Everything we have discussed in this chapter played a role in "winning" that night. As in the parable I recounted at the start of our adventure, hopefully the blind man could now "see the elephant."

1. https://www.artofmanliness.com/character/behavior/ooda-loop
2. Howe, Paul-Leadership and Training for the Fight, Skyhorse Publishing, 2011 p. 25
3. ibid. Howe, p. 38
4. op.cit. McKay
5. ibid., McKay
6. op.cit. Howe p. 37
7. Realistic De-Escalation- Kleim, V., www.forcescience.com, Force Science News, March 2020
8. Lewinski, William- New Research on Vision and Emotional Regulation for Effective Performance, Force Science News www.forcescience.com 12/8/21
9. Control of Visual Attention during the Baseball Free Throw-Vickers, J.N. American Journal of Sports Medicine, 24, (6th suppl.), s93-s97. 1996
10. Vickers, J.N. - Perception, Cognition and Decision Training: The Quiet Eye in Action, Human Kinetics pub., 2007 p.20
11. Ward, B.-The Eye and Seeing, Franklin Watts, London 1981 p. 16.
12. Gordan et. al.,World J Cardiol, 4/26; 7(4):204
13. ibid Gordon et.al.
14. ibid Gordon et.al.
15. ibid p.12
16. ibid. p.22

17. Milner, A.D. and Goodale, M.A. (2007) The Visual Brain in Action (2nd ed.) Oxford Psychology Series, 27, New York: Oxford University Press

18. Corbetta, M., Patel, G. and Shulman, G.L. (2008) The Reorienting System of the Human Brain: From Environment to Theory of Mind. Neuron, 58(3), 306-324

19. ibid. p. 306-324

20. Cavanagh, J.F. and Frank, M.J. (2014). Frontal Theta as a Mechanism for Cognitive Control. Trends in Cognitive Science, 18(8), pp. 414-421

21. Op. Cit. Vickers S93-S97

22. Mann, D.T.Y., Wright, A., & Janelle, C.M. (2016) Quiet Eye: The Efficiency Paradox- comment on Vickers. Current Issues in Sport Science, 1(1)

23. Cavanagh, J.F. and Frank, M.J. (2014). Frontal Theta as a Mechanism for Cognitive Control. Trends in Cognitive Science, 18(8), pp. 414-421

24. The Role of Mental Processes in Elite Sports Performance-Vickers, J.N. & Williams, M.A. (2019, The Oxford Research Encyclopedia, Sports and Performance, Oxford University Press

25. Seery, Mark-The Biospsychosocial Model of Challenge and Threat, Social and Personality Psychology Compass/Volume 7, Issue 9/ p.637-653, 9/2013

26. Folkman, S., Lazarus, R. S., Dunkel-Schetter, C., DeLongis, A., & Gruen, R. J. 1986. Dynamics of a stressful encounter: Cognitive appraisal, coping, and encounter outcomes. Journal of Personality and Social Psychology, 50, 992-1003

27. ibid. Folkman et.al.

28. Blascovich, J., & Tomaka, J. (1996). The biopsychosocial model of arousal regulation. Advances in Experimental Social Psychology, 28, 1-51.

29. Seery, M. D. (2011). Challenge or threat? Cardiovascular indexes of resilience and vulnerability to potential stress in humans. Neuroscience & Biobehavioral Reviews, 35, 1603-1610

30. Op. cit. Blascovich and Tenaka, 1996

31. Blascovich, J., Seery, M. D., Mugridge, C. A., Norris, R. K., & Weisbuch, M., Predicting athletic performance from cardiovascular indexes of challenge and threat. Journal of Experimental Social Psychology, 40, 683-688, 2004

32. Mendes, W. B., Blascovich, J., Lickel, B., & Hunter, S. (2002). Challenge and threat during social interactions with White and Black men. Personality and Social Psychology Bulletin, 28, 939-952

33. Seery, M. D., Weisbuch, M., & Blascovich, J. (2009). Something to gain, something to lose: The cardiovascular consequences of outcome framing. International Journal of Psychophysiology, 73, 308-312

34. Blascovich, J., Mendes, W. B., Hunter, S. B., Lickel, B., & Kowai-Bell, N., 2001, Perceiver threat in social interactions with stigmatized others. Journal of Personality and Social Psychology, 80, 253- 267

35. ibid. Vickers and Williams

36. Cavanagh J.F., and Frank, M.J. (2014) Frontal Theta as a Mechanism for Cognitive Control. Trends in Cognitive Sciences 18(8) pp. 414-421 Elsevier

37. Cooke, A. (2013). Readying the Head and Steadying the Heart: A Review of Cortical and Cardiac Studies of Preparation for Action in Sport. International Review of Sport and Exercise Physiology, 6(1), pp. 122-138

38. Op. Cit. Vickers and Williams

39. Op. Cit. Cavanaugh and Frank

40. Corbetta M. And Shulman, G.L. (2002) Control of goal directed and stimulus driven- attention in the brain. Nature Reviews Neuroscience, 3, 201-215

41. Smith, E.E., and Jonides, J. (1999). Storage and executive processes in the frontal lobes. Science, 283, 1657-1661

42. Bar-Haim, Y., Lamy, D., Bakersmans-Kranenburg, M.J., and van Ijzendoorn, M.H. (2007) Threat related attentional bias in anxious and nonanxious individuals: A meta-analytic study. Psychologu Bulletin, 133, 1-24

43. ibid., Bar-Haim, 2007

44. Hallet, P.E., (1978) Primary and secondary saccades to goals defined by instructions. Vision Research, 18, 1279-1296

45. Aveni, T.-A Critical Analysis of Police Shootings Under Ambiguous Circumstances, The Police Policy Studies Council Feb. 9, 2008

46. Academy Sharing Knowledge {ASK} Talks with Gary Klein, 2013

47. Stephens, D- Understanding the OODA Loop, Police Magazine 12/13

48. Klein, G. - A recognition primed decision (RPD) model of rapid decision making. Decision making in action, Models and methods, 5(4) pp. 138-147 1993

49. Hayes, A.-Game Theory, www.investopedia.com 9/29/22

50. Mann, D., Coombes, S.A., Mousseau, M.B., and Janelle, C.H.-Quiet Eye and the Bereitschaftspotential: visuomotor mechanisms of expert motor performance. Cogn Process, 12(3), pp. 223-234

51. Kleim, V. - U.S. Marshals Become Leader(s) in Modern Police Training, Force Science News, https://www.forcescience.com 6/28/22

52. https://www.forcescience.com/2023/09/heart-rates-performance-and-high-fidelity-training

53. https://www. Forcescience.com/2008/08/are-your-gaze-control-and-scan-pattern-linked-to your performance

54. Arble, E., Daughtery A.M. and Arnetz, B. (2019) Differential Effects of Physiological Arousal Following Acute Stress on Police Officer Performance in a Simulated Critical Incident. Front. Psychol. 10:759, doi 10.3389/fpsyg.2019.00759

55. https://www.forcescience.com/2019/05/is-heart-rate-a-predictor-of-police-officer-performance

56. https://www.forcescience.com/2022/08/top-experts-work-with-force-science-to-advance-police- related-research

57. Robert R. Horn, William J. Lewinski, Gustavo Sandri Heidner, Joshua Lawton, Craig Allen, Michael

W. Albin and Nicholas P. Murray (30 Nov 2023): Assessing between-officer variability in responses to a live-acted deadly force encounter as a window to the effectiveness of training and experience course, Ergonomics, DOI: 10.1080/00140139.20232278416

58. https://www.forcescience.com/2023/09/heart-rates-performance-and-high-fidelity-training

59. https://www.forcescience.com2023/12/accelerated-heart-rates-and-elite-performance

60. Ireland, C. A., & Vecchi, G. M. (2009). The Behavioral Influence Stairway Model (BISM): a framework for managing terrorist crisis situations? Behavioral Sciences of Terrorism and Political Aggression, 1(3), 203–218. https://doi.org/10.1080/19434470903017722

61. https://www.researchgate.net/figure/The-Behavioural-Influence-Stairway-Model-Vecchi-Van-Hasselt-Romano-2005_fig2_312458393

62. Azar-Dickens, John-Realistic De-escalation Instructor Course, Force Science Institute, 2022, p. 13.

63. Azar-Dickens, J. (2025), THE TEB MODEL, A new approach to crisis assessment and Intervention, Book logix, Alpharetta, Georgia, pp.22

Drug Related Risks

Martin Greenberg, MD

Drug related risks for law enforcement and the rest of us have dramatically changed in the last twenty years. Back then, the diagnosis of HIV or Hepatitis C was a death sentence. For law enforcement, needle sticks during frisks or body searches were the main culprits. In medicine, needle sticks handling improperly disposed sharps or in accidents suffered during procedures were most commonly involved. The fear of exposure to infected bodily fluids was equally concerning. Making matters worse, there is no glove protection against needle sticks. Aerosolized droplet infection through splatter, irrigation or drilling in the operating room was a further concern. "Space suits" were worn by operating room staff to filter inspired air in known HIV cases but they limited any use of magnification in hand or plastic surgery. This created both equity and standard of care issues as magnification using a microscope or eyeglass "loupes" became impossible using a spacesuit helmet. Special procedures were instituted in passing sharp instruments in the OR to avoid direct handoffs. Water pic type instruments called "pulse lavage" were banned. We were scared. Our hospital had an AIDS (autoimmune deficiency syndrome) unit where patients were basically sent to die. A sign at the entrance proclaimed "The Teddy Bear Trail" that seemed wildly inappropriate even then. A quilt's squares on the wall memorialized patients who had passed. Many immunocompromised patients developed a skin cancer called *Kaposi Sarcoma*. The smell of rotting flesh pervaded the ward. That smell is something one never forgets.

Luckily, times have changed since then. Today, it's common knowledge that type C (aka non-A/non-B) hepatitis is a curable problem. HIV disease can be indefinitely controlled at non-detectable levels. If treated, it will not progress to full blown AIDS. Rather than infections, today's life threatening drug related risks revolve around fentanyl poisoning.

Fentanyl is a synthetic opioid that was synthesized as a pain killer and as an anesthetic in 1959. It is legally manufactured here in the United States and is in current medical practice. A portion of this licit drug production is diverted through theft, fraudulent prescriptions, and illicit distribution. There were approximately 2,600 drug overdose deaths in 2012 but the number has dramatically risen yearly since then. (1) Fentanyl can be ingested in many ways as a pill, powder or liquid including injection, sniffing, snorting, smoking or taken orally via tablets, pills, effervescent buccal tablets (Fentora®), nasal sprays, fentanyl "lollipops" (actiq®) or sublingual tabs (Abstral®). (2) Duragesic® fentanyl patches are used as a strong transdermal analgesic. Even discarded patches may be reused in some form for their residual opiate. Its effects are identical to other opioids including analgesia, euphoria, sedation, pinpoint pupils and decreased respiration.

Signs of overdose include pinpoint pupils, decreased or unconsciousness and respiratory failure potentially leading to death. Fentanyl has many street names including Tango and Cash, Jackpot, China Town, Murder 8, Goodfellas, King Ivory and China Girl. (3) It may be clandestinely manufactured as a powder that can be cut (mixed) with other illicit drugs such as heroin, cocaine and even marijuana to amplify their effect or as "fake" (counterfeit) tablets mimicking other prescription opioids. These pills may be nearly identical to regular prescription meds. Xanax, Adderall and Oxycodone are commonly copied and are ordered by students and young adults over social media and internet sites using emoji code symbols. (4) The United States Controlled Substances Act of 1970 lists Fentanyl as a Schedule II controlled substance. Drugs in this category are dangerous with a high abuse potential and include Vicodin®, methadone, methamphetamine, Dilaudid®, Demerol®, oxycodone, Adderall® and Ritalin®. (5) Fentanyl is roughly 100 times more potent than morphine. (6) 2 mg. of fentanyl may be a lethal human dose. The Drug Enforcement Administration (DEA) states that 42% of illicit pills tested for fentanyl contained at least this lethal concentration. Fentanyl's customary powder one kg. distribution weight could potentially kill 500,000 people. (7) It is colorless, odorless and tasteless so it's impossible to know if fentanyl contamination is present in other non-prescription purchased drugs. 56,000 overdose deaths involving synthetic opioids occurred in 2020 (8) and 1 year later increased 55.6%. (9) Because fentanyl is frequently ingested inadvertently with other drugs the term poisoning rather than overdose is more accurate.

"A controlled substance analog is a substance which is intended for human consumption and is structurally or pharmacologically substantially similar to or is represented as being similar to a Schedule I or Schedule II substance and is not an approved medication in the United States." (10) Fentanyl analogs are drugs similar in chemical composition to Fentanyl. They include acetylfentanyl, furanylfentanyl and carfentanyl and are not detected with fentanyl detection tests. Carfentanyl is about 10,000 times more potent than morphine. (11) Fentanyl has become popular because it is inexpensive and boosts the euphoric and addictive effects of other controlled drugs. Many other synthetic opioids may have the same effect. A rising star in this category is U-47700. Its street names are "U4," "pink" or "pinky." It is white or light pink in color and is used as a powder or pills. (12)

In 2022, a number of mass fentanyl poisonings have been reported in our country. The DEA defines a mass overdose as three or more incidents related in time and location. Between February 28, 2022, and March 3, 2022, a total of seven incidents around the United States involving fifty-eight victims resulted in twenty-nine deaths. All of these poisonings involved opiates including oxycodone, cocaine and/or methamphetamine laced with fentanyl. (13)

Largely because of our open southern border and deteriorating geopolitics with China, the illicit importation of fentanyl through Mexico has become an increasing problem. Between July 2021 and June 2022, almost 73,000 opioid overdose (poisoning) deaths mostly related to fentanyl and its analogs occurred in our country. The history of Chinese importation of fentanyl and subsequent supplying of fentanyl precursors worldwide is a saga unto itself. Due to worldwide concern regarding fentanyl abuse, the United Nations (U.N.) placed the drug under its control in 1964. As we mentioned, the Controlled Substance Act (CSA) of 1970 regulates the domestic use of fentanyl. Multiple U.N. conventions since then have expanded the number of fentanyl analogs (30) to be placed under international control. The U.N. Convention Against Illicit Traffic in Narcotic Drugs and Psychotropic Substances of 1988 updated prior conventions and created lists of illicit drugs to be regulated (14) that did not include fentanyl precursors. In 2017, N-Phenethyl-4-piperidone (NPP) and 4-Anilino-N-phenethylpiperidone (ANPP) were added to Table 1 for the first time. The People's Republic of China (PRC) complied and instituted domestic controls in the next year. (15) Table 1, updated as of November 23, 2022, includes these precursors and 3 more; N-Phenyl-4piperidinamine (4-AP), tert-Butyl 4-(phenylamino) piperidine-1-carboxylate (boc-4-AP) and norfentanyl. (16) Unfortunately, there are over 150 fentanyl analogs with no known medical applications. (17) It is not documented that the PRC has complied with this latest Table 1 update. Currently, Mexican cartels, also termed Transnational Criminal Organizations (TCOs) receive fentanyl precursors from China to synthesize the final product(s) and deliver them to the United States. Controlling fentanyl synthesis requires controlling its precursor chemicals. A synthetic organic chemistry process called the *Siegfried* method was most commonly used in this process. A second route, the *Janssen* method, was felt by the DEA to be less popular as it was more technically involved. The Siegfried method required NPP and ANPP precursors that were both under U.S. domestic control by 2010. The PRC controlled these precursors in 2018. Presumably for this reason, the Janssen method using benzylfentanyl (not a controlled substance at the time) became more popular. Benzylfentanyl is converted to norfentanyl in a single step and then to fentanyl in a second step. Another unlisted fentanyl precursor becoming more commonly discovered in seizures at Mexican ports is 4-anilinopiperidine. This chemical can be converted to ANPP in a one-1 step process compared to the two-2 step reaction needed to convert NPP to ANPP. Thus, in 2020 the DEA declared a rule including benzylfentanyl and 4-anilinopiperidine in list one chemicals. (18) There has been at best mixed success collaborating with the PRC controlling fentanyl precursor sales. Some small victories include the PRC in 2019 adding all fentanyl related substances to its "Supplementary List of Controlled Narcotic Drugs and Psychotropic Substances with Non-Medical Use." This resulted in eliminating the direct importation of fentanyl and its analogs by July, 2022. Joint U.S.-PRC investigations resulted in conviction of a number of Chinese drug traffickers in China. Some seizures of these controlled substances in the Western Hemisphere resulted from Chinese information. The DEA was also allowed to maintain satellite offices in 4 Chinese cities. PRC Cooperation was limited by the U.S government's criticism of human rights violations in the Xinjiang Uyghur Autonomous Region, the PRC's Ministry of Public Security's (MPS) involvement in international drug exportation, and House of Representatives Speaker Nancy Pelosi's visit to Taiwan on August 4, 2022. (19) Furthermore, there is only minimal cooperation between the PRC and Mexican law enforcement that represents the major route of fentanyl precursors into Mexico where the final product is synthesized. Evidence exists of Chinese transnational criminal organizations in Mexico also involved in money laundering and "illicit value transfers" including the bartering of wildlife for fentanyl precursors. (20)

To complicate matters, Xylazine® (Rompum®, AnaSed®, Sedazine®) a non-opiate sedative, analgesic and muscle relaxant used in prescription veterinary medicine, has become increasingly popular as an adulterant in heroin, cocaine and fentanyl street drugs. It's produced as a clear liquid in 20, 100 and 300mg/ml concentrations. It is frequently also seen in the combination of heroin, cocaine and/or fentanyl known as a speedball. Xylazine can be smoked, snorted, ingested, inhaled or injected. As an alpha agonist drug, it inhibits the release of dopamine and norepinephrine at the neural synaptic level resulting in central nervous system depression. Xylazine potentiates the effects of the opiates with which it is mixed. It is legitimately sold in the United States and it is not a controlled substance. Xylazine is not approved for human use and even trace blood levels may prove fatal. It can be purchased online from Chinese sources for only $6-20 per kilogram and its low price allows its adulteration with opiates by illicit drug manufacturers increasing profits and their drug's effect. Used independently, Xylazine has many of the same effects as opioids and has a more persistent effect. In veterinary practice, it presents a one-to-four-hour duration of action in animals but in humans its duration is indeterminate. It cannot be detected in routine drug screening. The Drug Enforcement Administration has documented its presence in all four U.S. census regions and its prevalence has increased from 2020-2021. Just in the South, it has increased 193% during this period. The symptoms of its presence are basically the same as with opiates. Since it potentiates opiate effects, it increases the likelihood of a potentially fatal opiate overdose when combined with them. (21) As Xylazine cannot be identified on standard drug screens, its presence is underreported. However, from 2015-2020, the percentage of reported fatal drug overdoses involving Xylazine increased from two to twenty-six percent in Pennsylvania and nineteen percent in Maryland during 2021. Also known as "tranq," "tranq dope," or "sleep cut," it may cause severe skin ulcers and abscesses that may even lead to amputation. Its effects have been described as "zombification" due to its victims' zombie-like wanderings. It is especially prevalent in Puerto Rico where it is called "Anestecia de Caballo." The initial increase in blood pressure (hypertension) with its use may be followed by a precipitous drop so it is not recommended to aggressively treat the drug's hypertensive side effect for this reason. (22) Xylazine poisoning will continue to increase and only supportive medical care for humans is currently available.

Despite this gloomy situation, opioid overdoses and poisoning can be successfully treated using Naloxone (Narcan®). Naloxone is a safe, over the counter (OTC) medication that blocks opioid's effects. It is available as an injection or nasal spray. It works in two to three minutes if used promptly but multiple doses are usually needed with fentanyl poisoning. (23) It has no negative effects if symptoms are due to non-opiate causes. Specific medical training is not required to administer Naloxone. It will not reverse the opiate like effects of Xylazine but it may treat the effects of concomitantly used opiates. I have personally used ten nasal spray injections to reverse fentanyl's effects. Good Samaritan Laws generally exist in most states to protect both the poisoning victim and those helping them. Of course, immediately call 911 and remain with the victim until help arrives. If, for some reason help does not arrive, monitoring the victim for four hours is recommended. (24) Most fire and law enforcement agencies have Naloxone training and availability. Considering the prevalence of fentanyl poisoning in all our communities, it may be wise to have this medication personally available. It may be a simple way to save a life.

REFERENCES

1. DEA Drug factsheet, Fentanyl www.getsmartaboutdrugs.com)
2. April, 2020; Drugs of Abuse, A DEA Resource Guide, 2020, p. 50
3. ibid. Drugs of Abuse p. 50
4. https://www.dea.gov/fake-pills, 8/22
5. https://dea.gov/drug-information/drug-scheduling p.2
6. https://www.dea.gov/resources/facts-about-fentanyl, p.1
7. ibid. p.2
8. https://www.cdc.gov/drug overdose, p.1
9. Op. Cit. dea.gov. p.3
10. https://www.dea.gov/drug-scheduling
11. O'Donnell, J. Gladden, RM, Mattson, CL, Karlisa, M. Notes from the Field: Overdose Deaths with Carfentanyl and other Fentanyl Analogs Detected- 10 States, July, 2016-June, 2017
12. https://www.dea.gov/drug-information/drug-scheduling
13. https://www.dea.gov/mass-overdose-letter
14. https://www.crsreports.congress.gov.)
15. ibid. https://www.crsreports.congress.gov.)
16. ibid. https://www.crsreports.congress.gov.)
17. https://www.documents-dds-ny.un.org.)
18. Op. Cit. https://crsreports.congress.gov
19. https://www.federalregister.gov/documents/2020/04/15/2020-07064;
20. https://www.regulations.gov/docket/DEA-2020-0012
21. Op. Cit. https://www.crsreports.congress.gov.)
22. https://www.dea.gov/DEAintelligenceproducts/PRB-2022-25
23. https://www.nisa.nih.gov/research-topics/xylazine
24. https://www.brookings.edu/research/china-and-synthetic-drugs-control-fentanyl- methamphetamines-and-precursors.
25. https://www.harmreduction to.ca/naloxone)

A Brief Firearms Primer and Medical Ballistics

Martin Greenberg, MD

Scenario
The tactical team is called out to a barricade where a sniper is on a shooting spree with a scoped rifle from an upper floor window of a building on a narrow urban street. Multiple victims are reported. EMS vehicles cannot respond as they are in the field of fire. The street is isolated. Negotiators arrive but cannot communicate with the suspect. Tactical team members don their level IIIA tactical vests and helmets. They respond to the scene and stage at the command center around the blind B-C corner of the building. Marksmen take positions on rooftops surrounding the barricade but lack a clear view of the suspect because of the narrow street. The only building entry is on the A-B side in view of the sniper. The team decides to deploy in their assault vehicle with level IV armor. Proceeding down the street with eleven officers in the vehicle and seven walking behind, they immediately take fire. Multiple rounds hit the vehicle without apparent effect. An officer behind the advancing bear is hit in the helmet and immediately goes down. The vehicle reverses and retrieves the injured officer. The vehicle then backs up to the front door and empties

the eleven plus six team members into the building. Two teams then simultaneously clear the building. The apartment is reached and dynamically entered. The perpetrator is able to fire a handgun at the point officer, striking him in the center of his vest. Responding .223 caliber gunfire strikes the perpetrator's torso center mass in her ballistic vest and immediately immobilizes her. The point officer suffers only a chest wall contusion from the handgun round.

Introduction

We are all familiar with the Texas clock tower massacre when on August 1, 1966, ex-military marksman and University of Texas student Charles Whitman wreaked havoc from an elevated position with a high-powered, scoped rifle killing fourteen people and wounding more than thirty. This episode is credited to be a motivating factor for developing the modern SWAT team concept. Possibly readers have seen the movie *Phone Booth* (2002) where a sniper holds a hostage at bay from a distance. To understand the impressive level of destruction a single skilled rifleman can generate, we must understand the topic of ballistics. The American Heritage Dictionary defines ballistics as "The study of the firing, flight and effects of ammunition." (1) The obvious questions our scenario raises and which we hope to clarify here include what is the difference between handgun and rifle rounds, what type of protection does soft or hard armor provide, what types of gunshot injuries are most serious and how should they be treated? We will also address the issue of how we can avoid becoming the victims of gunshot trauma.

Nomenclature

A basic introduction to the various classes of handguns and long guns is needed to define the terms we will be using in the remainder of this discussion. Officers may already be familiar with this section of information. Basic handgun types include revolvers, semiautomatic pistols, single shot and multiple fixed barrel weapons. The revolver is the most common type of handgun in our country. It contains a rotating cylinder with five to eight chambers for ammunition. Single action revolvers require manually cocking the weapon's hammer after firing each shot. The classic single action revolver is the cowboy western six-gun that Samuel Colt invented in 1835. Double action revolvers rotate the cylinder and fire each time the trigger is pulled. They may also be manually cocked and fired. Solid frame (western style) revolvers are loaded sequentially through a cylinder gate. In break-top revolvers, the cylinder and barrel swing forward as a unit. Although common in Britain, this type of revolver is rare in the United States. The swing-out cylinder type of revolver is overwhelmingly the most common revolver we may encounter. Interestingly, the cylinder may revolve clockwise (Colt brand) or counterclockwise (Smith and Wesson brand). Semiautomatic, auto-loading pistols have an ammunition magazine in the grip of the pistol. Single action (SA) pistols such as the classic Colt Model 1911 type weapons require cocking before firing the first shot. Double action (DA) pistols fire the first shot by squeezing the trigger with a "heavy" pull followed by hammer back, "light" single action type firing. Double action only (DAO) pistols fire with the same heavier, hammer (or striker) down trigger pull for every shot. Semiautomatic pistols and rifles function through blowback, delayed blowback or recoil methods. In the first two, expanding gas from burning cartridge powder forces the unlocked pistol slide rearward causing empty cartridge case ejection and reloading. In recoil operated weapons (such as the popular Benelli shotgun) recoil inertia causes the locked bolt to unlock and move rearward. "Low capacity" pistol magazines offer about up to 10 rounds while "high-capacity" magazines offer twelve to over twenty rounds. Some autoloaders are equipped with a magazine safety that prevents firing the weapon with the magazine removed. A grip, manual, trigger safety or no safety at all may be present in modern autoloaders. Revolvers do not generally possess factory installed safeties although many have firing pin transfer bars to prevent discharge if dropped. Most law enforcement agencies today mandate high-capacity semiautomatic pistols as duty weapons although revolver use still occurs on duty and even more commonly off duty.

A rifle is a shoulder fired weapon with a rifled (not smooth) barrel. Federal law mandates that civilian rifle barrels be at least 16" long. Shorter barrels may be present on military/law enforcement models. Rifles may be single shot, bolt action, lever action, pump action or auto-loading. Bolt action rifles require manually activating a bolt which extracts the spent casing and loads a new round. Lever action rifles are the classic cowboy western guns we saw, for example, in the old T.V. series *The Rifleman.* These weapons are still in wide use and can be amazingly effective in skilled hands (recall how many miscreants Lucas McCain disposed of each week)! Pump action rifles require moving a barrel mounted slide to the rear to perform the ejection/loading cycle. Semi-automatic rifles function in the manner described above for pistols. High-capacity semi-automatic rifle magazines may contain up to thirty rounds and magazine drums may house up to 100 cartridges.

A shotgun is a shoulder fired weapon that has a smooth bore and fires pellets from shot-shells or solid slugs. The minimum legal barrel length is 18." Shotguns may be double barreled in "side by side" or "over and under" configurations. Firing mechanisms similarly include the single shot, pump action, semi-automatic, and less commonly lever or bolt action. A submachine gun is magazine fed and fires multiple pistol caliber rounds with each trigger pull. A machine gun is a shoulder mounted or crew served weapon capable of firing multiple center fire rifle rounds with each trigger pull. It is either magazine or belt fed.

Ammunition nomenclature can be quite confusing. Handgun and rifle barrels have spiral grooves throughout their length called "rifling." The areas between the rifling grooves are called "lands." The purpose of rifling is to make bullets leaving the barrel spin. The caliber of an American weapon is the measured internal diameter of the barrel from land to land. However, these measurements are inconsistent with other descriptive parameters frequently used such as bullet or groove diameter. Examples of such inconsistencies include both the .30-06 and .308 Winchester rounds having a diameter of .308 inches. The ".06" in .30-06 refers to the date of introduction of the round. Black powder cartridges may be named for the bullet diameter, the bullet weight, or the original black powder charge. ".45-70-405" denotes a .45-inch diameter bullet weighing 405 grains propelled by a seventy-grain black powder charge. Here, "grains" denote powder weight rather than granule numbers while in modern terminology grains refer to bullet weight. Even old smokeless powder cartridges may be designated this way. Thus, the over one hundred-year-old .30-.30 round has a .308" diameter bullet and was loaded with thirty grains of powder. A modern source of confusion is exemplified by comparison of the .38 Special and .357 Magnum rounds. These rounds have the same diameter bullets, but the magnum round has a longer case with more powder resulting in a more powerful cartridge. For this reason, .357 ammunition should never be fired from a .38 Special caliber revolver but a .357 revolver may fire all .38 Special caliber rounds. The more logical European system denotes the bullet diameter and the case length in mm. The classic American .308 Winchester cartridge translates to 7.62 (bullet diameter) x 51mm (case length). The AK-47 cartridge is a "short" (German: "kurz") .308 or 7.62 x 39 mm. Magnum classification denotes an extra powerful loading of a standard existing cartridge. A wildcat round is a specialty cartridge not in general production. Shotgun rounds (shot shells) are described using "gauge" with lower numbers indicating larger sizes. Common shotgun gauges in descending size order are

10, 12, 20, 28, and 410. The twelve-gauge shotgun is the most popular size hunting weapon and the exclusive size for the tactical/combat shotgun. Shot shells are currently filled with synthetic wadding and a variable number of pellets. The pellets may be either birdshot or larger buckshot. Buckshot pellets are numbered for size. The most common size is "00" or "double 0" (pronounced "ought") buck. Each "00" pellet is .32 caliber diameter. Twelve-gauge shells contain eight to twelve "00" pellets. Tactical shot shells usually contain eight to nine pellets with a lighter powder load for lower recoil. Shotgun "slugs" are solid projectiles that may take several shapes and are also "gauged." A .410 gauge shot shell is .45 caliber in diameter while a twelve-gauge slug or shot shell has a .70 caliber diameter.

A cartridge consists of a brass or aluminum case with a primer at its base filled with gunpowder and topped by some type of bullet. Pistol cartridge cases usually have straight walls with the exception of the .357 Sig round which is bottlenecked at the top. Most rifle cases are bottlenecked to improve cartridge feeding and to pack the maximum amount of powder into the case. (2) The base of a cartridge is called its head and may have several configurations to allow its extraction from the weapon's chamber. Most cartridges are rimmed, semi-rimmed or rimless. Civilian cartridges are marked with a head stamp stating the caliber and manufacturer. Military head stamps include the manufacturers code or initials and the two-digit year of production. A primer is set in the center of the case head (centerfire) or in its rim (rim fire cartridges). *Primers may be of the Boxer or Berdan* type. The American Boxer primer has a sensitive explosive in a brass cup that is struck with the weapon's firing pin or striker causing the small explosion to enter the less sensitive powder section of the cartridge through a single flash hole. European Berdan primers have two flash holes. Pistol and rifle primers may be large or small. Magnum primers are larger to better ignite a larger amount of powder. Old primers were made of mercury that was toxic and corrosive. Current rifle primers are made of lead styphnate, barium nitrate and antimony sulfide. Rim fire primers may contain any or all of these compounds. Gunshot residue tests may detect the presence of these primer compounds. Black powder propellant is a mixture of charcoal, sulfur, and potassium nitrate. It burns with a dense, white smoke. In 1884, smokeless powder was invented using nitrocellulose and nitroglycerine. Powder flakes are shaped like discs, flakes, or cylinders. In 1933, Winchester introduced ball powder. These powder grains are colored pale green and may be seen in skin powder burns.

The history of bullets could easily be the subject of an entire book. Captain Charles Minie invented the first bullet of barrel diameter to effectively seal propellant gases. (3) This was a wedge-shaped bullet whose propellant gases expanded it to fit the barrel's rifling. Breech loading rifles with metallic cartridges and bullets the size of the barrel soon followed. Bullets may be either lead or metal jacketed. Lead bullets are compounded with tin, antimony, or both to increase their hardness and to decrease fouling of the weapon's barrel and action. Lead bullets may be lubricated and may have one or more cannelures (grooves) to attach to the cartridge or to hold lubricant. They may be also "gilded" with a thin copper/copper alloy coating. Four configurations are common. The wad cutter bullet is a flat-topped bullet designed for target shooting. The semi-wad cutter has a truncated cone with a flat top. The round nose bullet has a conical shape and the hollow-point is a semi-wad cutter with a recess in the tip to facilitate expansion upon contact. Lead bullets are not used in centerfire rifle ammunition as the high velocities generated would melt the lead. Jacketed ammunition is used in semiautomatic actions to minimize feeding and jamming problems. It has a steel or lead core covered by a "jacket" of copper, zinc, aluminum, or steel. Bullets may be fully or partially jacketed. All military ammunition has a full metal jacket. The five types of military bullets include ball ammunition with a lead or steel bullet, armor piercing rounds with a steel core, bright or dim tracer bullets that burn when fired, and armor piercing (AP) incendiary bullets that combine these last two types. High velocity ammunition is generally partially metal jacketed. Its lead core is exposed at the tip. The two common types of these partially or semi-jacketed bullets are the soft-point and hollow-point. The tip may be secondarily jacketed by aluminum (i.e., the Silvertip) and may have the different bullet shapes described above. The partial jacket may also be scalloped to encourage hollow-point expansion. A major recent focus of the ballistic industry has been to create the perfect bullet that will expand in a maximal and reliable manner regardless of the bullet caliber or short length of the barrel through which it is fired.

Ballistic Energy Transfer
Ballistics is the study of bullets in motion. Subtopics include interior ballistics (bullet motion in firearms), exterior ballistics (bullet motion after leaving the barrel) and terminal ballistics (bullets' effect upon targets). *For our purposes, wound ballistics is the terminal ballistic study of living tissue.* Remembering high school physics, all objects in motion have kinetic energy that becomes potential energy as the object stops moving. The total kinetic energy of an object when moving equals its total potential energy at rest. A slowing object gives off its kinetic energy to its surroundings. A rapidly decelerating bullet dumps its kinetic energy rapidly into the object it strikes. The more kinetic energy that is almost instantly expended, the more energy the target must instantly absorb. The amount of tissue damage imparted by a projectile is in part determined by its ability to transfer ballistic energy to living tissue exceeding that tissue's ability to absorb it. Kinetic energy is defined by the formula: Kinetic Energy (K.E.) = ½ Mass (M) x Velocity (V) squared. This means that if the weight of the bullet dou-

bles, so does the kinetic energy. If the projectile's velocity doubles, its kinetic energy quadruples. Kinetic energy is most dependent upon the velocity of the projectile. Of course, the bullet must be able to come to rest within the target to impart all its kinetic energy. Dr. Martin Fackler, the "father" of wound ballistics, feels that projectile velocity 2,000 ft. /sec. is the threshold for high energy level tissue destruction. He pioneered the use of the ten percent ballistic gelatin medium as having similar penetration characteristics as living tissue. If a round passes through the target making a small hole and continues to travel through several sheetrock walls in an urban setting, a dangerous situation arises. Considering the width of a possibly heavily clothed human torso, about 12-18" of penetration seems ideal to achieve maximal safe energy transfer. Depending upon the location of the entry wound and the path of the projectile within the body, different organs may be struck. The projectile's effects will be directly related to the involved organ systems, their vascularity and anatomic characteristics (solid vs. hollow and liquid vs. air vs. bone consistency). The actual hole the bullet makes throughout its trajectory through the body is called the permanent wound channel. However, the projectile is actually pushing tissue away from it as it imparts its kinetic energy creating a temporary cavitation that has a lifetime of only 5-10 msec. The size of this temporary cavity and the effect of its accompanying shock wave on surrounding tissue vary with the amount of kinetic energy transferred and the local tissue's elasticity and cohesiveness. Low velocity rounds (most handgun rounds) lack the ability to expand tissue beyond its elastic limit. High velocity rounds (most centerfire rifle rounds) impart adequate energy to exceed local tissue's elastic limit and cause the tissue to "explode" or shatter. This is one reason for the explosive effects caused by high velocity limited penetration ammunition. Dramatic local occurrences when centerfire rifle rounds enter tissue include tail splash where tissue is violently driven backwards, the formation of a temporary cavity up to thirty times the diameter of the permanent cavity, undulating local pressures of up to 200 atmospheres (atm.) and the sucking into the wound of foreign matter and damage to distant vital structures including blood vessels, nerves, and even bones. Density and elastic cohesiveness of involved organs are other important wounding factors. (4) For example, DeMaio states that muscle and liver have about the same density. Liver, however, has much less elasticity or cohesiveness than muscle. A projectile traversing muscle will usually leave only a permanent wound channel while one traversing liver will create an explosive effect similar to shooting a gallon plastic water jug. Lung being highly elastic may sustain only little damage by a traversing projectile. Minimum critical velocities of 2,625 to 2,953 ft. /sec. are associated with supersonic wound shock waves and the large temporary cavities noted above. Each bodily tissue may have a unique level of kinetic energy needed to exceed its elastic limit creating explosive effects. Bullet factors also affect the loss of kinetic energy. Yaw, or "the deviation of the bullet from its line of flight" (5) will increase the amount of tissue contact with the projectile and cause tumbling within the target. The high velocity bullet may also fragment in predictable ways as tumbling deceleration strains the bullet to its failure point and increasing the energy dump and wounding effects through multiple projectile paths. The caliber, shape, and construction (jacketed, semi-jacketed, or lead projectile) will also play a role. The critical speed for hollow-point expansion varies but starts at about 705ft. sec. (5) Shotgun rounds create high velocity wounds as the multiple pellets and packing from any gauge shot shell create a contaminated wound requiring debridement. In the most common shot shell, 00 (double 0) buck pellets each measure 32 caliber. Shot patterns generally disperse 1"/ft. of travel from the muzzle. More pellets on target mean more wounding effects. As a twelve-gauge round will have eight to twelve of these pellets, imagine being shot with eight to twelve "00" .32 caliber bullets simultaneously! Shotgun slugs (twelve-gauge = seventy caliber) create a low velocity injury pattern.

Entry and Exit Wounds
Gunshot wounds may be penetrating or perforating. Perforating wounds exit the target. In contact wounds, the muzzle of the weapon is in hard or soft contact with the skin. In hard contact wounds, the skin under the muzzle is tattooed. In soft contact wounds, gas escapes around the muzzle creating a ring of removable soot. Angled contact wounds have an oval configuration and a radial, fan shaped, soot pattern on the side opposite to the muzzle. The radial soot is temporary as in light contact wounds. Incomplete contact wounds occur when the muzzle is in incomplete contact with the skin. Gases and soot then escape radially through the muzzle/skin gap. Microscopic elements from all parts of the cartridge are found within the permanent channel. Near contact wounds occur when the muzzle is close to the skin. They have a baked-in, tattooed appearance with a temporary surrounding soot ring that may be radial if the trajectory is angled. Here, the radial soot-ring points towards the muzzle. This is the case when the muzzle/skin gap exceeds 10 mm. (6) Angled light contact wounds may be differentiated from angled near contact wounds as the latter has a tattooed component. This is an important forensic distinction in discovering the direction from which a bullet was fired. Intermediate range wounds exhibit the classic powder tattooing pattern. This pattern begins at about a 10 mm muzzle/skin gap. There is therefore a continuum of overlapping wound patterns from hard contact to intermediate types. The density and distribution of tattooing depend upon many factors including the angle of trajectory, the quality of the target skin and overlying clothing. In angled shots, the tattooing is denser on the "muzzle side" of the wound. Tattooing is colored red, orange, or brown and is an ante-mor-

tem (before death) finding. These are punctate abrasions, not burns, and their color is due to the body's reaction of bruising or bleeding. Shooting dead people at an intermediate range causes a gray or yellow powder tattoo. Tattooing is permanent and does not occur on palms or soles. The term "powder burn" refers back to black powder wounds where the deposited powder actually burned the skin setting overlying clothing ablaze! Neither powder tattooing nor soot deposition will occur beyond a muzzle/skin gap of about 30 cm. With distant wounds, only the mechanical action of the bullet on the skin will occur. Entry wounds are characterized by a red abrasion ring surrounding the bullet hole. A fresh abrasion ring appears moist and granular. Eccentric abrasion rings do not describe a bullet's trajectory. Exit wounds at any distance generally appear larger and more irregular than entry wounds. They lack an abrasion ring. The deformation and tumbling of a non-stabilized projectile in the body explains the irregular shape of the exit wound. Abraded exit wound margins may rarely occur when the exit skin is braced or "shored" against a surface such as sitting in a chair or lying on the floor. The bullet's shape also does not correlate with the size of the exit wound.

"One Shot Stops"
The search for the "magic" handgun round that will produce instant incapacitation has been the subject of great debate over the last twenty years. Clint Smith, a nationally celebrated firearms trainer and the director of Thunder Ranch in Lakeview, Oregon, put the entire debate into focus by stating, "The purpose of a handgun is to fight your way back to your long gun." Handguns are convenient and portable but may not always be effective man-stoppers. In 1992, Evan Marshall and Benton County, Indiana Sheriff's Department Cpl. Ed Sanow published Handgun Stopping Power. (7) Here, they assembled a large number of actual, well documented shootings organized by handgun load and determined what percentage

occurred through "one shot stops." The actual mechanism of the stop or its fatality was not documented.

The "best of class" for each caliber revealed: one shot stops
.380 ACP-Federal 90-gr. JHP:	65%;
.38 Special (2" barrel)-W-W 158-gr. LHP+P	67%
.38 Special (4" barrel)-W-W 158-gr. LHP+P	75%
Federal 9mm. 115-gr. JHP+P+	89%
.357 Magnum-Federal 125-gr. JHP	97%
.44 Special-Federal 200-gr. LHP	72%
.44 Magnum-W-W 210-gr. STHP	89%
.45 ACP- Federal 230-gr. Hydra-Shok	91%

Steve Fuller created a computer program with this data dubbed "the Fuller Index." He predicted that a round with a kinetic energy of around 650 ft./lbs. could be expected to produce a one shot stop.

However, since that time, it has been well determined that *the most common reaction to being shot barring a significant neurovascular injury is no reaction.* In the old west, a famous saying was *"havin' your ten."* This means that even after sustaining a mortal vascular injury an accomplished pistolero would have about ten seconds to return fire. Another well-known Clint Smith quote explaining this was, "Just because you got to shoot doesn't mean you won. It just means you had your turn."

Ballistic Gunshot Wound Protection
"Ballistic body armor is designed to defeat projectiles in motion." (8) The National Institute of Justice (N.I.J.) has defined ballistic vest threat levels designed to defeat specific rounds. Soft body armor is made from polyethylene fiber (Spectra made by Allied Signal Company), Aramids (Kevlar made by DuPont, and Twaron made by Azko-Nobel). Soft body armor is basically a ballistic resistant fabric available as concealable

or tactical armor. The following threat protection levels are available for soft armor:

Threat level IIA must defeat a 9 mm full metal jacketed Remington (9mm FMJ Rem) fired from a 4" barrel traveling at 1,090 ft./sec. and a .357 Mag. 158 gr. semi-jacketed soft point Remington (.357 SJSP Rem) fired from a 4" barrel traveling at 1,250 ft./sec. Other non-mandated rounds this threat level stops include most non-FMJ 9 mm rounds, the .45 ACP, several .44 Magnum rounds and 12G 00 buckshot.

Threat level II stops the mandated 9 mm 124gr. FMJ Rem fired from a 5" barrel traveling at 1,175 ft./sec. and the .357 Magnum 158gr. SJSP Rem fired from a 6" barrel traveling at 1,395 ft./sec. (note increased velocity when a round is fired from a longer barreled weapon). Non-mandated rounds include 12G shotgun slugs, a variety of 9 mm FMJ rounds, and even the .50 Action Express round.

Threat level IIIA stops the mandated 9 mm 124gr. FMJ Rem fired from a 16" barreled carbine traveling at 1,400 ft./sec. and the .44 Magnum 240gr. SWC Rem fired from a 6" barrel at 1,400 ft./sec. Hard armor inserts usually made of steel, ceramics, aluminum or titanium are available for added frontal torso protection for this soft armor. More exotic armor plating in silicon carbide, boron carbide or cermets (ceramic/metallic combinations) also exist.

Hard armor is available as a threat level III and protects against centerfire rifle rounds 5.56 x 45mm (.223) and 7.62 x 51mm (.308). It is also available in level IV protecting against the 30.06 AP (armor piercing) round.

Fragmentation armor (FLAK Jacket) protects against shrapnel injury but possesses no official ballistic rating.

Puncture resistant vests are designed to defeat only edged weapons.

Reviewing Second Chance compiled statistics makes the obvious case for wearing a ballistic vest. FBI stats show that the odds of surviving a shootout are fourteen times higher if body armor is worn. These data also show that between 1980-1996, forty-two percent of the 403 officers killed with firearms could have been saved were they wearing body armor. Eighty-eight percent of all law enforcement officers were shot with bullets that would have been defeated by soft armor.

Central Nervous System (CNS) Incapacitation
Injuring vascular (blood containing) organs such as the heart and liver or disrupting major blood vessels such as the femoral or carotid arteries will result in major blood loss and rapid incapacitation within ten to fifteen seconds because of hypovolemic (blood loss) shock. (9) A low or high velocity gunshot injury to the Central Nervous System (CNS) above the shoulder blades, in the brain stem or within the cranial vault when properly placed may result in instant incapacitation. The frontal T-shaped area describes the eyes and nose and is currently called "the T box." The rule of thumb for CNS incapacitation is "the higher on the spine the better...the subject goes down precipitously as if you'd flicked a light switch." (10) This describes neurogenic (nervous system) shock and is the goal of the precision marksman. To achieve this result, the brain stem at the pons, medulla oblongata or upper cervical spine level must be severed or the cranial vault must be breached preferably by a high velocity round. The landmark for the medulla is in the "moustache" area just below the middle of the nostrils (nares) on the frontal view of the face. The landmark for the back side of the head is less distinct. It is a line drawn between the lower earlobes (tragus) in the midline of the head. A low velocity round may also be effective within the cranial vault but striking the frontal cortical motor strip assures the desired result. The landmark for this structure is located starting above the top of the ear (pinna) and extending toward the top of the head on its side view. Major John Plaster (Special Operations Group, ret.) likens this lateral area as similar to the area covered by wearing headphones.

Only the upper one-third of the head contains the cranial vault and brain. The liquid density of the brain accurately reproduces the effects of shooting a gallon water jug and transmits the temporary cavitation shock wave very well. This area is about four to five inches high and six inches wide. Intracranial gunshot wounds comprise one-third of all fatal shootings. (11) The entry wound punches out a relatively round skull fracture that drives bone fragments into the brain. High or even low velocity rounds may create shock waves causing secondary skull fractures. Intracranial bullets may ricochet ten to twenty-five percent of the time within the cranial vault, also creating fractures and/or more brain parenchymal (tissue) damage. Increased intracranial pressure because of bleeding or swelling may be a partial explanation for the devastating nature of these wounds. DeMaio states that forty percent of fatal civilian gunshot wounds involve the head (fifty percent involve the heart and great vessels while ten percent are miscellaneous). Bullets may follow the inner curvature of the cranial vault before coming to rest. A skull x-ray is always a good idea to document bony injury. The author has had personal experience with a head wound where midline anteroposterior entry and exit wounds were present in a lucid victim with no skull fracture demonstrating the tendency of bullets to track along the bones of the skull. The size of the permanent cavity within brain tissue bears no resemblance to the caliber or kinetic energy of the round. The time needed for "instant incapacitation" may be calculated, per Plaster, to be approximately .12 seconds for a .308 round to travel 100 yards from the weapon to the subject and another ½ millionth second to divide the brain stem. The realistic marksmanship ability to accomplish these shots is a relevant question. If an acceptable level of marksmanship accuracy is one Minute of Angle (M.O.A.) or one inch off target/100 yards, it would be impossible to make the cranial vault shot beyond about 300-400 yards. As most tactical scenarios occur within seventy-five yards, this shot may be a realistic goal. The ability to successfully make a brain stem shot is more questionable. As the angle of elevation increases, the trajectory may miss the medulla with an elevation angle of only five degrees although the pons (lower brainstem) and upper spinal cord could still be struck successfully if the shot remains midline.

Gunshot Wound Medical Care
Despite the foregoing analysis, do not despair. Actually, only about ten percent of gunshot wounds are fatal. Gunshot victims should be reassured they won't die. It is important to avoid the pessimistic mindset that you will die if shot if for no other reason than if you stop fighting you really may die. If injured, don't be sad-get mad! No one should be allowed to take you from your family and loved ones! If you make it to a Trauma Center, you have a ninety-eight percent chance of survival.

The first priority in providing medical care to the civilian or law enforcement gunshot victims is to search and completely disarm them. For officers this includes all primary, secondary, and backup firearms. The weapon search includes edged weapons. Do you know where your co-workers secrete all their weapons? An injured, disoriented team member may think he is being attacked by the treating teammate and respond violently. If they are not disarmed, further unnecessary injury may result.

The victim should be evacuated to a safe location for care if possible. The bare minimum care in the inner perimeter should be provided including a quick A, B, C (Airway, Breathing, Circulation) first aid evaluation. A wound dressing may be applied as needed. An ambulatory victim may walk to safety. A non-ambulatory victim may be carried into a safe area via a carry technique or a litter. The staging of appropriate medical care should conform to the Tactical Combat

Casualty Care (TCCC) guidelines. That algorithm is beyond the scope of this discussion. However, all armed individuals would be well advised to have a tourniquet on their person to control significant extremity bleeding. Arms and legs can well tolerate up to two hours of tourniquet use. Approved tourniquets, if possible, should be strictly monitored by the person who applied them. Documentation of tourniquet application time must accompany the victim. Extremity wound care may also include the application of a compression dressing and the use of hemostatic agents. Remember, the survival rate after sustaining a gunshot wound is ninety percent!

Avoiding Gunshot Training Injuries
There truly are no "accidental discharge" firearm injuries. All unintended shootings are the result of some type of human error and are therefore avoidable but unintended. *The correct term for an unintended firearm discharge should therefore be just that- an unintended discharge.* One's brain is the most effective firearm safety. Following the National Rifle Association's (NRA's) Four Rules of Firearm Safety religiously should go a long way to eliminate negligent discharge firearm injury.

They are:
1. Keep your weapon pointed in a safe direction until you are ready to fire it;
2. Keep your finger off the trigger until you are ready to fire the weapon;
3. Do not point your weapon at anything you are not willing to destroy;
4. Know your backstop and what is beyond it (will the ballistic characteristics of your rounds allow them to travel beyond the intended target? (12)

A fifth rule known to officers might be included: "Never relinquish your firearm."

Summary

Understanding ballistics requires an understanding of kinetic energy transfer and the difference between low and high velocity gunshot injuries. The medical care of these two categories of gunshot trauma differs greatly. Rifle and shotgun wounds always require surgical debridement while low velocity handgun wounds are not considered "open" injuries (including fractures) and do not automatically require surgery.

We should do everything within our power to eliminate unintended discharges and friendly fire ballistic injury. If the unthinkable should occur while on duty or in training, an understanding of medical ballistics and prompt execution of appropriate first aid skills may save a life.

REFERENCES

1 American Heritage Dictionary, third ed. Houghton Mifflin, USA p.141
2 DeMaio, Vincent-Gunshot Wounds, CRC Press, Boca Raton, 1993 p 12
3 Butler, D.F.-United States Firearms: The First Century 1776-1875. Winchester Press, New York 1971
4 ibid. DeMaio, p. 43
5 ibid. DeMaio, p.46
6 Bruchey, W.J. et al., Police Handgun Ammunition, US Gov't. Printing Office, 1984
7 Op. Cit. DeMaio, p.57
8 Marshal, E. and Sanow, E.-Handgun Stopping Power, Paladin Press, Boulder Colorado 1992
9 Second Chance Live Fire Demonstration Notes presented by Lt. A. Kulovitz (Cook County Sheriff's Police, retired)
10 Plaster, J.-The Ultimate Sniper, Paladin Press Boulder, Colorado 1993 p.131
11 ibid. Plaster, p.131
12 https://www.NRA.org/NRAgunsafety rules

Heat Stress

Martin Greenberg, MD

Eighteen people died in the summer of 2001 in the Chicagoland area from heat-related stress. As tactical activities frequently occur outdoors, it is in the officer's self-interest to have a working knowledge of heat stress related issues.

Heat Stress Factors
1. *Metabolic Rate-* The higher the intensity of activity, the higher our metabolic rate becomes. This raises our core body temperature. We measure the production of metabolic heat in calories.
2. *Ambient Temperature-* The outside (ambient) temperature is directly related to our core temperature.
3. *Hydration-* Evaporation of sweat from the skin is our major means of thermo-regulation. Dehydration limits our ability to freely perspire and to benefit from its cooling effect.
4. *Humidity-*The amount of moisture in the air and a major factor in heat stress. Sweat evaporation is inversely related to humidity. The more humid it is, the less our sweat evaporates. In a water saturated or humid environment,

there may be no evaporation of perspiration. It is the evaporation of perspiration that is responsible for its cooling effect.

5   *Clothing* -Tactical clothing is usually heavy and black. This significantly hinders our ability to lose heat from our skin's surface to the environment. Up to seventy percent of the cooling effect of sweating may be lost by wearing heat retaining clothing.
6   *Fitness-* Unfit and/or unacclimated individuals will sweat less than their fit/acclimated counterparts. Obesity (excess adipose/fat tissue) acts as a natural insulator.
7   *Concurrent Medical Risks-* Older age, chronic medical problems including heart disease, vascular occlusive diseases such as diabetes, illnesses involving fluid loss from vomiting or diarrhea, and ethanol use all magnify the effects of heat stress.
8   *Acclimatization-* Our bodies lose heat more efficiently as we are gradually exposed to warm ambient temperatures over one to two weeks. A heat acclimated individual may perspire twice as much as a non-acclimated person.

The Heat Index

The heat index combines the effects of ambient temperature and humidity to describe the apparent temperature. This describes how hot it actually feels outside, or the true effect of temperature and humidity in producing heat stress. This value can be obtained from the Heat Index Table:

any value *less than eighty* is comfortable;
any value *greater than ninety* is extreme;
any value *greater than 100* is hazardous;
any value *greater than 110* is extremely dangerous.

The Heat Index Table
HUMIDITY %
RELATIVE AMBIENT TEMPERATURE (DEGREES F.)

	70	80	90	100	110	120
0%	64	73	83	91	99	107
10%	65	75	85	95	105	116
20%	66	77	87	99	112	130
30%	67	78	90	104	123	148
40%	68	79	93	110	137	
50%	69	81	96	120	150	
60%	70	82	100	132		
70%	70	85	106	144		
80%	71	86	113	OVER 140		
90%	71	88	122	OVER 140		
100%	72	91	OVER 120			

As an example, you go for a run on a sunny, summer afternoon after having a few beers the night before. You are slightly dehydrated, but don't realize it. You planned to run eight miles but on this hot, sticky day, you feel like you've run ten miles after only two are completed. You later find out that the temperature was 100 degrees. With the humidity greater than seventy percent, 100 degrees feels like (or has the effect of) 144 degrees. When the humidity is ninety percent, 90 degrees feels like 122.

Heat Production
When we exercise, heat is produced in direct relation to the energy we expend. An elite runner may expend 1,500kcal/hour while a novice runner may only generate 500 kcal/hour. In full gear, it is a reasonable assumption that the officer may fall within this spectrum. Since body metabolism as a means of energy production is estimated to be only twenty-five percent efficient, seventy-five percent of this energy is generated as heat.

The sun's radiant energy is responsible for generating up to 150 kcal/hr. inside us on a clear, summer day.

Convective Heating is the increase in heating of an object due to wind effects above about 72 degrees Fahrenheit. (The opposite effect occurs below 32 degrees.) Standing in a wind above this temperature doesn't cool you; it "cooks" you.

Conductive Heating represents the increase in heating an object due to direct contact. Most commonly, this would represent the heat transferred from a hot ground surface through your boots to your feet. Using this example, heat production alone would generate a heat burden of about 1200 kcal/hr. If no means of heat dissipation were present, core body temperature would rise 1 degree centigrade for every five to eight minutes of activity.

Heat Loss

An acclimated individual perspires twice as much as a non-acclimated individual. Perspiration and its evaporation are the body's prime means of heat loss. Skin blood flow results in cooling by convection and conduction. Older individuals can expect a decrease of twenty-five to forty percent in skin blood flow and a corresponding deficit in body cooling potential. Our sweat glands become active as the core body temperature rises. One liter of sweat is produced during the expenditure of 500 kcal. Training increases skin blood flow and sweating. An acclimated individual also begins to sweat earlier, allowing for more efficient heat dissipation. Each gram of evaporated perspiration cools the body by 0.6 kcal. Acclimated individuals may perspire at a rate of 30g/min. resulting in considerable, potential cooling. The environment has a major impact on our body's heat loss. Humidity decreases the evaporation of perspiration and limits our primary heat loss mechanism.

Heat Regulation

Core body temperature is the result of a balance of the bodily processes that produce and dissipate heat. The body's thermoregulatory balance is expressed is expressed by the formula:

$S=M+R+Cd+Cv-E$ (Winslow, 1937) where;
S=stored heat
M=metabolic heat production
R=amount of heat gained or lost by radiation (sunlight)
Cd=conductive (surface contact) heat gain or loss
Cv=convective (wind) heat gain or loss
E=evaporative (sweat) heat loss

Our body's heat balance is thus determined by the amount of heat produced by muscle activity, heat gained or lost from the environment, and heat lost through perspiration. Please note that sweat dripping from the body does not significantly contribute to heat loss (no evaporation), but air flow over the body (through wind or motion) does. Loss of air-flow is one reason why you start to sweat more when you stop moving.

Heat-related Illnesses

*Heat Rash-*Heat rash is also known as prickly heat, and is caused by excessive exposure to hot, humid air. The resulting rash can substantially reduce the skin's ability to sweat. This potential sweat deficit makes heat rash more than just an annoyance. First aid includes cleansing the involved area with a plain soapy water and drying thoroughly. Calamine lotion provides itching relief.

*Heat cramps-*Heat cramps may occur after prolonged heat exposure and include abdominal and other voluntary (under our control) muscle spasms. They usually occur after profuse sweating and are the result of electrolyte (sodium and potassium) imbalance. First Aid consists of resting in a cool, shady area while getting plenty of water or electrolyte drinks.

Heat Exhaustion-Heat exhaustion is caused by dehydration. Symptoms include chills, lightheadedness, nausea/vomiting, and headache. Body temperature is elevated to about 100-102 degrees Fahrenheit. Sweating is profuse. First Aid for heat exhaustion also consists of rest and fluids. Intravenous (I.V.) fluids may be considered should serious vomiting occur.

Heat Stroke-Heat stroke is a POTENTIALLY FATAL ILLNESS caused by a sudden failure of the body's thermo-regulatory system. It may lie on a continuum with worsening heat exhaustion. It may at first appear similar to heat exhaustion but quickly manifests more serious symptoms including disorientation, seizures, and then loss of consciousness. The body temperature may rise over 104 degrees F. Sweating is absent, but the skin may be moist from prior perspiration. A rapid heartbeat (sinus tachycardia) is frequently present with a pulse rate of over 160 bpm (beats/minute). The blood pressure may be low (hypotension), and kidney damage may occur. Emergency Care for this life threatening problem includes removing the victim from the heat, removing all clothing except underwear, and transporting to a medical facility as quickly as possible. While waiting for or during transport, start intravenous fluids (if available) and apply ice bags to the groin area, the axillae (armpits), and head. Sponge the remainder of the body with cool water or alcohol. Improvise one or more fans to allow for maximum evaporative cooling.

THIS IS A MEDICAL EMERGENCY!

How to "Beat the Heat"

1. If possible, *SLOW DOWN*. Increase "downtime" and decrease time on duty proportionally to heat risk factors. With all other factors equal, short, high intensity activity may be better than long, drawn out heat exposure.

2. *HYDRATE!* Drink fluids before, during, and after a mission. Before heat exposure drink about a pint (16 ounces) and 6-8 ounces every 15 minutes during aerobic exercise. Water weight loss should not be confused with fat weight loss. A pound of fat equals 3,500 calories. Running a marathon, for example, loses only 2,500 calories (less than a pound). Replace each pound of water weight loss with sixteen ounces of water replacement.
3. If the mission lasts over an hour, consider fluid/electrolyte replacement drinks (FRDs) such as Gatorade. During heat stress, blood glucose falls and electrolytes (sodium, potassium, and chlorine) are lost in sweat. Electrolytes are critical in maintaining body fluid balance and promoting fluid absorption from the small intestine. Sodium also helps maintain blood volume which is important in responding to dehydration/heat stress. Please don't include caffeinated or alcohol containing drinks as they act as diuretics (drugs causing increased urine fluid loss) resulting in a net deficit in fluid balance. Don't use salt tablets as they may cause gastric (stomach) distress and require precious fluid for digestion.
4. *ACCLIMATIZE* by increasing heat exposure intervals over 1-2 weeks. The physiologic adaptations to gradually increasing heat exposure include an increase in blood plasma volume, an earlier onset and increased volume of perspiration, a reduction in lost sodium, and a reduction in skin blood flow. This allows increased blood flow and oxygen delivered to the working muscles that need it. Remember

that the non-acclimatized operator maximally sweats only about 0.6 liters/hour. This potential increases to 1.5 liters/hour when fully acclimatized. Evaporating sweat is the body's main cooling mechanism.

5 *AVOID DIRECT SUNLIGHT. Wear 30 SPF sunblock.* Use shaded cover whenever possible.

6 *WEAR LOOSE, LIGHT COLORED, HIGH TECH, COOLING FABRICS.* Dark colors absorb light and heat; light colors reflect them. Black has been shown not to be the most camouflaging color in any environment. Better choices from a heat fighter's perspective would be lighter patterns such as desert, desert camo, or urban camo. Official issue Air Force Nomex® flight suits are sage (light green). Are the benefits of Nomex, Kevlar, or Polypropylene fabrics so overwhelming that they should replace simple cotton in extreme heat? The tactical operator will definitely reap the benefit of cotton as a cooling fabric but may only rarely need the fire or cut protection of heavier Nomex/Kevlar. A loose hat is also an important piece of clothing protecting the head and central nervous system. Shed all non-essential gear and lighten essential gear (for example, more modern ballistic vests or light Kevlar helmets). Consider using Gore-Tex containing footwear such as Matterhorn Acadia boots that keep feet at a comfortable 83 degrees Fahrenheit.

7 *LISTEN TO YOUR BODY.* Little or no sweating in a hot environment is an ominous sign of moderate to advanced dehydration. Nausea, vomiting, or muscle cramps are frequently a

sign of serious heat related illness. If they occur, stop all activity, remove excess garments, get out of the heat, hydrate, and seek medical attention. Check your (radial) pulse periodically at the wrist level. It is located at the palm and thumb side of the wrist crease. Practice feeling it in advance. Remember that your body's workload increases with the temperature and humidity. Your heart rate, as a reflection of workload, increases about 1 beat/minute for each degree of temperature over 77F/25C. Think of increasing heat and humidity as increasing the grade of your exercise treadmill.

Protecting yourself in the heat is a MIND WITH BODY, NOT MIND OVER BODY activity.

Officers/Operators are trained to ignore adversity in completing their mission. Do not allow your tactical mindset to make a fatal mistake in dealing with the silent enemy of heat stress.

Cold Stress

Martin Greenberg, MD

Scenario
Your tactical team is called out on a windy mid-winter night to a hostage barricade. The ambient outdoor temperature is 5 degrees F. With wind chill correction, it is −15 degrees. The team surrounds a small rural home without any natural wind barriers for six hours. There is effectively no place to seek shelter. After 1 hour, you notice your toes becoming painful and then numb. At the indoor debriefing, you remove your all season boot and see that three toes are blue. As your foot warms slowly, it becomes increasingly painful. The blue toes eventually die, mummify, and are amputated. Your foot remains chronically painful. The officer's appreciation of the spectrum of cold related injury is mandatory for mission success in cold environments.

Introduction
This chapter will discuss the challenge of managing cold stress in the tactical environment. It will review the body's reaction to cold stress, environmental factors, cold related illnesses, and safety recommendations. The officer must be prepared to effectively function in cold weather. How does our body respond to cold stress?

Physiology of Cold Exposure

For normal functioning, our body core temperature must remain within a few Fahrenheit degrees of 98.6. Several factors affect our body's ability to gain and lose heat. *Metabolic Heat Production (MHP)* varies proportionally with activity. With greater activity, your body will produce more heat. At rest, the average male generates 80-90 Cal/hr. (about the same amount as a 100W light bulb). Maximal aerobic exercise can increase MHP to 1,000 Cal./hr. for short periods. Sustained hard work can increase MHP 4-5X, while shivering can increase MHP 6X the basal rate. Radiation is the gain or loss of heat in the form of electromagnetic radiation. Radiation heat loss is the source of the thermal imaging signature. Of course, in cold environs heat loss will exclusively occur which can be limited by insulation. Conduction represents heat loss through physical contact between 2 materials of differing temperatures. Increasing the area of surface contact increases the amount of heat loss. If other variables are equal, an individual lying on cold ground will lose more heat than when standing. Convection is responsible for heat loss from contact with cold moving air. Evaporation of sweat also causes heat loss. Each liter of sweat "loses" 540 Cal. of heat. Sweating diminishes in high outdoor humidity. When we are acutely exposed to cold, skin temperature is reduced to minimize its temperature gradient with the environment. Heat production is increased by shivering. Vasoconstriction (blood vessel narrowing) diverts blood from the skin and extremities providing a cooler shell of tissue to minimize heat loss. Vasoconstriction's protective effect is about equal to wearing a light business suit. The degree of vasoconstriction depends both on skin and core body temperature. Interestingly, skin sensors respond to absolute ambient (outdoor) temperature and its rate of temperature change. A sudden temperature change will trigger vasoconstriction and transient shivering. Peripheral (skin and extremity) vasoconstriction will increase central blood volume triggering a reflex loss of volume through increased urination. This phenomenon is called "cold diuresis." The body is wrongly "tricked" into thinking too much blood volume is present. This diuresis, or loss of fluid, may cause dehydration and hypovolemia (low blood volume). If vasoconstriction is insufficient to protect core temperature, heat production through muscle contraction (shivering) occurs. First, muscle tone increases which doubles the body's basal (base) metabolic rate. If the core body temperature continues to fall, shivering continues through cyclic muscle contraction and relaxation. Maximal shivering occurs at a core body temperature of 94-97 degrees F. Its dramatic effect is to increase MHP up to 6X! Shivering is an important emergency method of heat production and is sustained only at a considerable cost. Shivering disables purposeful coordinated muscle activity (i.e., marksmanship skills), increased muscle activity stimulates increased extremity blood flow and heat loss, and it requires increased caloric intake to sustain itself. Although vasoconstriction protects core body temperature, it places the peripheral or *acral* body parts at risk of severe cold injury. This potential injury is limited by the phenomenon of *Cold Induced Vasodilation (CIVD)*. This phenomenon begins in water below 50 degrees F. and in air below 32 degrees F. CIVD bypasses closed arterioles (smallest arteries) by opening arteriovenous connections in ten to twenty minute cycles of constriction and dilation. The effectiveness of CIVD may vary individually and increases the rate of heat loss at about 40 Cal./hr. If this mechanism fails to maintain core temperature, it stops and the extremities are sacrificed to protect the core. Although ingenious, the effect of compensatory, heat conserving mechanisms is small. Protection must then come from familiarization with the environment, cold avoidance skill development and equipment selection.

Risk Factors in Cold Injury

Risk factors worsening cold injury include tobacco use, alcohol consumption, responsibilities in the tactical situation and African American race. Fatigue may generally decrease the tactical operator's awareness of his/her surroundings including the associated cold injury risks. Dehydration may accompany cold exposure as water requirements in this setting are high. Cold air is generally dry and it will increase the amount of fluid lost through respiration. Muscle activity required to work in the cold also increases water demand. To avoid dehydration, operators should drink at least four quarts of water/day. This is the same recommendation made for desert survival. Nutrition requirements in cold environments may increase easily to 4,000-5,000 Cal./day. Operators must increase their food intake accordingly. Warm drinks provide the added benefit of heat and calories.

Cold injury prevention knowledge includes common sense measures such as:

-Stand on rocks, boards, or brush rather than in water or mud;

-Be aware that if extremity numbness occurs, immediate re-warming is crucial;

-Keep clothing and footgear clean, dry, and loose enough to permit easy circulation;

-Use sunscreen. Reflection of snow and ice can cause sunburn that is unpleasant, causes long term skin cancer, and may prevent the use of protective gear (i.e., helmet, balaclava, gloves);

-Use eye protection. Sunglasses will protect against glare and goggles may protect the cornea from freezing.

-Avoid contact freezing injury. Local frostbite (freezing living tissue) can occur in seconds when touching frozen objects with unprotected skin. Risky objects include vehicle door handles, metal tools and weapons, and cold liquids such as antifreeze that exist in the liquid state at below freezing temperatures.

-Avoid illness and injury by avoiding falls on icy surfaces. This may mean illuminating the ground or choosing alternate entry plans.

-Avoid carbon monoxide fume exposure while resting/sleeping in vehicles.

-Avoid burns from fires started to keep warm in the training setting.

Nicotine is a potent vasoconstrictor associated with tobacco use. It will aggravate injury caused by cold induced extremity vasoconstriction.

Alcohol use generally increases the risk of all forms of cold related injury. Some of its adverse effects are impairing judgment and coordination, reducing shivering, reducing the pain of cold exposure, increasing diuresis (worsening dehydration) and limiting the production of needed blood glucose (sugars).

Genetically, African Americans are more prone to cold related injury and should exercise special caution in this regard.

Wind Chill Factor

Wind chill is an estimate of the cooling potential of still air that would equal the combination of ambient outdoor temperature and wind speed. For example, the ambient outdoor temperature is 30 degrees F, but it feels like 15 degrees in a strong wind. The risk of cold exposure is stratified into three *levels of danger*. Estimates are based on dry, healthy individuals.

Little danger - Safe to have exposure for up to five hours with dry skin.

Increasing danger-exposed skin may freeze in one minute.

Great danger - exposed skin may freeze in thirty seconds.

Wind chill work recommendations are based upon the Army Work Intensity Equivalents:

High- digging a foxhole, running, marching with a load, making, or breaking camp;

Low- walking, drill, and ceremony;
Sedentary- performing sentry duty or clerical work.

Wind chill work intensity recommendations in the *Little Danger Zone* are:
High Work Intensity- Surveillance needed by team leader; gloves mandatory below 0 degrees F.; increase hydration.
Low Work Intensity- surveillance needed; skin covered and dry; mittens or gloves with liners; no facial camo below 10 degrees F; full head cover below 0 degrees F.
Sedentary Work Intensity- full head cover; no facial camo below 10 degrees F; vapor barrier boots below 0 degrees F; shorten duty cycles; provide warm facilities; use the Extreme Cold Weather Clothing System (ECWCS).

Wind chill work intensity recommendations in the *Increased Danger Zone* are:
High Work Intensity- ECWCS with gloves/mittens with liners; no facial camo; all skin covered and dry; warm shelter for rest periods; vapor barrier boots below 0 degrees F.
Low Work Intensity- Thirty to forty minute work cycles.
Sedentary Work- Postpone nonessential training; Fifteen to twenty minute work cycles; enforced buddy system; no exposed skin.

Wind chill work intensity recommendations in the *Great Danger Zone* are:
High Work Intensity- Postpone nonessential training; allow essential tasks with less than fifteen minutes exposure; buddy system with no exposed skin.
Low Work Intensity- Cancel outdoor training.
Sedentary Work Intensity- Cancel outdoor training.
General Clothing Recommendations- Common sense cold weather clothing recommendations include wearing a warm hat, covering exposed skin, wearing multiple dry clothing layers and using appropriate footwear. There are many high-

tech fabrics currently available in the tactical market. The gold standard in cold weather clothing is the Army mil-spec *Extreme Cold Weather Clothing System (ECWCS)*. This is a tri-laminar system composed of long underwear to wick body moisture, an intermediate layer polar fleece jacket and overalls and an outer Gore-Tex hooded jacket and pants. Generation one and two varieties are currently commercially available. High tech footwear options include waterproofing, Gore-Tex lining to wick moisture, and even a boot that maintains a constant interior temperature throughout a range of ambient temperatures (Danner ® Acadia boots).

Cold Related Injuries
Cold related injuries include freezing injuries (frostbite), non-freezing cold injury (NFCI), hypothermia and other cold related problems.

Frostbite- Frostbite is the most common cold related injury. It often occurs with a sudden drop in temperature. Extremity survival depends upon its early recognition and treatment. Frostbite occurs when living tissue freezes. This occurs at 28 degrees F. Interestingly, pigmented cells have a greater susceptibility to freezing than non-pigmented cells. This explains the increased frostbite susceptibility of dark skin. With slow re-warming of a frozen part, blood supply returns (reperfusion) and injury is increased. Some frostbitten tissue may recover. If re-freezing occurs, tissue will usually be irreversibly damaged. Immediately after the injury, all frozen tissue looks alike: cold, hard, and bloodless. Usually, the degree of frostbite injury may not become clear until days or even weeks later. There are four degrees of frostbite injury:

1. *First degree frostbite-* usually involves only the outer layer of skin (the epidermis). Skin appears yellow or white and with thawing it quickly becomes red and painful. The involved

part swells but does not blister. Motion remains normal. Healing usually occurs in seven to ten days.

2 *Second degree frostbite-* involves the epidermis and the underlying dermis (the whole thickness of the skin). It initially looks the same as the first-degree injury, but limitation of motion and clear blisters develop. Although tissue usually survives, healing may take up to a month. The involved part may have long term cold sensitivity.

3 *Third degree frostbite-* Here, freezing occurs into the subcutaneous tissues that are stiff while frozen. As thawing occurs, motion briefly returns and vanishes when limited by rapid extremity swelling. Bloody blisters form and then slough (outer or epidermal skin falls off). Healing is slow and permanent tissue loss may occur. Cold hypersensitivity is common.

4 *Fourth degree frostbite-* The entire extremity may solidly freeze! Reperfusion (blood supply return) with thawing is poor. Blisters and swelling do not develop. The affected area may die and mummify, appearing hard and black. Living and dead tissue will eventually demarcate (clearly separate), and amputation may become necessary.

5 *Corneal frostbite-* is a rare, disabling injury that may be found in helicopter aircrews where the cornea permanently opacifies (becomes cloudy). Treatment is a corneal transplant. Goggle use may prevent this problem.

Frostbite first-aid- A "*high index of suspicion*" of the problem is most important. Immediately stop further cold exposure! If re-freezing is a risk, do not thaw the affected part.

If not, place the affected area on warm axillary or groin skin. Do not expose the frozen skin to temperatures of >103 degrees F. The injured part will be numb and inadvertent burning (i.e., exposure to light bulbs, open flames, car exhausts) should also be avoided. Get to a hospital E.D. quickly! There, if tissue is frozen, or cold and anesthetic it will be warmed. Thawed tissue, however, should not be re-warmed. Active re-warming describes the process where hands and/or feet are immersed in a temperature-controlled water bath at 102-105 degrees F. The face and ears can similarly be covered with a wet towel at the same temperature. Warming continues until improvement in motion and circulation plateaus at about 15-45 minutes. After re-warming, carefully dry the area and apply a bulky dressing. Elevate the extremity above heart level. The use of a burn cream such as Silvadene ® is optional.

In serious cases, hospital admission will occur. Other treatment measures may also include core temperature probe monitoring, IV re-hydration, tetanus toxoid immunization updating, narcotic pain control, anti-inflammatory medication to decrease re-perfusion injury, and the use of antibiotics such as Penicillin and Clindamycin. Infection must be treated aggressively and vasospasm fighting medication alpha-adrenergic receptor blockers might be used where extensive, reversible tissue damage is present. Of course, tobacco products are forbidden during treatment and recovery! Serious long term side effects may include tissue loss, contractures (loss of joint motion), pain, cold hypersensitivity, increased susceptibility to re-injury, and hyperhidrosis (unusual sweating).

Non-Freezing Cold Injury
Non-freezing cold injury (NFCI), also known as trench foot or immersion foot, results from prolonged exposure to wet, cold, but above freezing temperatures. This injury occurs when extremities cool to below 65 degrees, but above freezing temperatures. Cooling may damage all tissues, but selectively

affects blood vessels and nerves. Blood vessel damage impairs local blood flow and worsens the injury. Wet conditions also worsen the problem as water cools more effectively than air. Constricting clothing, immobility, hypothermia, and a crouched posture may all further decrease extremity circulation. Generally, NFCI affected tissue will appear pale, anesthetic, pulseless, and lack voluntary motion but is not frozen. The skin may be macerated and the extremity looks unchanged after re-warming. In twenty-four to thirty-six hours, redness and burning pain will develop.

NCFI is classified into four stages:
1. *Minimal (Class A)*- Hyperemia (redness) and slight sensory changes lasting two to three days occur. By one week, recovery is complete. Residual cold sensitivity is unusual. Regular activity is resumed by one to two weeks.
2. *Mild (Class B)*- Edema (swelling), hyperemia and sensory changes are present two to three days after injury. The swelling lasts one to three weeks; the pain lasts two to four weeks; the numbness lasts four to nine weeks. There are no blisters or skin loss. Hyperhidrosis and cold sensitivity persist in half of affected individuals. Returning to unrestricted activity can take two to four months.
3. *Moderate NFCI (Class C)*- This is a more serious problem where edema, hyperemia, blisters, and mottling (patterned, bluish skin color) occur two to three days post injury. Anesthesia may be present for over one week, edema lasts two to three weeks, and pain/redness last up to three and a half months. Some of the blisters may slough, but no deep tissue loss occurs. Many sufferers may experience permanent disability of some type.

4 *Severe NCFI (Class D)-* Bloody drainage and gangrene (dead tissue) are present at two to three days after injury. Paralysis of foot muscles occurs. Deep tissue loss with possible amputation is likely. Pain lasts four months or longer.

NCFI Treatment
If NCFI is noted, seek urgent medical attention! Treatment includes tetanus prophylaxis, re-hydration, pain control, no active warming, aggressive infection control, and non-weight bearing until circulation is fully restored.

Preventive measures include: early inspection and detection; inspect feet every eight hours; don new dry boots and socks only after feet become warm with normal feeling; active warming is not needed, and massaging feet may worsen the injury.

Hypothermia
Pathophysiology- The initial response to a drop in core body temperature is vasoconstriction followed by an increase in muscle tone and metabolic rate. As described previously, a continued core temperature drop will trigger shivering, tachycardia (rapid heart rate) and hypertension (high blood pressure). These compensatory effects will reach their maximum at a core body temperature around 95 degrees F (35 degrees C). Below this temperature, compensatory mechanisms fail and the victim will become obtunded after a period of confusion, withdrawal or combativeness. The medic should be aware that some danger may be present when dealing with a hypothermic officer or bystander/perpetrator in this state. Below 95 degrees F, the rate of core temperature drop will increase. At 85 degrees, the metabolic rate is fifty percent of normal. At 68 degrees, the metabolic rate is around twenty percent of normal. Metabolic rate will no longer keep up with tissue demands leading to a progressive shutdown of all organ systems.

Medical Conditions That Interfere with Thermoregulation- Many medical conditions can interfere with thermoregulation (temperature control). These include hypothyroidism (low thyroid function), hypo-adrenalism (low adrenal function) and situational issues such as malnutrition, trauma, significant burns and intoxication. Those victims in any of these categories need special attention. Knowing the victim's medical history is especially helpful in this situation.

Factors That Influence the Rate of Cooling- These factors include ambient temperature and wind chill factor, tactical clothing, precipitation, amount of physical activity, and availability of shelter.

Degrees of Hypothermia- Hypothermia is characterized as mild, moderate, or severe in nature.

It is probably unrealistic to expect the medic or the tactical team to have a rectal thermometer handy to measure core temperature of a hypothermia victim. These temperature ranges are only a guideline for care. It is wise to assume the worst when categorizing a victim as suffering from mild, moderate, or severe hypothermia.

1. *Mild hypothermia-* Mild hypothermia is associated with a core body temperature of 90-96 degrees F. (32-36 degrees C). Spontaneous re-warming occurs without medical complications.
2. *Moderate hypothermia-* This level of hypothermia is associated with a core temperature of 82-90 degrees F (28-32 degrees C). Spontaneous re-warming slowly occurs, and atrial cardiac (upper heart chamber) non-life-threatening arrhythmias (abnormal rhythms) may occur.

3. *Severe hypothermia-* This life-threatening disorder is evidenced by a core body temperature below 82 degrees F. little spontaneous re-warming occurs. Life threatening arrhythmias including ventricular fibrillation where the heart stops pumping is a significant risk. Below about 70 degrees F, heart and central nervous system (CNS) electrical functioning ceases. Also, be aware that severe bleeding problems (coagulopathy) may occur.

Hypothermia First-Aid- Anyone suspected of hypothermia is at risk of sudden death! Handle the victim gently. Remove wet clothing and add much warm, dry insulation. Cover the mouth with a scarf to warm ambient air.

Sudden Death in Hypothermia- This phenomenon can be due to ventricular irritability (electrical irritability of the lower heart muscle chambers), hypovolemia and sudden intraventricular cooling.

Ventricular Irritability- The hypothermic heart muscle is electrically unstable and discharges in an uncoordinated manner.

Hypovolemia (low blood volume) - this problem is caused by insufficient fluid intake and cold diuresis. Reflex contraction of large leg veins is absent allowing blood to abnormally pool there. Muscular exercise increases blood flow to the extremities reducing central blood volume. These factors combine to cause hypotension (low blood pressure).

Sudden intraventricular cooling- With re-warming, blood flow returns to the extremities and stagnant, cold, hyperkalemic (high potassium containing), acidotic (acidic) extremity blood returns to the heart possibly resulting in ventricular fibrillation (heart contracting asynchronously like a "bag of worms" and not pumping blood).

Sudden death may be prevented by keeping the victim quiet and supine. Avoid sudden movements during rescue and passively re-warm the victim by providing enough insulation to prevent heat loss. Re-warming will occur even from a core body temperature of 80 degrees F. at a rate of 0.25-1.0 degree/hour. *Active re-warming* occurs in the hospital setting and includes surface techniques for mild and moderate hypothermia. These include baths, blankets, and wet towels at 104 degrees F. Core re-warming for severe hypothermia or during cardiac arrest management includes the use of heated, humidified air at 112 degrees F, direct vascular warming (hemodialysis or cardiac bypass), and intra-luminal (stomach) or intra-peritoneal (abdominal cavity) lavage. *If cardiac arrest should occur...you don't know the victim's core temperature. Don't stop CPR and note the elapsed resuscitation time to later communicate with paramedics.*

-take the pulse for a full minute before beginning CPR (Cardio-Pulmonary Resuscitation). Make sure ventricular fibrillation is present as ventricular fibrillation may be caused by inappropriate CPR use;

-*continue CPR* when the core temperature is between 42-79 degrees F. and the patient has had no vital signs for five hours or more;

-*continue CPR* when the core temperature is 79-90 degrees F, no vital signs are present for more than twelve hours.

That's right! Continue CPR for five to twelve hours!

-the normal cardiac drugs will not work below core body temperatures of 90 degrees F.

Remember: NO ONE IS DEAD UNTIL THEY ARE WARM AND DEAD!

Summary

Humans cannot sense core body temperature. Skin is sensitive to cold and will be painful until it cools to 50 degrees F. or lower. Cessation of pain requires immediate visual inspection of the extremity. Extremities below 50 degrees F. (10 degrees C.) are paralyzed. These hypothermia victims cannot help themselves. The most important adaptation to cold is awareness of the spectrum of cold related injuries. Learning and applying skills, clothing and equipment appropriate to the weather is crucial to mission success and to survival.

The Silent Enemy of Police Suicide

Martin Greenberg, M.D.

True Scenario (1)
January 17, 1994: "Twenty-seven-year-old Joseph Cibarelli. Seventeen months with the 46th Precinct of the NYPD. After an evening of dining and discussing plans for the future with his wife, he went home and shot himself in the head. He used his off-duty revolver, a chrome-plated S&W handed down from his father to his uncle and finally to him. Fellow officers described him as a sensitive individual who would "take personally things that happened in the rough-and-tumble world that should not have been taken that way." (1)

True Scenario (2)
September 6, 1994: "Thirty-year-old Steven Laski. An eight-year veteran, he was one of eleven patrolmen in his precinct who were transferred to desk jobs the previous May as a result of an ongoing corruption investigation. In April, fourteen officers had been arrested from the same precinct on drug, robbery, assault, and civil rights charges. Laski's handgun and his badge were taken away. He was divorced and living with his mother. He drove his blue Mustang to a deserted street and shot himself in the mouth with a .22 rifle He died in civilian clothes." (2)

Police Suicide: A Difficult Problem

Police agencies and especially tactical teams expend great effort, time and money training their officers to avoid falling victim to homicide. We expend almost no resources combating a much greater problem. In the year 1995, 162 officers were killed in the line of duty nationally. In that year, the NYPD lost one officer to that fate, but seven NYPD officers committed suicide. In that year, the FBI lost one agent to homicide and five agents to suicide (www.policestress.org/suicide.htm). Each year, two to three times the number of officers have been lost to suicide as to homicide. The goal of this article is to review some aspects of police suicide, and some common sense solutions to address this difficult problem.

Police Suicide: An Epidemic?

Approximately 300 police officers commit suicide annually. Disagreement exists about the true frequency of police suicide as compared to the general population. As a profession, law enforcement has been judged to have the third highest suicide rate of 130 occupations. The surgeon general's report on mental health lists suicide as the ninth leading cause of death in America. The average suicide rate of the American public is 12/100,000. The suicide rate in the American military is 13/100,000. The suicide rate in law enforcement is 18/100,000. (3) The highest suicide subgroup includes white males over seventy-five years old. Police officers commit suicide fifty-two percent more often than the public in general. Unlike the military, there is no law enforcement "mission acceptable" homicide rate. This same distinction should be equally true for suicide. Obtaining accurate data regarding suicide is difficult. In a Chicago Police Department study (FBI, 1983), it was discovered that sixty-seven percent of police suicides had been misclassified. A University of Buffalo study suggests that police officers are eight times more likely to kill themselves than to be killed. This study also found that police suicides are more likely to be misclassified as death due to accidents, poisonings, violence, external causes, or undetermined causes. (4) It is possible that misclassification represents an attempt by fellow officers to preserve the fallen officer's dignity, funeral/burial honors, and financial/insurance benefits. Allen Kates (5) points out that statistics don't reflect the number of retired officers who commit suicide and suggests that the police suicide rate is at least twice the national average. Unfortunately, there is no scientific way to pinpoint the true number. Unlike the mourned victims of homicide, officers lost to suicide are often forgotten.

What Is Stress?
Police work is constantly referred to as a high stress profession. Stress is likewise held responsible for the suicide response. To understand the role of stress in the complex problem of suicide, we must first understand the physiology of stress.

Stress may be defined as outside forces affecting the individual. Although we think of stress as a negative factor, it is the force driving natural selection and has created the plant and animal kingdoms as we know them. Man is the most adaptable creature on the planet as a result of the stresses he has successfully faced.

Historically, the French physiologist Claude Bernard described the concept of maintaining the internal environment of the body, or *"milieu interieur."* Equilibrium exists in the body that is threatened by external stressors such as temperature changes, predators, or diseases that must be reacted to and successfully managed. The neurologist Walter Cannon used the term "homeostasis" to describe this relationship and to recognize that emotional stressors existed. He described the "fight or flight" response and traced it to the release of *norepinephrine* (nor-adrenaline) from the "medullary" section of the adrenal gland. This is the hormone responsible for the critical incident stress responses of tunnel vision, auditory exclusion, and slowed time perception that the tactical community has heard so much about. Hans Selye described the pituitary gland (the master gland) and its control of the hormone *cortisol* secreted by the "cortical" section of the adrenal gland. He coined the term "stress" and performed experiments exposing rats to constant adverse stimulation. In this environment, rats displayed enlarged adrenal glands, gastrointestinal ulcers and a degradation of the immune system. He called this negative state *"The Stress Syndrome."* It became clear that over-stimulation of these adaptive bodily reactions could act like a disease and damage the body faced with too much external stress.

Normally, the stress response involves the brain that signals the adrenal medulla to release nor-epinephrine. The hypothalamus and the pituitary glands mediate the intermediate, maintenance stress response including the release of cortisol and other hormones. The resulting behavioral response includes increased arousal, focused attention, a diminished pain response, and shutting down of the gut. How does the stress response actually happen? The "hardware" mediating the stress response includes the interaction of two systems: the *hypothalamus-pituitary-adrenal (HPA) axis* and the *sympathetic nervous system (SNS)*. The SNS releases nor-epinephrine when triggered by an area of the brain called the locus coeruleus. A feedback loop exists between the systems that are both interactive and affected by an individual's genetics. No two people respond to stress identically.

Within the HPA axis, the hypothalamus releases a hormone called Corticotrophin Releasing Factor (CRF). CRF travels through the bloodstream to the pituitary where it causes the release of another hormone, *Adreno-Cortico-Trophic Hormone or ACTH*. ACTH travels similarly to the adrenal cortex to release stress hormones including cortisol. Cortisol is a steroid that in continued high blood levels causes the stress response. A feedback loop normally exists in the presence of high cortisol levels to cause the pituitary to shut down ACTH production and moderate the blood cortisol level. The locus coeruleus activates the sympathetic nervous system (SNS) that releases nor-epinephrine and controls "automatic" bodily functions such as heart and breathing (respiratory) rate, blood pressure and preferential large muscle blood supply. The link between the HPA axis and the locus coeruleus (SNS) is an area of the brain called the limbic system. This is the brain's emotion and memory area. An activated SNS can be moderated by reassuring memories or the emotional relief of realizing a situation is actually non-threatening. The limbic system is like a computer that in milliseconds performs a stress analysis based upon current information to decide if a stressor is truly dangerous. Prolonged experimental stress in lab animals causes dysfunction in this system and causes the stress syndrome including high blood pressure, muscle wasting, decreased appetite, sexual dysfunction, ulcers, immune system suppression and depression. The stress syndrome seems to duplicate many officers' depression and medical problems. Drugs like cocaine and amphetamine hyper-sensitize the stress response. Chronic maternal stress can even affect her fetus with resulting life-long dysfunctional stress responses. Unpredictable/uncontrollable stress maximizes the stress syndrome.

In summary, uncontrollable, unpredictable, constant stress may cause profoundly negative effects including all aspects of the stress syndrome. The stress syndrome may be a cause of depression and health problems in law enforcement officers. A final bad consequence of experiencing prolonged, uncontrollable, negative situations is a learned helplessness and hopelessness leading to anxiety and clinical depression.

Post-Traumatic Stress Disorder (PTSD)
"The sword must be plunged into the fire 10,000 times before it is tempered." (Chinese proverb)
Post-traumatic stress disorder (PTSD) is a term most of us have heard. It refers to a psychological state where the sufferer

is in a current state of anxiety based upon past experienced stress. It may represent the dark side of the warrior virtues of self-sacrifice and stoicism. Officers are taught to be constantly strong and in control. Internalizing stress for fear of appearing weak is a psychological formula for disaster. Eventually, pent up stress will be expressed in a possibly uncontrolled manner. Traumatic events such as being involved in a mass casualty incident, placing your life in immediate jeopardy or using lethal force are examples of situations that may create anxiety disorders later if they are not psychologically laid to rest. Even repeated smaller traumatic events such as experiencing bullying may develop the same problem. While the dysfunctional "re-living" of a traumatic acute event is called Post Traumatic Stress Disorder (PTSD), the chronically recurrent problem is termed *Prolonged Duration Stress Disorder (PDSD)*. According to the American Psychological Association, these disorders affect hundreds of thousands of Americans yearly. Amazingly, ten percent of the population experiences this problem at some time during their lives. Previously, PTSD was alternatively called "shell shock" or "battle fatigue syndrome." It affects women more than men. It is the reaction to a deeply shocking and disturbing experience. It is important to be aware of PTSD/PDSD because, through suicide and stress related medical problems, they are responsible for taking twice the number of lives as the traumatic events that created them.

Consider PTSD/PDSD if two or more of the following problems are present for more than three months:
1. Recurrent and intrusive (involuntary) thinking about a traumatic event;
2. Distressing dreams of the event;
3. A sense of reliving the event including flashbacks and hallucinations (hearing/seeing the event);
4. Experiencing intense psychological distress

when exposed to cues relating to the event (for example, being in the rain after being attacked in the rain);
5   Making efforts to avoid thoughts, feelings, or conversations relating to the trauma;
6   Making efforts to avoid people, places, or activities that recall the trauma;
7   Traumatic amnesia (not remembering the event);
8   Experiencing diminished interest and participation in important life events;
9   Experiencing an estrangement/detachment from others;
10 Being unable to have strong emotional/love feelings for others;
11 Feeling a sense of a foreshortened future (impending doom);
12 Difficulty falling or staying asleep;
13 Difficulty concentrating;
14 Experiencing a feeling of distrust for most other people (everyone is crazy but me);
15 Avoid being touched and / or experiencing a strong "startle" reaction when being unexpectedly touched.

Prompt counseling should be obtained if these symptoms are recognized. However, a clear line should be drawn between sensitivity to PTSD and wrongly assuming that it must occur after every traumatic event. Coming to grips in advance with the unpleasant moral necessity of possibly using lethal force may neutralize much of its psychological impact. Train your mind to successfully visualize the possible event just as you train your body to successfully respond to it. Cognitive therapy trains one to separate the intrusive thoughts of PTSD from their associated anxiety. Stress inoculation therapy gradually exposes the sufferer to triggering stimuli using techniques to successfully manage the stress. Medications for PTSD are in the Selective Serotonin Re-uptake Inhibitor (SSRI) class. Low Serotonin hormonal brain and cerebrospinal fluid {CSF} levels are depression related.

Ethical Considerations
Ethical behavior is defined by Webster's II New Riverside University Dictionary as "behavior conforming to accepted principles of right and wrong that govern the conduct of a profession." (6) Ethical behavior is linked to stress for several reasons. We believe that cynicism grows from hopelessness in discovering we cannot dramatically change the negative situations that we regularly observe. Personal or witnessed unethical behavior certainly worsens that cynicism and the stress accompanying it. The performance of an unethical act is stressful because of the criminal penalties and social stigma attached to its discovery (see scenario #2). Consider also the stressor of knowing one has violated an ethical norm. The loss of one's job and identity as a police officer may be the expected but often intolerable result of not telling the truth, violating the law or department policy. There can be no denying that an internal stressor results from denying the positive internalized norms we hope that all officers have developed to some degree.

The exact description of expected ethical behavior by police officers was well summarized by *The Law Enforcement Code of Ethics of the International Association of Police Chiefs (1957):*

"As a Law Enforcement Officer, my fundamental duty is to serve mankind; to safeguard lives and property; to protect the innocent against deception, the weak against oppression or intimidation, and the peaceful against violence or disorder; and to respect the constitutional rights of all men to liberty, equality, and justice.

I will keep my private life unsullied as an example to all; maintain courageous calm in the face of danger, scorn, or ridicule; develop self-restraint; and be constantly mindful of the welfare of others. Honest in thought and deed in both my personal and official life, I will be exemplary in obeying the laws of the land and the regulations of my department. Whatever I see or hear of a confidential nature or that is confided to me in my official capacity will be kept ever secret unless revelation is necessary in the performance of my duty.

I will never act officiously or permit personal feelings, prejudices, animosities, or friendships to influence my decisions. With no compromise for crime and with the relentless prosecution of criminals, I will enforce the law courteously and appropriately without fear or favor, malice, or ill will, never employing unnecessary force or violence and never accepting gratuities.

I recognize the badge of my office as a symbol of public faith, and I accept it as a public trust to be held so long as I am true to the ethics of police service. I will constantly strive to achieve these objectives and ideals, dedicating myself before God to my chosen profession...law enforcement."

Using this canon, Larry Jetmore describes the officer as ideally concerned with the welfare of others, a protector of the weak, a behavior model for others: brave, loyal, self-disciplined, law abiding, honest, honorable, pious, and trustworthy. (7) While few or no police officers may actually achieve this ethical ideal, we are all probably aware of it. When we fall short of it, we know it. Stress is the usual result. The degree of experienced stress is proportional to the magnitude of the ethical lapse. In other words, the greater the ethical violation, the worse we should generally feel.

Luckily, the subject of professional ethics and stress is in the curriculum of most police academies and departmental corruption is certainly much less prevalent now than in the past. The absolute intolerance of both personal and witnessed corruption will hopefully continue this positive trend.

Police Culture and Suicide

In Eastern cultures, suicide has historically had a cultural role. (6) In ancient Japan, seppuku, the ritual art of self-disembowelment, was an accepted way to deal with personal or public dishonor. Indian widows engaged in suttee, or self-immolation on their husbands' funeral pyre as an expression of extreme grief. In the modern Western world, suicide has been prohibited with religious and civil penalties. In Illinois, while coercing or assisting in a suicide is a Class 2-4 felony (720ILCS5/12-31), no specific criminal offense for attempting or committing suicide exists. Those who fail at suicide are usually considered mentally ill and are placed in psychiatric confinement until they are judged to be sane by 2 psychiatrists. The stigma of a suicide attempt will usually follow one for life. Therefore, a failed suicide attempt may have profound negative consequences.

The professional model of police culture is distinguished by a paramilitary, vertically oriented chain of command that limits avenues of expression and presents a strict list of general orders. Weapons are readily available. Officers are taught to be in control at all times. It is their job to be the regulatory element in all situations where they are professionally present. Physical control is required when verbal control fails. When all else fails, lethal force represents the ultimate physical control. The officer's sidearm symbolizes physical control. Intense stress may accompany this responsibility. New police officers may experience their idealism replaced by cynicism because of the inability to exert problem solving control in many situations. "The police culture may create an (armed) individual trained in the use deadly force to maintain control, who is stressed and cynical." (8) In this light, suicide conforms to the control dictum-a way of exerting control when other options don't exist. It may be part of the dark side of the double-edged sword of control. Hopelessness, as a result of loss of control, may slowly worsen insurmountably. Loh summarizes the process as follows: (the) "graduate is frequently exposed to blood, gore, and danger. (He/she) does not unburden these horrors on spouse. Spouse wouldn't understand. A few drinks with the guys after work to help unwind. Fellow cops don't understand. Can't trust civilians. Can't admit troubles, even to fellow cops; would be considered a wimp. Can't trust fellow cops. Drinking increases. Spouse takes off. Gun is handy." (9) Although the subject of "first responder" depression may be presented in police training academies, law enforcement suicide is generally not discussed. Violanti states "suicide is (viewed) as particularly disgraceful to the victim officer and to the profession." (10) To compound the problem, law enforcement suicide is rarely viewed as an agency administrative problem. Multiple past police administrators have stated that police suicide was not job related. Gale Scott quotes a NYC Police Foundation study stating that these suicides are due to non-job related issues including personal problems, substance abuse, and depression. (11) Many agencies disavow acknowledgement of the police suicide issue by not keeping or releasing statistical data on this subject.

Warning Signs of Suicide
A voluminous literature exists regarding the motivational factors to commit suicide.

A suicide survivor group, SOLOS, (the Survivors of Loved One's Suicides) feel that the goal of suicide is to end pain and suffering but not necessarily to end life. The person may not be a controller, but a victim; they may be acting involuntarily, not voluntarily. About eighty percent of suicides are related to depression or mental disorders. Remember that the stress syndrome causes anxiety and depression. Underlying what may seem to be a rationally thought out act, is a desperate effort to escape extreme anguish. (12)

Michael Connor (13) summarizes suicide motivational issues as follows:

1. *Change-* A way to change how one feels about their life situation.
2. *Choice-* A way to make a life choice when no other options seem available.
3. *Control-* A way to stop the victim's negative behavior, to control events, or to effect other change.
4. *Self-Punishment-* A way to relieve guilt or punish oneself.
5. *Punish Others-* A way to inflict harm or punish others.
6. *Psychosis-* The result of a loss of contact with reality.

Connor presents a brief list of "Critical Suicide Risk Factors" including:
1. Wishing one didn't exist.
2. Thinking one would like to go to sleep and not wake up.
3. Dwelling on death.
4. Feeling one would be better off dead.
5. Thinking about suicide.
6. Planning suicide.
7. Suicidal gestures (physically injuring oneself or participating in dangerous behavior.)

Contributing factors for suicide include:
1. Alcohol or drug abuse.
2. Impulsive behavior.
3. Explosive Anger.
4. All or nothing thinking.
5. Depression.
6. Isolation and Withdrawal.
7. Feelings of hopelessness, rejection, helplessness.

8   Giving away important belongings.
9   Sense of loss/abandonment.
10 Anniversary or recent death of someone close.
11 Unusual behavior with pre-existing depression.
12 Marital or parental separation or divorce.
13 Loss of important relationships.
14 Unsuccessful efforts to ask for help.
15 Psychiatric history.
16 Health problems.
17 Poor communications and ongoing conflicts in personal relationships.
18 Background in the military or law enforcement.
19 Loved one(s) committed suicide.
20 Can't or might not be able to meet obligations.
21 Loss (potential loss) of face.

If a Critical Suicide Risk Factor is identified (especially in the presence of contributing factors), a possible situation is present. Your agency's crisis intervention plan should be activated (hopefully a plan exists and you know who to call). The involved person should not be left alone during this process. This may become a difficult or even confrontational situation. Trust your instincts. If you feel strongly about it, follow through. An analogous situation might be taking away an intoxicated friend's car keys.

Appropriate actions interacting with a potential suicide victim also include (14):

1   Be direct. Speak openly.
2   Be willing to listen. Allow expressions of feelings.
3   Be non-judgmental. Don't debate or lecture.
4   Show interest and support.
5   Never dare someone, even jokingly, to commit suicide.

6 Don't act shocked.
7 Don't be sworn to secrecy. Seek help immediately.
8 Offer hope and take action. Remove dangerous articles in the immediate vicinity.

Consider calling 988 or visiting http://www.988lifeline.org/. This is the national 988 Suicide and Crisis Lifeline service. It was begun in 2005 and is administered by the U.S. Substance Abuse and Mental Health Services Administration (SAMHSA) and respected private partners. Both the hotline and website are available 24/7 throughout the country and provide life saving information and contacts.

You've done the right thing; you may be thanked for it later.

What's An Agency to Do?
Law enforcement is recognized as being one of the highest stress producing professions. (15) High rates of suicide, alcoholism, divorce, and health problems such as heart disease and strokes are commonly present. According to one study, the average officer may only live 5 years past retirement.

The five general categories of stress include:
1 One's personal life;
2 Law enforcement work tension;
3 The public's non-supportive attitude toward law enforcement;
4 The dysfunctional aspects of the criminal justice system;
5 Stresses caused by employing law enforcement agencies.

An organizational approach to law enforcement stress reduction may improve department morale and positively impact the other general stress categories. In response to negative publicity from a rash of 8 officer suicides in five years, the Philadelphia, Pennsylvania Police Department created the position of Stress Manager in 1995. This job description examines general orders and seeks revisions to reduce line officer stress. Decreasing stress might logically decrease officer replacement costs by improving morale, productivity, and departmental efficiency. Specific areas of concern might include job assignments, shift scheduling, training scheduling and reimbursement, and court scheduling. Command level adjustments include supervisory support and availability, humane Field Training Officer (FTO) programs and the crucial area of managing critical incident stress. The Michigan State Police Behavioral Science Unit trains all MSP sergeants in critical incident stress management techniques. It is crucial to establish a formal program for managing suicide related issues. If such an emergent situation arises, an action plan must exist that is known to all officers so that they may respond appropriately. Even expressions of concern, follow-up phone calls to family members, and paperwork assistance following a critical incident may reap rewards in productivity down the line. Some method of allowing or even encouraging officer constructive criticism is suggested. A small step such as providing a suggestion box may be appreciated. As recent legal decisions have placed the responsibility for officer stress squarely in the agency's lap (Mogel v. Arizona, 12/19/92), it is the wise administrator who will develop policies to address the management of depression, stress related complaints and suicidal behaviors. A standardized policy regarding victim family support after successful suicides might also be helpful.

What's An Officer or an Involved Individual to Do?
There are no easy answers to this question. It is certainly a good idea to keep in mind the larger perspective or your role in society beyond law enforcement. You may be a husband, wife, father, mother, son or daughter. Your family loves and needs you. Don't be afraid to share your fears and frustrations with them. You may be surprised by their understanding and

support. Avoid the "Stress Syndrome." There is a life off duty. Enjoy it! Make non-law enforcement friends. Turn off the scanner at home. Volunteer in religious or school activities. Develop a hobby. Don't be jaded by your negative experiences. Importantly, keep your sense of humor! Humor is truly a stress safety valve. Decreasing stress with humor may actually improve performance. (author's note-as a retired trauma orthopedic surgeon, I've noticed that in the most life threatening situations, humor is frequently present.) Rocco Mazza (16) recommends practicing the 6 "R's":

1. REFLECTION - Be sensitive to the stresses that affect you.
2. RELAXATION AND EXERCISE - Have fun and stay fit. Don't take yourself too seriously.
3. RELATIONSHIPS - Have a set of guiding values. Love God, love your family, and love yourself!
4. REFUELING - You are what you eat. These days I recommend limiting carbohydrates and sugars.
5. RECREATION - Have fun with the people you care about. This especially includes your family and non-police friends.
6. RESPONSIBILITY - Take responsibility for your life choices and direction.

Remember, as Dave Smith points out, to "love your profession, not your department." Your department is a thing. It can't love you back. Gain satisfaction from loving your work and the relationships it creates. Your family loves you: your community needs and respects you.

Summary
There are no glib solutions in dealing with the reality of police suicide. Even one suicide is unacceptable. Although eliminating

suicide is highly unlikely, this should still be our goal. Neither individuals nor agencies have done nearly enough in this effort. A multi-dimensional approach is needed including:

1. *Admission that a problem exists* - Get law enforcement suicide out of the closet! All law enforcement agencies should openly accept that a special problem regarding an increased suicide rate among police officers exists compared to the general public. Hiding the problem through misclassification of suicide as accidental death harms our profession more than it may help any individual victim. We need to know the true scope of this problem. Misclassification should be absolutely forbidden. The knowledge that suicide will be recognized as such may hopefully discourage it. Gun cleaning kits dropped at the suicide scene in an effort to reclassify the suicide as an "accidental discharge" should never occur and should meet severe sanctions. Such a cover-up occurred in the suicide of twenty-eight-year-old Massachusetts State Trooper Catherine Galvin on Oct. 29, 1994. (17) We also need to know accurate statistics regarding race/gender data, and the true number of police retiree suicides.

2. *Education-* Law enforcement suicide and Post Traumatic Stress Disorder must receive adequate coverage at both the police academy and at agency in-service levels. Formal stress reduction training is available through many avenues including the Central Florida Police Stress Unit Training Institute. Their phone number is 1-800- SUICIDE.

3. *Continue the battle* against law enforcement corruption as a source of stress.

4. *Agency efforts-* All agencies should adopt separate and formal critical incident, stress reduction, and suicide risk response programs. Hopefully, in the future these types of programs will be standardized nationally. Agency efforts at stress reduction including officer feedback, flexible shift assignments, community policing concepts, humane FTO programs, and requiring officer participation in stress reduction training are a possible few avenues to investigate. There should be no professional sanction against an officer obtaining help from an agency response program. Through existing policy, victim's families should know where they stand. Agencies partnering with their work force to seek creative and effective solutions to stress management will benefit both groups.

5. *Individual efforts-* Be aware of the Critical Suicide Risk (and contributing) Factors. If a suicide related issue develops, don't hesitate to pursue it. Remember the "appropriate actions" suggested in approaching someone considering suicide. Immediately contact the designated police administrator to set your agency's formal response plan into action. Try to be as well rounded a person as possible. Compartmentalize police work into its proper place in your life. Be able to laugh about life and don't take yourself too seriously (we know...you're the police).

REFERENCES

1. http://www.tearsofacop.com/police/articles/turvey.html
2. http://www.tearsofacop.com/police/articles/turvey.html
3. Police Magazine /2003
4. Suicide and Life Threatening Behavior, 26(1):79-85, 1996
5. Kates, A.-https://www.copshock.com
6. https://www.policestress.org/ethical.html, Central Florida Police Stress Unit
7. Jetmore, L.- The Path of the Warrior, Looseleaf Law Publications, Flushing, N.Y., 1997
8. "Police Officers: Control, Hopelessness, and Suicide," Knowledge Solutions Library, http://www.corpusdelecti.com/suicide.html, April 1995
9. Ibid. Turvey, 1995
10. Loh, J.-The Oregonian, January 30, 1994, p. A24
11. Violanti, J.- "The Mystery Within, Understanding Police Suicide" FBI Law
12. Enforcement Bulletin, February 1995, pp. 19-23
13. Scott, G.-"Job Not Guilty in Cop Suicides," New York Newsday, September 15, 1994, p. A23
14. https://www.solos.org
15. https://www.crisiscounseling.com/Suicide/SuicideRisk.html
16. https://www.policestress.org/reduce.html Central Florida Police Stress Unit
17. Mazza, R.- Behind the Heavy Badge, Guns, and Weapons for Law Enforcement
18. Armstrong, D.-Suicide Epidemic Spreads Through Police Ranks, Boston Globe, Aug. 23, 1998

Dental and Facial Injuries

Martin Greenberg, MD

SCENARIO
A high-risk warrant service callout occurs involving a dynamic entry. As the team quickly enters the darkened structure, the lead officer trips over an obstruction on the floor and falls forward face first. As he lands, he instinctively protects his long gun, and his chin forcefully strikes the carry handle of the AR-15 carbine. The tactical team continues in and completes the entry within a few seconds. The injured point officer then spits out blood and an upper front tooth. Within thirty seconds of the call "medic up!" the lost tooth is irrigated with sterile saline solution and gently replaced in its socket. The operator is instructed to bite down on a sterile gauze sponge to aid in the tooth's alignment and splinting. He is then immediately transferred to the emergency department where the hospital dentist wires the tooth to its neighbors and prescribes a tetanus toxoid injection, pain meds and antibiotics. The tooth eventually survives.

INTRODUCTION
The law enforcement officer or really any of us may encounter a wide variety of traumatic, blast, burn, chemical, and missile type facial injuries. Hausamen makes the clear case that the "management of cranio-maxillofacial trauma includes treatment of facial bone fractures, dento-alveolar (dental-gum)

trauma, and soft tissue...injuries of the head and neck."(1) The head, face, and neck tissues can be subject to injury from various types of projectiles including bullets, shrapnel, bone, and teeth. Trauma to the orbital, nasal, maxillary (upper jaw) and mandibular bones can cause these bones to break in several different ways requiring a variety of repair techniques (Picture One). Injuries to the eyes and their muscles, nerves and blood vessels may also occur if the facial bones or teeth are broken or avulsed. Trauma to the nose can even send bone fragments into the front of the brain! Though generally stronger than the upper jaw, the lower jaw or mandible may be dislocated and/or broken. If the mandible is broken it becomes unstable and is easily separated from the temporomandibular joints (TMJs) that attach the mandible to the skull. The soft tissue of the cheeks and lips can also then even be stripped from the jaw.

All craniofacial and maxillofacial trauma research efforts (1-6) report a concurrence of broken cervical vertebra with craniomaxillofacial trauma. Cervical vertebra number two appears the most common fracture of the neck associated with blunt trauma to the midface. (2, 3)

Along with bullets, shrapnel, and other projectiles, teeth may be knocked out completely (avulsed), partially fractured, and/or loosened. Tooth fragments can turn into missiles and with enough velocity, puncture and lacerate (cut) through nerves and blood vessels. Broken teeth and facial bones turned into secondary missiles can embed into the nasal and maxillary sinuses, throat, cheeks, tongue, and lips.

Facial and lower jaw trauma has an associated likelihood of laryngeal trauma and airway damage. The facial bones are the thickness of an eggshell. When fractured, they have the potential to collapse and compromise the airway. When lacerations accompany oral and maxillofacial trauma, bleeding and swelling is often profuse. Swelling of the tongue may also present a particularly difficult airway problem.

In summary, oral and maxillofacial trauma refers to any injury to the face, nose, jaws, and teeth. It may be severe enough to cause a concussion, a cervical spine (C-Spine) injury or a brain injury. Secondary missile injuries due to bone and tooth fragments accompany oral and maxillofacial trauma. Finally, oral, maxillofacial, and periodontal (gum) trauma may compromise breathing.

Incidence of Maxillofacial Trauma
In discussing maxillofacial trauma, it is necessary to define some basic anatomic structures and fracture patterns around the face.

  A. Key Anatomical Regions:

  Cricoid Cartilage: durable circular ring of tissue located below the thyroid cartilage, and in between the thyroid and cricoid cartilage.

  Infraorbital Rim: area of face that forms the bony, protective circular ring around each eye.

  Nasal-Orbital area: region of midface that encompasses the nasal bones, the bridge of nose, and bony orbital rims surrounding the eyes.

  Nasal Pyramid: the two delicate bones that attach directly to the frontal process of the upper maxillary jaw which help to form the bridge of the nose.

  Pterygoid Plates: wing shaped bones of the base of the skull, behind the maxilla (upper jaw). These bone plates serve as attachments for several muscles that help to direct and guide the mandible during movement in multiple directions and when clenching down.

  Thyroid Cartilage: primary cartilage of the larynx, made of two broad, flat plates that form a V-shaped structure called the "Adam's Apple."

  Temporomandibular Joints: bilateral joints of the mandible (jaw) that insert into rotating sockets on the skull in front of the ear.

Zygomatic (Malar) Bone: the bone on either side of the face below the eyes.

Zygomatic Arch: the bone formation of the zygomatic process of each malar bone joining the skull temporal bone.

B. Fracture Definitions:

Blowout Fracture: a fracture of the base of the eye sockets that is also called an orbital floor fracture (see Picture 1).

LeFort Type I Fracture: a fracture in which the maxilla (upper jaw) separates from the midface below the nasal-orbital area and through the nasal pyramid. The medic can usually determine when the upper jaw (hard palate) seems to be floating in the mouth when he/she grasps the upper front incisor teeth (see Picture 2).

LeFort Type II Fracture: (pyramidal fracture) describes a fracture across the nasal root and through the infra-orbital rim but below the zygomatic (malar) bone (see Picture 2).

LeFort Type III Fracture: upper jaw fracture involving the complete separation of the upper jaw and the zygomas. The face may look "longer" or stretched and flattened. All of these types of fractures involve the fracture of the pterygoid plates. The maxilla often is displaced posteriorly causing an open bite. Here, all of the facial bones but not the skull will be mobile (see Picture 2.)

Mandibular (Jawbone) Fracture: This is one of the most common facial fractures. The mandible can fracture in the areas of the condyle, the body, and the bony midline (see Picture 1.)

Nasoethmoidal (NOE) Fracture: NOE fractures extend into the nose through the ethmoid bones, the frontal sinus, ethmoid sinuses, anterior cranial fossa, orbits, frontal bone, and nasal bones. Fractures through the ethmoid area are prone to cerebrospinal fluid (CSF) leaks from tears leading to CSF rhinorrhea (leaking into the nose).

Orbital Floor Fracture: This type of fracture usually occurs when a blunt object strikes the eye and its surrounding bones.

Interestingly, the eye itself usually does not rupture and the pressure of the blow is transferred to the delicate bones of the orbital floor. This is a serious fracture that can lead to double vision, loss of vision or eye paralysis.

Step-off Fracture: Feeling the palate from inside the mouth may reveal an irregularity called a step-off fracture. Eye injuries may be associated with these fractures. A thorough eye exam with concurrent facial trauma is important for this reason.

Tripod Fracture: A tripod fracture is a fracture of multiple facial bones (usually the malar, the inferior orbital rim, and the lateral orbital wall). Suspect it after blunt force to the cheek with physical findings of marked periorbital (around the eyes) swelling and bruising. Malar flattening may be seen early but marked swelling of overlying tissues often obscures this finding. Facial numbness due to an infraorbital nerve injury may also occur.

Zygoma Fracture: Physical findings of a depressed malar eminence with tenderness suggest a zygoma or zygomatic arch fracture. Local swelling may obscure the depression. The patient may complain of pain in the cheek on movement of the jaw. The patient may have trismus (difficulty opening the mouth) from impingement of the temporalis muscle as it passes under the zygoma.

Reports regarding the incidence of cranio-oral-maxillofacial trauma are few (1, 2, and 3). Clinicians may use different descriptors to describe facial trauma. For example, there are three types of LeFort type jawbone fractures of the maxillofacial (upper) jaw structures (Picture Two). Leading to confusion, all of these maxillofacial fractures can be reported as LeFort fracture types 1-3 or they may be described generally as "mid-face fractures."

The second reason that it is difficult to establish reliable reports on the occurrence of oral and maxillofacial trauma is that several types of health care providers treat these injuries including physicians (MD, DO), oral surgeons (DDS) and combined physician-oral surgeons (DDS, MD). Up to seventy-five percent of people involved in auto-accidents will sustain at least minor maxillofacial trauma. (6) Automobile airbags may decrease this percentage. Hackel and colleagues (2) report that over forty percent of patients involved in motor vehicle accidents (MVAs) with maxillofacial trauma also have cervical spine injuries. Gassner and colleagues (3) report facial injuries in twelve to forty percent of automobile accidents. Facial trauma may occur with cervical spine fractures. Again, the most common associated cervical spine fracture involves the second cervical vertebra. This is potentially serious as spinal cord injury at this level may be fatal. In fact, a type of fracture of this vertebra is called "the hangman's fracture."

We live life "face first." Despite training, many officers still "lead with the face." Sports trauma accounts for almost forty percent of facial trauma. Lateral mid-face fractures are the predominate type of sports related maxillofacial fracture. Other studies suggest that about twenty-two percent of maxillofacial fractures are seen during activities of daily life (ADL) and about eleven percent occur during assaults. (2) Similarly, up to seventy-four percent of maxillofacial trauma patients sustained soft tissue injuries including lacerations, concussions, and hematomas. The incidence of dento-alveolar (tooth related) trauma as a component of facial trauma ranges from eight to fifty percent. (3)

Data on gunshot injuries to the face is also limited. Military (7) and civilian reports (8, 9) demonstrate that bullets account for significant cosmetic and soft tissue damage to the mouth and face. Larger bullet caliber, higher projectile kinetic energy and the use of hollow point, pre-fragmented or fragmenting rounds are also factors affecting the amount of resulting facial trauma, bleeding, and potential airway loss. Surgical correction is required in ninety-eight percent of these serious maxillofacial injuries with a 2.2% mortality rate.

Maxillofacial Trauma Emergency Treatment

Trauma is the leading cause of death during the first forty years of life. (3) A rapid and focused assessment is required in all trauma cases. *The officer or medic should check for Deformities, Contusions, Abrasions, Punctures, Burns, Tenderness, Lacerations, and Swelling with the mnemonic known as "DECAP-BTLS." (6)*

The major signs of physical trauma to the oral and maxillofacial structures include swelling, bleeding, bruising, and black eyes. Other signs include jaw crepitus (a sign of dislocation and/or fractures of facial and jaw bones, redness and blisters in burn patients, possible airway blockage due to swelling and bleeding and loss of the physical structure of parts of the face. Symptoms may also include pain, paresthesia (tingling), blurred or double vision, decreased mobility of the eye, numbness in the area of the eye or loss of vision. Double vision can linger for months after maxillofacial injuries. Symptoms of traumatic brain injury include problems with thinking, memory, judgment, mood swings, and difficulty with coordination and balance. These symptoms can linger for long periods of time. Trauma to oral and maxillofacial structures can lead to loss of airway, hypotension (low blood pressure) and shock.

After the primary survey (DECAP-BTLS), the secondary survey should be performed. The secondary survey is a step-by-step *CRASH PLAN*. (10) The primary objective for the medic during maxillofacial emergency care is to maintain an open airway (4-8) and secure cervical spinal stability.

The mnemonic *"A CRASH PLAN"* stands for:

A is for Airway: Is the airway patent and is adequate air exchange occurring?

C is for Cardiovascular: Is the heart rate normal or abnormal?

R is for Respiration: Is the patient breathing normally and effectively? Is breathing labored? Are breath sounds symmetrically present?

A is for Abdomen: look for signs of obvious trauma and use your stethoscope to listen for bowel sounds.

S is for Spine: Is the victim moving all his extremities? Are obvious spinal deformities present?

P is for Pelvis: Is the pelvis stable to manipulation?

L is for Limbs: Are the limbs symmetric or deformed? Are they being protected or are they used normally?

A is for Arteries: Is bleeding present? Are carotid and femoral (groin) pulses present?

Inspect face for any obvious asymmetry. Inspect all open wounds for embedded foreign bodies. Gently palpate for bony injury. Palpate bony structures of the eye's supraorbital ridge and skull frontal bone for a step-off fracture (see Fracture Definitions). Thoroughly examine the eyes for injury, abnormal ocular movements, and visual acuity. Inspect the nose for any widening and palpate for tenderness and crepitus (a crackling sensation). Inspect the nasal septum (separation of the nostrils) for a septal hematoma and clear rhinorrhea (cerebrospinal fluid leak through the nose). Palpate the zygomatic bone (see Anatomical Definitions) along its full length. Check for facial instability by carefully manipulating the teeth and hard palate. Avoid being bitten. Gently push back and forth, then up and down. Feel for movement or instability. Test the teeth for stability and inspect for any frank bleeding at the gum-line. This is a sign of periodontal trauma and possible fracture through the alveolar bone around the teeth. Check the teeth for malocclusion and step-off fractures. Palpate the mandible for tenderness, swelling, and step-off (see Picture 1). Check for localized edema or ecchymosis in the floor of the mouth under the tongue. Does the officer feel any facial numbness? Inspect the area just in front of the ear for bruising and feel for tenderness. This is the condyle of the mandible and the site of an often-missed fracture. A mandibular fracture is suggested by the inability to open the mouth, malocclusion (mal-alignment) of teeth or palpable bony step-offs. Gingival bleeding at the base of a tooth suggests a fracture, especially if teeth are malaligned. Edema or ecchymosis may be present in the floor of the mouth. Gently palpate the face for any sign of injury. Always assess for symmetrical eye movement. Never push on the eyes directly. Evaluate the ears for hemotympanum (blood behind the eardrum) that can signify a temporal bone skull fracture. Check the facial nerves by having the victim smile.

Foreign objects such as dentures, orthodontic appliances, avulsed teeth, fractured pieces of bone, or even projectiles (glass, shrapnel, and earth) may be encountered. (1-9) These objects can obstruct the airway. A digital (finger) sweep and suction of the oral cavity and oropharynx (upper throat area) are essential during the primary survey. If dentures are in place, unbroken, and secure in the mouth, leave them. Unbroken dentures can act as a temporary splint for injured bones and teeth. Remove broken dentures. The force required to break a denture is significant so suspect accompanying facial fractures. Retain the broken dentures for forensic records as all modern dentures will have the patient's name embedded in the plastic. Dental surgeons may later use these denture fragments as surgical splints to restore alignment of the jaws during operative procedures.

An emergency room visit should be immediately obtained for all suspected skull or facial fracture victims!

Palpate the orbital (eye socket) rims to make sure a tripod fracture has not occurred. A tripod fracture involves the fracture dislocation of the facial bones around the eyes. Make sure there is no double vision that can occur when an orbital blowout fracture occurs. An orbital blowout fracture is a break of the back wall of the eye socket. The inferior or medial rectus eye muscles can become entrapped in the fracture and limit eye motion. Make sure that there is no infra-orbital nerve hypesthesia (diminished sensation). The infra-orbital nerve supplies sensation to the facial area just to the side of the nose.

This can also occur with a blowout fracture or a tripod fracture. Finally, another technique to determine whether the conscious patient has oral and maxillofacial fractures is to ask them to bite down. Broken teeth always create a high index of suspicion for a facial fracture.

Once the A, B, Cs (Airway, Breathing, and Circulation) of field medical care have been completed, the oral/maxillofacial trauma patient can be transported to a hospital for definitive care. A victim sustaining enough trauma to break maxillofacial bones may have sustained a cervical spine fracture unless proven otherwise (2, 3, 6, 9).

Basic Tooth Anatomy
Individual teeth are actually a specialized type of individual bones that extrude through the skin of the mouth. Teeth have two general anatomic parts. The hard, durable, calcified, glass-like enamel "crown" is the portion of the tooth that you can see covering the top of the tooth above the gums. The remaining hidden part of the tooth is usually called the "root." The majority of the body of the tooth is composed of dentin. Dentin has a composition almost identical to bone. The root does not have the hard enamel protective covering of the crown. Some teeth have one root while other teeth will have up to five roots. The saying, "long of tooth" means that one can see both the crown portion and the root portion of the tooth. Root protrusion above the gum line is a normal part of aging. The center of each tooth has a hollow portion that houses and protects the dental nerves and blood supply also called the pulp (Picture 4). Typically, we have "baby teeth" and then thirty-two "adult" teeth. The wisdom teeth are the last to erupt, usually at ages eighteen to twenty-two.

As teeth grow and erupt out of the bones of the jaw, they push through the gums and into the mouth. The gums are known as the gingiva and alveolar mucosa. The eruptive process of teeth includes the formation of a ligament type tooth suspension called the periodontal ligament. The periodontal ligament with its associated ligamentous structures called Sharpie bundle fibers completely envelope each individual tooth. The periodontal ligament binds the tooth and connects the tooth to the surrounding alveolar bones of the jaw (Picture 4). The periodontal ligament apparatus acts like other ligaments in the body absorbing shocks and stresses through a trampoline suspension system able to handle the stresses associated with chewing and grinding. (11)

Field Management of Tooth and Gum Injuries
The officer or medic should expect to encounter loose and partially attached implants, bridges, or other prosthetic materials. The medic may consider adding a simple Dental Trauma Kit to their trauma bag. A sample kit could include: 4X4 sterile gauze sponges, saline packs, cold packs, gauze pressure packs, roller gauze, a set of orthodontic wire cutters, a set of upper and lower universal extraction forceps, topical anesthetics and universal sports bite guards.

Tooth and gum injuries may involve the crown, the root of the tooth, the surrounding gums and soft tissue lip attachments. Teeth may be damaged in the following ways (see Picture 4).

Class 1 Fractures (breaks)- involve only the enamel portion of the tooth. The fracture edge may be rough but only minimal pain will be present. The officer may remain on duty and seek dental care later at his discretion.

Class 2 Fractures- include the enamel and the dentin but not the pulp. The visible yellow color of dentin will help to demonstrate this injury. The tooth will also be more sensitive to water or air contact. The officer can remain in action after sustaining this injury but should seek dental care as soon as possible.

Class 3 Fractures- include the enamel, the dentin, and extend into the pulp chamber. Here, much more pain will be present than with a Class 2 fracture. The tooth may bleed as the artery nurturing the tooth may be injured. Bleeding should be locally controlled with pressure and the officer should be taken out of service and sent for dental consultation.

Class 4 Fractures- are fractures of the tooth's root. They may be oriented in a vertical or horizontal direction and may de-stabilize the tooth. The officer with a class 4 tooth fracture should be taken out of action and sent for dental care.

Lip lacerations may occur with tooth fractures and may be packed with a sterile gauze dressing or even repaired by a physician or dental surgeon at the scene if they are properly trained and equipped. The tooth may also sustain alignment injuries in its bony (alveolar) socket. In a luxation injury, the tooth is displaced within the socket usually as a result of a direct blow to the front of the mouth. Luxation may only be minimally painful and the tooth may appear misaligned. A soft diet and a dental consult within twenty-four hours are recommended. Buddy splinting the tooth with dental floss is a temporary first aid measure. Immediate dental consultation is recommended to treat the luxated tooth.

Tooth extrusion is the incomplete loss of a tooth from its socket. This is a more serious injury than a tooth luxation and usually involves tearing of the tooth's periodontal ligaments, artery and nerve. It may not be very painful. If mandated to do so, the officer or medic may reposition the tooth by asking the operator to bite down on a gauze pad. The officer should be taken out of action. Definitive care involves a soft diet, tooth wiring and possible endodontic treatment (root canal).

Tooth avulsion represents the complete loss of a tooth. Tooth avulsion is a dental emergency. The tooth must be returned to its socket as soon as possible. Wisniewski states that the success rate of tooth re-implantation after fifteen minutes is ninety percent. After thirty minutes, re-implantation is seventy percent successful. After one hour, the tooth survival rate drops to thirty percent. It may be necessary to replant the tooth at the scene as it will usually be impossible to obtain dental care within this narrow time window. The medic should not scrape, scrub, or disinfect the tooth. Rather, rinse the tooth with sterile saline, local anesthetic solution, milk, or Hank's solution (a commercially available dental solution). Don't clean the alveolar (tooth) socket. Replace the tooth into its socket and have the officer bite down on a sterile gauze pad to assist you. If re-implantation cannot be performed at the scene, Wisniewski recommends that the tooth be placed into a sterile plastic sealed container bathed in sterile saline, cold milk, local anesthetic solution, or even saliva. Don't transport a dry tooth or use tap water as it may damage the tooth. If such containers or media are not available, the tooth may be wrapped in gauze and placed in the conscious officer's mouth next to the gum or under the tongue during transport. The Save a Tooth System (www.smartpractice.com) is a self-contained, commercial tooth transfer system. Definitive treatment for this serious dental injury includes a soft diet, tooth splinting, root canal and antibiotic therapy. (12)

Look for any broken teeth or dental prostheses/appliances lying about in the immediate environment. The medic should be aware that tooth fractures or avulsions, orthodontic wires, orthodontic traction devices, dentures, and porcelain prosthetics (crowns and bridges) can obstruct the airway as well as contribute to secondary trauma. The best course of action is to remove anything from the oral cavity that is loose, floating, or broken. An officer's field scissors are usually adequate to cut through orthodontic wires.

Any prosthetic dental parts encountered during the scene survey should be collected. Gather and store these items in a Ziploc bag for forensic studies. Intact but completely avulsed natural teeth have the potential to be re-implanted. The officer or medic should assume that any unaccounted for natural or prosthetic teeth were aspirated or swallowed. A chest and/or abdominal x-ray may demonstrate the errant tooth.

The vast majority of lacerations and bleeding on the exterior face and lips can be stabilized successfully with trauma pack and pressure dressings provided by an Ace® Wrap, Emergency Bandage® or Olaes® Bandage. Lacerations and tears within the oral cavity such as the buccal (cheek) mucosa, gums, lips, and tongue can also be dressed with gauze. The easiest manner to manage these injuries is to place the gauze between the teeth and the laceration using the natural pressure of the muscles within the lips and cheeks to apply direct pressure on the laceration while against the jaws and gums. Though the face and mouth bleed profusely, pack dressings are usually sufficient enough to stabilize the wound during transport from the field to the Urgent Care, emergency room or a dentist's office.

Oral Hygiene Rationale and Recommendations
The oral and maxillofacial trauma victim has the potential for significant post injury problems. Surgical repairs of maxillofacial fractures utilizing titanium mini-plates, orthodontic wires and endosseous titanium dental implants require anywhere from eight weeks to six months to fully heal. Soft tissue repairs (nerve and skin grafting) and bony repairs may require longer healing periods. Damage to the optic nerve (cranial nerve two) can lead to vision disruption and blindness. Damage to the facial nerve (cranial nerve seven) or the trigeminal nerve (cranial nerve five) may occur. Paresthesias (constant tingling), anesthesia (constant numbness), loss of facial muscles or their control and excessive drooling are other potential problems. Broken teeth often require endodontic (root canal) therapy to remove the damaged neuro-vascular bundle within the root and eliminate tooth based dental pain. Daily oral hygiene becomes very difficult for the post trauma individual who has dental wires, mini-plates and/or external fixation. Most oral and maxillofacial trauma and surgery patients will have soreness, limited range of jaw movement, limited access to the oral cavity and greatly reduced oral hygiene skills for

extended periods of time. Oral flora (bacteria, fungi, virus, and protozoa) thrive in the oral cavity with inadequate daily hygiene. Without proper oral hygiene, the remaining undamaged oral and maxillofacial structures are at higher risk for the onset of cavities (bacteria dissolve the enamel and spread into the dentin) and periodontal disease. Health care professionals play a significant role in the care of the trauma victim by correcting the damage and in assisting the patient to maintain oral health and tissue integrity during healing.

Summary
The officer or medic can expect to encounter a wide variety of traumatic, missile, and burn type injuries during their career. Research demonstrates that injuries to the maxillofacial, oral, and periodontal structures account for ten to seventy percent of all injuries. Cervical spine fractures are common life-threatening injuries associated with oral and maxillofacial trauma. Airway maintenance is always a key concern. Prompt re-implantation of avulsed teeth may salvage them. Emergency Medical Services (EMS) personnel can provide Basic or Advanced Trauma Life Support skills to save teeth and even lives until victims can receive definitive care.

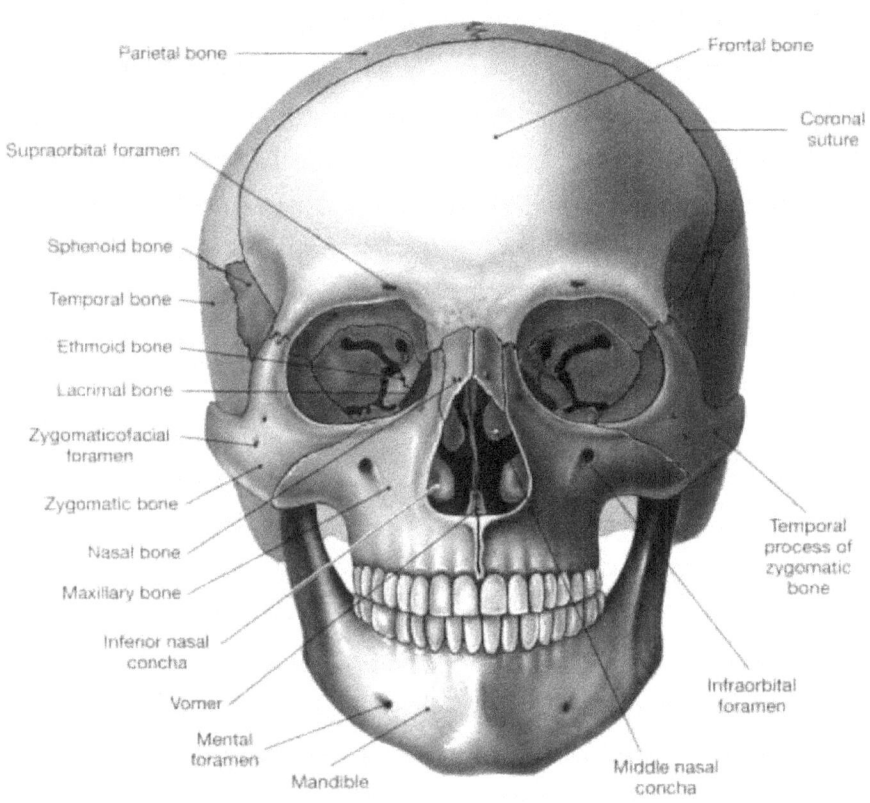

Oral and Maxillofacial Trauma Zones: (Martinia F, Human Anatomy, 2nd Ed, (1995), Prentice Hall, New Jersey, pg., 145.

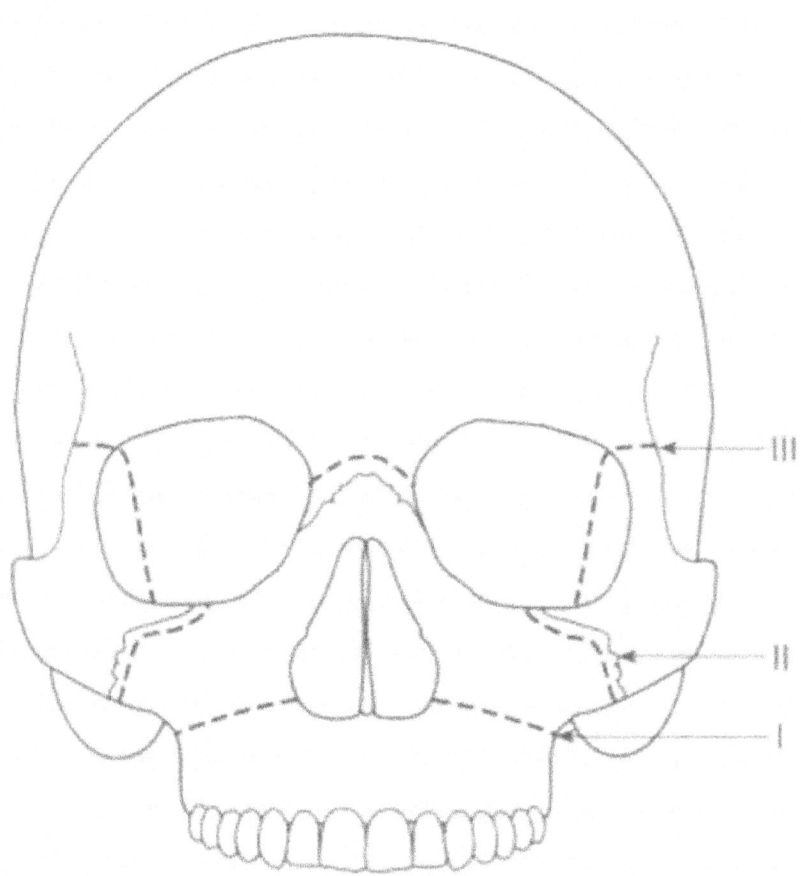

LeFort I, II, and III Fracture zones (6). Courtesy of Dr Joel Epstein, DDS, MSc, FRCDS (Can).

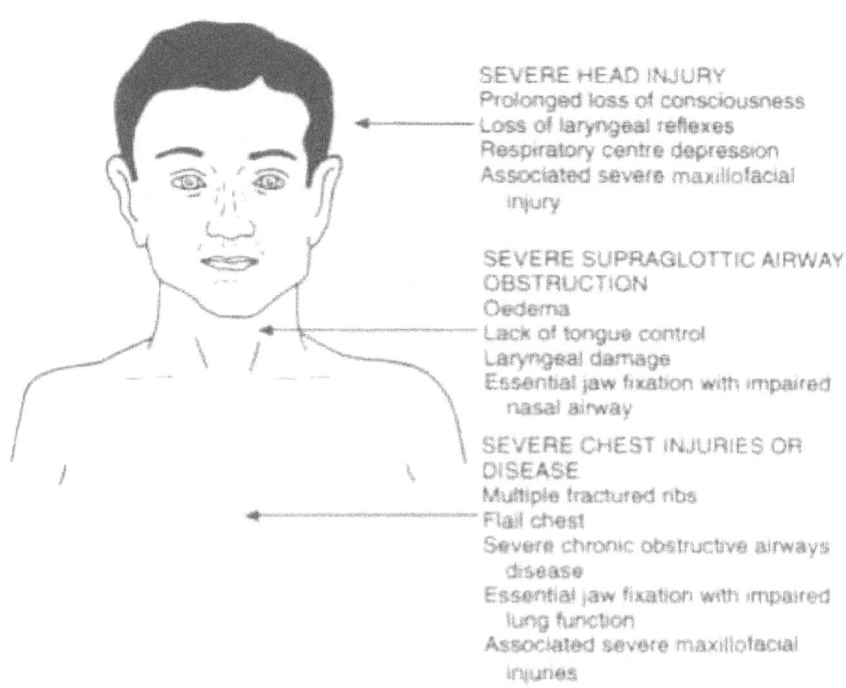

Maxillofacial surgical indications for intubations and or tracheotomy (6): Courtesy of Dr Joel Epstein, DDS, MSc, FRCDS (Can).

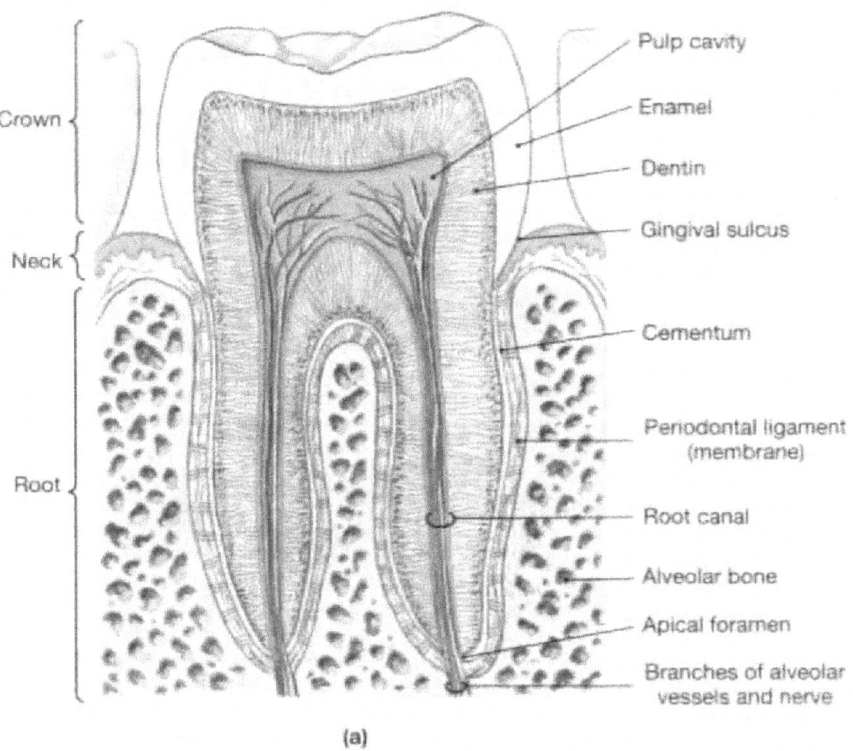

TYPICAL ALVEOLAR BONE, PERIODONTAL LIGAMENT AND TOOTH ANATOMY PICTURE. Courtesy of Dr. Michael Colvar.

REFERENCES

1. Hausamen J. The scientific development of maxillofacial surgery in the 20th century and an outlook into the future. (2001) Journal of Cranio- Maxillofacial Surgery, 29:2-21.
2. Hackl W, Hausberger K, Sailer R, Ulmer H, Gassner R., Prevalence of cervical spine injuries in patients with facial trauma. (2001). Oral Surgery, Oral Medicine, Oral Pathology. 92:370-375.
3. Gassner R, Tarkan T, Hachl O, Rudisch A, Ulmer H., Cranio-maxillofacial trauma: a ten year review of 9543 cases with 21067 injuries. (2003) J of Cranio- Maxillofacial Surgery, 31:51-61.
4. The Oxford Handbook of Dental Patient Care. (2003), Scully C, Epstein J, Wiesenfield D. Oxford University Press, Oxford, Chapter 8.2.
5. Emergency Care, 9th Ed. (2001). Limmer D, O'Keefe M., Grant H., Murry R., Bergeron J., Brady/Prentice Hall, New Jersey, pp. 765 -792.
6. Pre-hospital Emergency Care (7th Ed), Mistovich J, Hafen B, Karren K. (2004). Brady/Prentice Hall, New Jersey, pp. 757 -776.
7. Pilcher R., Management of missile wounds of the maxillofacial region during the 20th century. (1996) Injury, 27:81-88.
8. Hollier L, Grantcharova E, Kattash M., Facial gunshot wounds: a 4-year experience. (2001) J of Oral Maxillofacial Surgery, 59:277-282.
9. Motamedi M., Primary management of maxillofacial hard and soft tissue gunshot and shrapnel injuries. (2003) Journal of Oral and Maxillofacial Surgery, 61:1390-1398.
10. Heiskell, L. and Tang, D. (1996) Medical Management of K-9 Emergencies-Part Two, The Tactical Edge, winter, pp. 44.
11. Color Atlas of Dental Medicine: Vol 1: Periodontology (1989) Rateitschak K, Rateitschak E, Wold H, Hassell T., Thieme Publishers, New York.
12. Wisniewski, J. F.- Dental Injuries in Manual Of Sports Medicine, Safran, M., McKeag, D., and Van Camp, S., editors, Lippincott-Raven Publishers, Philadelphia, Penn., 1998, pp. 500-505.

Understanding the Threat of Radiologic/Nuclear Weapons

Martin Greenberg, MD

Scenario
Imagine that terrorists explode a homemade one-kiloton nuclear device in an urban area. A 300-ft. diameter blast area is ignited leaving a 120-ft. crater and vaporizing everything within this area. Buildings within one-fourth mile are totally destroyed, while all others within miles are heavily damaged. All humans and animals within ¼ mile are instantly killed or maimed, many simply vaporized in the intense heat and blast. The dark red color of blood, a radioactive mushroom cloud extends over 10,000 ft. high. Radiation exposure kills a majority of humans within a one-fourth by nine-mile area within two weeks and spreads hundreds of miles downwind. Cancer rates rise for the next several generations in the surrounding area with many other long-term effects.

Introduction
This material describes the physics, medical effects, history, mechanics, and current global status of nuclear weapons. Although no nuclear terrorist attack has ever been documented, it still is important to understand this devastating potential

threat. Please do not feel that this subject is too terrifying or overwhelming to consider. This is a reference chapter whose goal is to provide a general overview of nuclear weapons in the twentieth and twenty-first century.

Thermonuclear Physics
Uranium fission is most effectively caused by one neutron striking a uranium nucleus. This nucleus splits and releases two or three neutrons and a tremendous amount of energy. These freed neutrons can then potentially strike other nuclei and continue the chain reaction. A baseball-sized sphere of fissile (able to produce a chain reaction) plutonium will produce an explosion equal to 20,000 tons of TNT. An adequately sized sphere of fissile material is needed to sustain a chain reaction. Too small a sphere will allow too many neutrons to escape the sphere without striking nuclei. The minimum sphere size needed to sustain a chain reaction is termed the critical mass. The actual mass of material needed depends upon the purity of the material. Uranium that is enriched to greater than twenty percent U-235 is termed Highly Enriched Uranium (HEU). Weapons grade uranium has been enriched to greater than ninety percent U-235. Its pure critical mass is said to be 25 kg. The critical mass for Pu-239 is 8 kg. Plutonium can therefore be used to make smaller/lighter weapons. Less than this amount is called a sub-critical amount. A dense, non-fissile envelope called a tamper usually surrounds the fissile material. The tamper prevents neutron loss and optimizes the chain reaction. In a bomb, creating a super-critical mass is not practical as it would immediately explode. Instead, two sub-critical masses are separated and become critical when a conventional explosive fires the sub-critical masses at one another. This firing tool is called a gun-assembly device. Alternatively, an implosion weapon utilizes chemical conventional explosives surrounding a core of fissile material. The detonated conventional explosive uni-

formly compresses the sub-critical mass into a dense super-critical mass. Implosion weapons can use Uranium or Plutonium and are more complex to construct than gun-assembly device type weapons. The implosion impact welds the sub-critical pieces together that then become critical.

The nuclear explosion takes a millionth of a second to occur. In contrast, nuclear fusion is a reaction in which lighter elements are joined to form heavier elements. The end product weighs less than the sum of its parts. The difference is converted to energy. As hydrogen isotopes are used in these high temperature reactions, fusion devices are called hydrogen or thermonuclear bombs. In a *hydrogen bomb*, an atomic bomb is surrounded by a layer of lithium deuteride and a tamper. The resulting explosion produces neutrons that impact the lithium, "fissioning" it into helium, tritium, and energy. This energy creates the high temperature needed for the fusion of deuterium and tritium, and tritium with itself. "Advanced thermonuclear weapons" include an outer shell of HEU that combine the fusion and fission reactions to greatly increase weapon yield. The *cobalt bomb* includes cobalt in its shell that is converted by fusion neutron bombardment to the 5-year gamma emitter cobalt (Co)-60. Other isotopes such as gold (gamma emitter for days) or zinc (gamma emitter for months) can be used for shorter effects. The operative tactic is to make strategically valuable areas like the nation's capital or large cities uninhabitable for variable periods of time. The general term for an area denial weapon is a *salted bomb*. Enhanced radiation weapons or "*neutron bombs*" are small fusion devices that allow the explosive burst of neutrons to escape and act to destroy personnel but not local structures.

A Brief History of Nuclear Weapons

The dawn of the nuclear age revolved around a race against time between Germany and the United States to develop the atomic bomb during WW2. The United States was entering a battle for its very survival when on August 2, 1939 Albert Einstein informed President Franklin D. Roosevelt of efforts in Nazi Germany to purify U-235 and to develop an atomic bomb. Soon after, a massive research endeavor named the Manhattan Project was begun to develop a viable atomic bomb. From 1939-45, over 2 billion dollars were spent (translated into 37.7 billion 2022 dollars) in this project led by physicist J. Robert Oppenheimer. A key problem was the production of adequate amounts of enriched uranium to sustain a nuclear chain reaction. It was difficult to extract this isotope as the ratio of uranium metal to its compounded ore was 1:500. An ore is a combination of elements containing the desired metal. The 1 part thus obtained that was over 99% U-238 which was useless in bomb production. Scientists at Colombia University were ultimately able to resolve this problem and a massive enrichment plant was constructed at Oak Ridge, Tenn. using a gas centrifuge to separate the 2 uranium isotopes. The great question was would atomic fission actually work? Everyone knew that they were engaged in a life or death race to deploy an atomic weapon. The first atomic bomb was code-named "The Gadget" and finally on July 16, 1945 at 0530 hours, The Gadget's explosion marked the beginning of the nuclear age. A breathtaking fireball, white to orange and rising at 360 feet/second presented its then unexpected mushroom cloud 30,000 feet over the Los Alamos desert. All that remained of the sand under the blast were fragments of jade green radioactive glass, named Trinitite after the operation's code name Trinity and formed by the heat of the reaction. So bright was the flash that residents of distant communities thought "that the sun came up twice that day" and a blind girl reportedly saw the flash 120 miles away. Upon seeing it, Oppenheimer quoted the Indian prophet Bhagavad Gita: "I am become Death, the destroyer of worlds." A petition was even signed by a number of these scientists not to unleash this destructive power upon the world. It was ignored and on August

6, 1945 a 12.5 kiloton gun-assembly type Uranium bomb weighing 4½ tons named "Little Boy" was loaded on a B-29 bomber, the Enola Gay, and dropped on Hiroshima at 0815 hours. Ground Zero was set at 1,980 feet. Its target, the Aioi Bridge, was narrowly missed. In an instant 66,000 people were killed with 69,000 additional casualties. Total vaporization from the blast was ½ mile in diameter. Total destruction occurred 1 mile from the blast. Everything flammable was ablaze to 2 ½ miles with blast effects extending a total of 3 miles. On August 9, 1945, a second plutonium bomb named "Fat Man" was dropped on Nagasaki, Japan. The 22 kiloton implosion bomb leveled half the city, killing 39,000 inhabitants and injuring 25,000. Today, physicists studying these detonations retrospectively feel they were so crude that by current standards they utilized only 0.1% of their potential explosive capability.

The Global Picture
The Nuclear Nonproliferation Treaty (NPT) is an international agreement designed to prevent the spread of nuclear weapons; to verify that the peaceful use of nuclear energy is not being subverted to weapons development; to promote the peaceful uses of nuclear energy and to eventually lead to the complete nuclear disarmament of existing nuclear powers. It entered into force on March 5, 1970. By 2016, 191 countries were parties to the treaty. Parties that do not have nuclear weapons must negotiate individual agreements with the International Atomic Energy Agency (IAEA) to protect the peaceful use of nuclear energy and to detect/defer its military uses.

Atomic powers (the U.S, U.K., France, Soviet Union, and China) are allowed to possess nuclear weapons but must make progress towards total nuclear disarmament. The NPT and the IAEA may be at least partially responsible for containing nuclear weapon's growth. The IAEA is responsible for promoting the growth of the peaceful use of nuclear energy and for monitoring non-nuclear powers to ensure that they do not develop nuclear weapons programs and was also concerned more with the use of nuclear materials than nuclear site development. If it were not in actual use, nuclear infrastructure could be created without notifying the IAEA until its completion. North Korea informed the IAEA 7 years after nuclear material was transferred to a new site. The NPT is also inherently unfair as it creates an environment of "haves" and "have-nots." This inherent inequity naturally encourages infractions.

The global proliferation of a black market nuclear WMD trade is especially worrisome. In May, 1993 the Lithuanian police raided the Innovation Bank on an anonymous tip and discovered 4000 kg of the mildly radioactive and non-fissionable element Beryllium. Apparently, a Swiss buyer offered $24 million (ten times the market rate) for the cache. Beryllium may be used as a neutron reflector in a nuclear weapon. Ultimately, it was revealed that its source was the Institute of Physics and Power in the Russian region of Obninsk. The Beryllium was purchased by the Russian Mafia and the sale had been approved by senior government officials!

Organized crime is rampant in the Baltic States and many borders are extremely porous. Most of the nuclear smuggling is centered in former soviet installations. More troubling than amateur nuclear theft is evidence that organized crime is serving as a go-between for high level government and military officials disposing of dangerous nuclear material to third parties. Organized crime and the government may be one and the same as Nordex, an Austrian metal trading firm, was founded with KGB funds and was involved in the Beryllium transaction.

The Russian military was also in chaos. At least 500 officers committed suicide in 1996 and corruption is common. General Alexander Lebed stated that 84 of 132 "suitcase bombs" (model RA-115; weight 30kg; yield 2 kilotons) were missing. (1) There are many more examples of lost or stolen Russian nuclear material, of inadequate nuclear security and of unemployed physicists seeking third world employment.

Medical Management of Acute Radiation Sickness
The adverse effects of ionizing gamma radiation are termed *the Acute Radiation Syndrome. The clinical course of radiation injury is described in 4 phases.*

In the *Prodromal Phase (Phase 1)*, nonspecific symptoms mimic an acute viral illness including fever, malaise, and possibly nausea/vomiting for about 24 hours.

The *Latent Phase (Phase 2)* is an asymptomatic period lasting from only hours to over 3 weeks. During this time, blood and gastrointestinal related problems are worsening but are not yet clinically evident. The duration of this phase shortens with an increasing radiation dose.

The *Manifest Illness Phase (Phase 3)* represents the period of time that clinical symptoms are present.

The time during which *recovery or death* ensues *is termed Phase 4.*

The severity of acute radiation syndrome is radiation dose dependent. It is divided into 5 stages.

Stage 1 occurs after a whole body absorbed dose of 50-150 rads. Victims may be asymptomatic or may display viral like symptoms that may include nausea and vomiting for up to forty-eight hours. Complete spontaneous recovery is expected.

Stage 2, the Hematopoietic (blood-forming) Syndrome, occurs after a whole body exposure of 150-400 rads. In this stage, bone marrow suppression occurs. The bone marrow produces white blood cells that are responsible for immune system function. Platelet levels also drop. Immunosuppression causes "opportunistic" infections (infections that would not generally occur) while thrombocytopenia (low platelet levels) approaching 20,000-30,000 cause spontaneous bleeding. The

LD50 / 30, or the dose that will kill fifty percent of exposed victims without medical care in thirty days varies from 250-450 rads.

Stage 3 represents a dose of 400-600 rads and is a *severe Hematopoietic Syndrome* requiring heroic, life-saving measures such as bone marrow transplantation. Obviously, during a Mass Casualty Incident (MCI) such heroic efforts would be generally unavailable as medical resources become strained. This rationing of care would be reflected in a lowered LD50 and more fatalities would be expected.

Stage 4 occurs after a whole-body exposure of 600-1500 rads. Here, the loss of gastrointestinal lining cells causes severe diarrhea with fluid and electrolyte losses. This stage is termed the Gastrointestinal Syndrome. Life-saving measures include fluid and electrolyte replacement and gut sterilization with Neomycin. Don't forget that the Hematopoietic Syndrome is also present requiring bone marrow transplant. Stage 4 LD50 / 30 with maximal heroic care is about 1100 rads.

Stage 5 occurs after an exposure of greater than 1500 rads. One would expect to succumb to this radiation dose within about forty-eight hours regardless of treatment. Confusion, ataxia (loss of balance) and sensory deficits that occur with massive whole-body exposure are termed the Central Nervous System Syndrome. It's occurrence during the first 48 hours post exposure is ominous usually indicating a supra-lethal dose. The Latent Phase during Stage 5 exposure is also short to non-existent. (2)

Since the outcome of the Acute Radiation Syndrome is dose dependent, it is important to use the presence or absence of symptoms to estimate the stage and thus the expected treatments and outcome. For example, if the Gastrointestinal Syndrome is not present, it is likely that less than 600 rads of whole-body exposure has been absorbed. Alternatively, if the Hematopoietic Syndrome is present, anywhere from 150-600 rads may have been absorbed. Another good dosi-metric marker is the total lymphocyte blood count measured forty-eight hours after exposure. This figure is obtained by adding the absolute number of all the types of white blood cells (WBC's) in a complete blood count (CBC). A total lymphocyte count (TLC) of greater than 1200 indicates a minor exposure. A 300-1200 count indicates a serious problem warranting heroic measures. A TLC count of less than 300 indicates a grave prognosis.

It is also important to differentiate between local and whole body exposure. The former is usually caused by particulate (alpha/beta) exposure while the latter is caused by gamma radiation. Local external exposure of about 500 rads will cause a superficial skin burn similar to a sun burn. 1000 rads will cause a partial thickness skin burn, and 2000 rads will cause a full thickness burn. Even a 20% radiation burn might be fatal as opposed to a conventional 50% skin burn because of greater underlying tissue/organ damage. Realize that a victim of ionizing radiation is NOT radioactive and cannot endanger first responders. A contaminated victim, however, CAN contaminate contacts with alpha/beta particles. Internalized alpha particles will cause local long-term damage. Beta particle damage is more far-reaching, and beta particles may also emit gamma radiation. The contaminated victim should be wrapped in a nonporous material. This procedure is termed cocooning. Medical care is provided by removing the cocoon as needed. Geiger counter monitored decontamination at the scene is recommended. Communication with the treating facility is critical.

Nuclear Explosion Effects
The damage caused by a nuclear weapon result from blast energy, thermal and ionizing radiation and nuclear fallout. Blast energy and thermal/ionizing radiation are released within a microsecond. Local residual radiation (fallout) occurs over about forty-eight hours.

Blast damage accounts for about sixty percent of released nuclear energy. Static overpressure describes the sharp increase in air pressure caused by the shock wave. The blast wave weakens structures that are then torn apart by blast winds. Dynamic pressures describe the damage caused by blast winds forming the blast wave.

There are four possible types of nuclear blasts and their effects:

Air bursts are nuclear explosions detonated below an altitude of 30km. The fireball does not touch the ground. Injuries occur from blast pressure, burns and radiation. No fallout occurs. A significant local electromagnetic pulse (EMP) effect (see below) is expected.

A *surface burst* occurs with a detonation at ground level. The fireball touches the ground or water and creates a base surge associated with local and/or worldwide fallout (see below). Damage is less than with an equivalent sized air burst.

Subsurface bursts occur below the water or ground. Local shock effects will occur including heavy fallout and all other surface burst effects if the air or water surface is breached.

High altitude bursts occur above 30 km. altitude. Fireballs are larger than air bursts and EMP effects are maximal. Thermal and pressure effects are greater than with air bursts. No fallout occurs and no appreciable adverse radiation health effects are noted. Thermal radiation is responsible for about thirty to fifty percent of the total released energy. Thermal radiation results in heat and light extending beyond the blast range. Objects will absorb and reflect portions of this energy. Light colored objects may reflect much of the thermal energy. Absorbed energy creates heat causing burns and firestorms with gale force winds blowing inwards towards the center of the fire.

Gamma rays resonate in the upper atmosphere after a nuclear explosion creating an *electromagnetic pulse (EMP)* that may damage unshielded electronics and will disrupt communications. Radiation is only responsible for about five percent of the energy released in a nuclear blast. It consists of neutron and gamma radiation. The larger the yield of the bomb, the less important the radiation component becomes in comparison as it does not rise proportionately with weapon size.

"Nuclear winter" is the hypothetical climate condition described by Carl Sagan and others resulting from a large scale nuclear war. Here, the upper atmosphere would be covered by a uniform belt of smoke and soot from the 30th to 60th latitude. The sun's light would be diminished and the temperature would theoretically drop up to 20 degrees C. Darkness, killing frosts and radiation would damage animal and plant life. The protective ozone layer would also be significantly degraded with further negative effects on land and ocean plant life. In conjunction with infrastructure collapse, nuclear winter could lead to a massive loss of life secondary to starvation and disease. More recently, many scientists feel that these predictions may be exaggerated.

Nuclear fallout is the residual particulate matter falling to earth after a nuclear explosion. The residuals include radioactive isotopes with varying half-lives, unfissioned nuclear material, and environmental elements made radioactive by neutron bombardment. If the detonation exceeds ten kilotons (KT), small particles 0.01-20 micrometers in diameter may rise into the stratosphere causing worldwide fallout distantly settling back to earth even over years. Larger particles from a large detonation or most particles from a smaller one will fall back to earth in the area of the blast as local fallout. The exposure risk from the alpha, beta, and gamma particles of a standard fission bomb will substantially decrease after forty-eight hours. After that, alpha and beta contamination represent a long-term inhalation and ingestion risk through bioaccumulation. Bioaccumulation is the ingestion of radiation contaminated plant and animal foods. Strontium (Sr)-90 and Cesium (Cs)-137 are long half-lived isotopes of special concern for causing late human cancers through bioaccumulation. Strontium is "mistaken" by the body for calcium and is incorporated into bone. Meteorological effects such as precipitation above the nuclear cloud may worsen local fallout. Subsurface land or water blasts may create a cloud of contaminated water or soil at the base of the explosion called a base surge that may also increase local fallout. If possible, sheltering in place for the 48 hours immediately following a nuclear detonation is recommended to minimize local fallout effects. Also, do not consume locally produced plant, animal, or water products for an indefinite period following the attack.

Within reason, protect yourself using time, distance, and shielding.

Make time your ally by limiting exposure intervals and rotating staff. Understand that radiation exposure decreases proportionally to the square of the distance from the source. Obviously, maximally distance yourself from the source. Even small increments of distance are beneficial as protection accrues logarithmically. Shielding effects are particle dependent. *Alpha particles* are stopped by a sheet of paper. *Beta particles* may be stopped by clothing, aluminum foil, or the outer layer of skin. *Gamma particles* will penetrate up to four to six inches of lead or two to four feet of earth. To protect oneself from alpha or beta particles, avoid ingesting or inhaling contaminated dust or material. Use a particulate mask, gloves, and personal protective equipment (PPE). The inhalation or ingestion of radioactive particles will result in those particles emitting ionizing radiation inside the body and causing radiation poisoning. It is statistically unlikely for death to immediately occur from massive gamma radiation. The United States Army has published expected performance levels for troops exposed to varying levels of gamma radiation. A Level C suit will probably provide adequate protection from alpha and beta radiation. Decontamination is a common sense procedure that involves physically removing and disposing of contaminated clothing, washing skin and equipment, and cleaning all wounds. Avoid unnecessary exposure to contaminated rescue personnel. Be aware that any radioactive dispersion incident is a Haz-Mat emergency. Remember that if your patient transport vehicle (helicopter, ambulance, etc.) becomes contaminated it will be useless for transporting other victims to a clean location.

Summary
Attempting to deal with any nuclear/radiation related event is an unpredictable, hazardous undertaking. Protect yourself and realize that all victims should be evaluated, treated and transported in a safe, Haz-Mat protocol driven manner. An interesting unanswered legal question regards the commission status of surviving sworn officers if their municipality no longer physically exists. Common sense disaster preparation includes storing an adequate personal supply of "clean" food and water at the shelter-in-place location. Important personal documents should be kept available. A particulate mask and a nonporous outer garment worn outdoors for at least two days after the blast provide significant alpha/beta protection. Medical treatment for acute radiation sickness victims will be limited. Protecting remaining medical structures from looting by a radiation-sickened citizenry hopelessly seeking care may be part of the tactical team's or officer's role. However, treatment does exist for many aspects of the nuclear threat. Interagency teamwork including the EMS and Incident Command Systems is mandatory. The Federal agency investigating nuclear weapons incidents is the Department of Defense Joint Nuclear Accident Center (phone #: 703-325-2102). A nuclear attack is probably the most frightening of all the weapons of mass destruction scenarios. As in all other WMD arenas, a response plan is still needed. The Naval Reserve Damage Control Service School of the Great Lakes Naval Base (phone #: 847-688-3550) and the National Guard Civilian Support

Teams (CSTs) are readily available for education and consultation services. Illinois' CST #5 is based in Bartonville at the Joint Armed Forces Reserve Center. Their contact number is 309-697-3635. Please research the resources available in your state. It is our responsibility to face this threat in the same knowledge driven manner we have employed in other WMD areas.

REFERENCES

1. Parrish, Scott-Are Suitcase Nukes On The Loose? The Story Behind the Controversy, Center for Nonproliferation Studies, Monterey, Ca. 1997, pp.1-14
2. Radiation Poisoning, http://www.wikipedia.com
3. Nuclear War Survival Skills- Kearny, C., Oak Ridge National Laboratory, 1987 http://www.oism.org/nwss
4. The Medical Implications of Nuclear War- http://www.nap.edu/openbook/0309036925/html/171.html, copyright 1986, 2000, The National Academy of Sciences.
5. Stern, Jessica-The Ultimate Terrorists, Chap. 6-The Threat of Loose Nukes, Harvard Press, Boston, Mass., March, 1999
6. Wikipedia Online Encyclopedia- Nuclear Weapons, http://www.wikipedia.com
7. Naval Reserve WMD Damage Control Service School Course- Given to the South Suburban
8. Emergency Response Team (SSERT), 2003
9. Nuclear Winter and Other Scenarios- http://www.thespa.com/jon.roland/vri/nwaos.html
10. Counter-Terrorism for Emergency Responders- Burke, R., Lewis Publishers, Boca Raton, 1999
11. The U.S. Armed Forces Nuclear, Biological and Chemical Survival Manual- Couch, D., Basic
12. Books, New York, 1993
13. Explosives and Demolitions- FM5-25, Headquarters, Department of the Army, p. 104, 1967
14. Terrorism: An Investigator's Handbook- Dyson, W., Anderson Publishing Co., Cincinnati, OH, 2001

Biowar Considerations

Martin Greenberg, MD

This chapter is intended to provide an analysis of the biological weapon (BW) threat. Please use this as a reference guide. Specific descriptions, treatments and drug regimen are provided for completeness purposes only. Please do not be deterred by them unless they are of specific interest. Unlike a Chemical Weapon (CW) attack, here no crime scene generally exists. Rather, tactical containment teams and first responders may likely be present at hospitals and triage/holding areas. Memorizing disease symptoms and antibiotic protocols is not relevant to the law enforcement community. Relevance lies in understanding the magnitude of the threat.

Imagine that a terrorist cult or government successfully releases the Ebola virus. Within days, large numbers of people develop fever and joint pains. The tissues connecting our musculoskeletal system and major organs liquefy. If touched, the skin bleeds. We choke on our sloughed tongues. Our eyes fill with blood that leaks down our cheeks. Near death, we convulse, splashing infected blood on anyone in the vicinity. This blood remains contaminated for a month. Ninety percent of us are dead within a week.

Definitions
Biological agents are defined by the United Nations as "living organisms...or infective material derived from them, which are intended to cause disease or death in man, animals and plants,

and which depend for their effects on their ability to multiply in the person, animal, or plant attacked." Toxins are the poisonous by-products of these organisms. Surprisingly, biological agents are more toxic than chemical agents. Microgram (10 to the -6th power) toxin doses are lethal. Picogram (10 to the -12th power) biological agent doses are lethal. BW agents are more specific than CW (Chemical Weapon) agents. They attack a single host class (humans, plants, or animals). They are hard to control, dependent upon weather conditions, geography and vectors (carriers such as birds and insects). BW agents act within days. CW agents act within minutes, while toxins act immediately. Anthrax spores may survive for years in the soil, but aerosolized BW agents are generally non-persistent. Ideally, a BW agent should be infectious, hearty, and able to reproduce quickly and easily. The target audience defines the appropriateness of the agent. Staphylococcus, for example, is appropriate to infect a salad bar, but inappropriate for widespread aerosol dissemination. Different types of living organisms may be used as biological weapons. Viruses are "a collection of genes wrapped in protein."

A virus enters a cell and usurps the cell's RNA (ribonucleic acid) forcing it to reproduce the intruder's genetic material and thus causing infection. Among others, BW viruses include Ebola, Marburg, encephalitis, yellow fever and dengue fever. Most lethal viruses have difficulty surviving outside the host. Generally, a virus' lethality is inversely proportional to its transmissibility. In other words, it's more difficult to catch the Ebola virus than a cold. Bacteria are living organisms that can survive outside the body. These include the infection causing organisms with which we are most familiar including anthrax, brucellosis, glanders, plague, and tularemia. Fungi are plant-like organisms that usually attack plants. Toxins are chemical by-products of living organisms. Botulinum toxin is the most toxic substance known. Ricin is a toxin produced from castor beans. Venoms are toxins obtained from reptiles and insects.

The Biological Warfare Convention

The convention on the Prohibition of the Development, Production, and Stockpiling of Bacteriological (Biological) and Toxin Weapons and on Their Destruction (the Biological Warfare Convention or BWC) bans the production, development, transfer, acquisition, and use of BWs. It entered into force on March 26, 1975. 183 countries have signed and/or ratified the BWC. Ten states/countries have neither signed nor ratified it (mostly African nations and Israel.) The U.S. pledged to ban BWs in 1969. The BWC unfortunately lacks verification protocols, but negotiations have been underway to add them to the agreement.

The Fear of Disease

Historically, epidemics have killed many more people than those killed in conflicts. It is reasonable to fear this killer. However, exotic illnesses such as the Ebola and Marburg viruses which killed 800 and 10 people respectively are feared more than malaria which routinely kills one million people yearly. Fear of the unknown imbues disease with an almost supernatural horror. The mid-fourteenth century Black Death decimated one-fourth of Europe's population and was thought to be due to the supernatural. The fear of disease and its actual effects have changed the course of many wars. The Mongols, for example, won the Battle of Caffa (a port city in Crimea) by catapulting plague infested cadavers into the walled city. The Japanese killed 3,000 prisoners of war (including Americans) in WW2 BW experiments. They also attacked eleven Chinese cities with plague and killing 700. Fear, too, is generated by the fact that frequently no specific agent antidote, vaccine, or countermeasure is available. By genetically combining virulent viruses such as Ebola or hemorrhagic fever with an easily spread, common virus such as influenza, it has been hypothesized that viral dissemination would be facilitated.

BW Planning Considerations

Jane's Information Group feels that four components are necessary to create a successful BW attack. They include: the agent, the munitions, the delivery system, and target meteorological conditions. These elements must be addressed in any successful strike.

The BW agent may be a toxin or an organism. Toxins usually have no, or limited incubation periods. The target area is limited. An organism has a longer incubation period of up to several days with a wider target area of even hundreds of square kilometers. Agents may be deemed "incapacitating" or "lethal" for obvious reasons. As previously mentioned, they should be infectious/toxic, easy to produce in quantity, and stable from production through dissemination. BWs are deployed in liquid or dry form. Liquids are produced easily but are difficult to disseminate in a respirable mist of five microns diameter. Dry agent is difficult to produce, requiring sophisticated drying and milling technology. However, once produced they are easily disseminated. Luckily, no agent is both easy to produce and disseminate and no standard appearance exists. All liquid agents regardless of production techniques should have a viscosity of five to fifteen centipoises. Solid/liquid content should be five to twenty percent. Its viscosity would be between whole milk and light pancake syrup. The colors of liquid agents are variable but those derived from fermentation are colored opaque amber to brown. Agents grown in egg media will be yellow or pink/red. Viruses grown in sophisticated tissue culture technology would likely be processed into a dry powder. They would ideally contain particles one to five microns in diameter. Containing a strong static electric charge, these agents would be difficult to handle. Less sophisticated processing would yield a ten to twenty micron diameter particle that would be easier to manage but would tend not to remain aerosolized. Dried agent has the same color as its liquid counterpart. Dying, however, could effectively change the dry agent's color. Munitions designed to release BW agent as an infectious, respirable mist may vary widely. They are termed "point source" munitions. Alternatively, "line source" munitions release agent along a line perpendicular to prevailing winds to disseminate agent across a very large downwind target. Domestic terrorists would more likely employ crude garden style sprayers. This single fluid device requires 600 psi to work effectively. A two fluid nozzle is ten times more effective and only requires a working psi of 90. Explosive devices might also be used but would kill much of the agent through blast effects. If the difficult task of producing high concentration, small particle, neutrally charged dry agent was overcome, a simple delivery system such as the ABC fire extinguisher would be highly effective. Meteorological conditions must be considered when attacking an outdoor target. To keep agent at ground level (3-15') an air inversion is needed where a cold air layer prevents vertical air currents and keeps the agent at ground level. Inversions are present at night, daybreak, and sunset. Sunlight also destroys live organisms, but spores and toxins are not affected. A prevailing wind speed of 5-25 MPH is also an important factor. A lower speed will limit coverage while a higher speed will disperse the agent excessively. Dry agents work best in dry climes: liquid agents work best in a moist/humid environment. Temperature and precipitation may have only minor effects upon BW delivery. The urban outdoor environment may degrade agent effectiveness as vertical air current eddies between buildings create "micrometeorological effects" and disperse agent. Snipers are well aware of these air eddies when firing from an urban location. For about one minute after release, BW agent equilibrates with the atmosphere. Heavy particles of greater than 15 microns diameter fall to the ground while those of one to five micron diameter remain suspended in the aerosol and act as a gas. This gas is termed the "primary aerosol." Since it acts as a gas, it is unimpeded by objects in its path. It will not adhere to trees, buildings, or clothing. Individuals at risk, breathing at ten to twenty liters per minute are likely to suffer inhalation infection. Biological agent decay will also occur and is expressed in percent death/minute of aerosol age. It is a geometric progression. In Jane's example, a twenty percent per min. degradation rate implies aerosol content is halved every 3.5 minutes after release. Delivery systems other than inhalation may be effective on a much more limited basis. Ingestion of agent causes only limited damage. Contaminating municipal water supplies is unrealistic due to agent dilution/diffusion. Chlorination is effective in its intended role as a bactericide. Reverse osmosis filtration, coagulation, and flocculation systems are effective against a host of toxins including ricin, microcystin, T-2 mycotoxin, and sagitoxin. Small-scale contamination of a water supply directed at a small target such as a building is possible if the water is contaminated as it enters the target. Isolated attacks on food sources such as salad bars (1984 Rajhneeshee cult Salmonella typhimurium salad bar poisonings) and product tampering (1982 Tylenol scare) have severe psychological effects.

The Agents
It is certainly not necessary to memorize the symptom complex of each potential BW agent as this information has little bearing in the pre-hospital environment. Rather, several agents will be described to demonstrate the most common examples of these organisms.

Anthrax - Anthrax is caused by the gram positively staining (an identification technique) rod shaped bacterium called *Bacillus anthracis*. Its BW application is as a pulmonary agent. The spore form would be released via sprayer and would be inhaled. The disease incubation period is one to seven days. After two to four days, symptoms of shortness of breath, exhaustion, tachycardia (rapid heart rate) and shock occur. Death occurs after one day. The mortality rate is ninety percent. 8,000-10,000 spores are necessary to cause an infection. There is no effective treatment. The World Health Organization (WHO) estimated in 1970 that if anthrax was sprayed over a city of 500,000 inhabitants, that 125,000 would become infected and that 95,000 would die. No effective treatment is available. In other words, if you develop a symptomatic infection, you will die. No wonder that BWs are called the "poor man's nuclear weapon." The dramatic implications for the health care community are that people stricken with anthrax, coming to hospitals for treatment will instead be triaged and observed while asymptomatic (healthy appearing) individuals will require antibiotics. It is likely that a treatment vacuum will occur where the medical community will be unaware that the problem exists for several days and by then treatment would no longer be effective. An anthrax vaccine is available which has recently been the subject of much controversy. A number of troops have refused inoculation under penalty of court martial claiming that it was responsible for Gulf War Syndrome. The vaccine consists of six doses over eighteen months with yearly boosters. Should this vaccination be given to the entire population in the expectation of a BW attack? Non-vaccinated, potentially exposed individuals need ciprofloxin 500 mg. BID (twice a day,) or doxycycline 100 mg. BID for a month and require vaccination with at least three doses prior to discontinuing antibiotics. Effective treatment also assumes that non-genetically modified anthrax has been disseminated.

Plague- Plague is caused by the aerobic, gram-negative rod-shaped organism *Yersinia pestis* (formerly called Pasturella pestis). It is a non-spore forming organism that clinically causes bubonic or pneumonic plague. The latter form would be seen in intentional dissemination first affecting the lungs. It results from inhalation of the organism and causes hemorrhagic pneumonia that is fatal unless treated. Although it is extremely infective as a respirable mist, agent degradation and instability are barriers to its successful weaponization. As mentioned, it was termed "the Black Death" and was responsible for killing one-fourth of Europe's population in the mid-1400s. It can be successfully treated within twenty-four hours of symptom onset with streptomycin 30mg/kg. IM in two divided doses/daily for ten days, or doxycycline 200mg. IV followed by 100mg. IV every twelve hours for ten to fourteen days. Post Exposure Prophylaxis (PEP) for asymptomatic individuals is doxycycline 100mg. by mouth BID (twice a day) for a week or for the exposure duration if longer than seven days. Decontamination is affected by boiling or dry heating above 130 degrees F. steam for fifteen minutes or treatment with Lysol. It is also killed by sunlight exposure for five hours. A vaccine is available administered at zero, three, and six months. Booster doses every six months times three and yearly afterwards are protective for individuals in high-risk settings. Unfortunately, it is not protective against pneumonic plague.

Tularemia- This disease is caused by the gram negative, non-spore forming coccobacillus, *Francisella tularensis*. The two most common forms of tularemia are the ulceroglandular form (caused by the inoculation of infected mosquitos, ticks, or deerflies,) and the typhoidal form (caused by the inhalation of contaminated dust, or the ingestion of contaminated food or water.) In the former, an ulcer appears at the site of inoculation with local lymph node swelling followed by fever and nonspecific systemic symptoms. The latter presents with weight loss, fever, and collapse. No lymphadenopathy (enlarged lymph nodes) is present, and the diagnosis is difficult due to its nonspecific symptoms. This organism is extremely infective. Even 1 organism may cause clinical infection. The likelihood of contracting this disease is almost 100%. Every exposed unprotected individual would develop clinical disease. The choice route would be an aerosol causing pneumonia. Tularemia is treated with the antibiotic streptomycin 1G every 12h IM (Intra-Muscular) for two weeks. Gentamicin is also effective but runs the risk of kidney damage. An investigational vaccine is also available.

Smallpox-The *variola virus* causes smallpox. This disease was conquered, or declared eradicated, by the World Health Organization in 1980. Two known virus banks retained variola samples; the Centers for Disease Control (CDC) in Atlanta and Vector in Koltsovo, Russia. However, an unknown number of clandestine banks may possibly retain viral samples. The virus is highly infective. The incubation period is about twelve days; quarantine is required for sixteen days after exposure. Symptoms include fever, headache, muscle pain, and vomiting. Delirium may occur in fifteen percent. About three days later, a rash about the face, forearms, and hands appears. The rash then spreads to the trunk and becomes pustular. After one to two weeks, the pustules form scars. A vaccine is available administered intra-dermally (within the skin) that leaves a permanent scar. This Wyeth brand vaccine is effective if given up to one week post exposure. Immunity lasts between three and ten years and booster injections are recommended for repeat exposures. Vaccine immune globulin (VIG) is given to pregnant or immunosuppressed individuals (0.6mg/kg within 24h).

Toxins- Toxins are effective and specific poisons produced by living organisms such as bacteria, algae, fungi, and plants. Many toxins produced for military purposes were sensitive to heat and light and thus made unstable and impractical weapons. In the late 1970s, development of gene and biotechnology allowed toxins to be produced in larger amounts or even synthetically. Genetic modifications allow them to be less sensitive to light. Using bio-regulators (naturally occurring peptides participating in bodily activities) it is possible to target specific body organs. Microencapsulation technology makes it possible to protect unstable toxins when dispersed. Because most toxins are unstable in alkaline solutions, 1-2% hypochlorite decontamination solutions effectively destroy them.

Botulinum toxin is produced by the bacteria clostridium botulinum. It is the most toxic substance known. The organism grows on improperly preserved food and causes the disease botulism. The incubation period is one to three days after which suffocation by respiratory paralysis eventually occurs. If untreated, it is fatal in sixty percent of cases. The toxin occurs in 7 different forms. The most lethal is type A (molecular weight 150,000) with a lethal dose of 1 microgram if ingested. A vaccine is available, but if poisoning occurs no antidote exists. Facial muscles are affected first, followed by symmetric, downward paralysis. When the diaphragm and chest muscles are paralyzed, breathing ceases. The respiratory LD50 is not known (the amount needed to kill fifty percent of subjects) but it is extrapolated from rhesus monkey experiments as 4.88 microns for a 70kg subject. Treatment includes the use of assisted ventilation and antitoxin (20ml IV.) Antitoxin does not reverse paralysis that may take months to resolve. The pentavalent vaccine (types A-E) is an investigational drug.

Castor oil seeds can be used to extract ricin which is also classified as a lethal toxin. E. coli bacteria have also been genetically modified to produce this toxin. It is easy to naturally produce in large quantities and became notorious when it was used in the 1978 London "umbrella murder." A ricin treated bullet was used to kill a Bulgarian defector. In 1995, 4 members of the Minnesota Patriots Council militia were discovered possessing ricin. Its mechanism of action is to block bodily protein synthesis. Death occurs through multi-organ failure. Congestive heart failure is a major feature, and treatment is supportive only.

Staphylococcus enterotoxin B (SEB) is produced by the Staphylococcus aureus bacteria and is classified as an incapacitating toxin. It is the bacteria most commonly associated with food poisoning. Because it is very stable and requires only a small dose (ED50=.025 mcg) to cause symptoms via the respiratory route, it is a potential inhalation agent as well. SEB is a protein (molecular weight=28,500D) and is water soluble. It can withstand boiling for several minutes and can survive freeze-dried for over a year. Ingestion of 20-25g causes food poisoning symptoms after a few hours including nausea, cramps, diarrhea, and vomiting. Spontaneous recovery usually occurs within twenty-four hours. Inhalation symptoms occur within one to six hours following exposure including fever, chills, headache, myalgia (muscle pain,) and a cough which may persist for one to four weeks. Nausea, vomiting, and diarrhea may also occur. Despite the more severe symptoms caused by the inhalation route, the mortality rate is only 2%. Fluid replacement therapy may be needed in severe cases.

Viruses - Ebola is a viral infection that causes death in fifty to ninety percent of cases. It is transmitted through contact with any infected organs or body fluids. The virus has a variable incubation period of up to twenty-one days. Symptoms include sudden weakness, fever, headache, and sore throat followed by kidney and liver failure, a rash, vomiting and diarrhea, and internal/external bleeding. The bleeding begins on about the fifth day. Because of its virility, Ebola is assigned a likely status as a BW. The *Marburg virus* is a cousin of the Ebola virus and was first described when an epidemic severe hemorrhagic illness occurred in Germany at the same time as the importation of African green monkeys to where the disease was traced. Cases have also been reported in sub-Saharan Africa. Little else is known about the virus. Symptoms develop about a week after exposure and are similar to Ebola. They also include conjunctivitis (irritated eyes) and photophobia (light sensitivity). There is no vaccine or effective anti-viral therapy available to treat these infections. The Marburg mortality rate is twenty-five percent.

Putting it all together; a biological warfare treatment scenario

A BW attack may be overt or covert. A crime scene will exist only in the overt scenario. In a covert (unwitnessed) attack, evidence it has taken place will initially be epidemiological, or retrospective, as large numbers of similarly affected casualties flood medical facilities over the first few days. Unfortunately, this initial, asymptomatic time interval may also be the "golden period" during which treatment may have been effective. Cross contamination also occurs with a number of BW agents, and we thus unwittingly may become "the vectors of our own destruction." Such a real time reenactment was aired on the ABC News show Nightline episode production "Biowar" on 10/1-8/99. It dramatically and realistically portrays the panic and social disintegration that is the "true force multiplier effect" surrounding an unfolding BW incident.

Sidell, Patrick, and Dashiell also relate the following scenario:

"An intermediate-sized strategic hypothetical target could be represented by the typical city and its surrounding network of suburbs-about 400 to 800 square miles. One jet fighter could disseminate 100 gallons of Francisella tularensis (the causative organism of tularemia) along a fifty-mile line starting northwest of Rockville, MD, and ending southwest of Vienna, VA. The attack would be expected to produce fifty percent casualties in four to seven days in metropolitan Washington, D.C., and could result in severe pneumonia in 1.9 million people, of whom twenty percent would be expected to die without antibiotic treatment. This level of casualties would destroy the ability to function of a significant and vital section of the U.S. and would severely stress the remainder of the country to provide the resources needed to limit the biological disaster." (JAVMA, Vol. 190, No.6, 1987, p.716) Over an average of the first 3 days, casualties of inhalational tularemia would experience the sudden onset of chills, fever, headache, muscle aches, extreme

fatigue (prostration), and loss of body fluids. The diffuse nature of symptoms would significantly delay diagnosis. The conventional diagnosis would rest upon a sputum/blood gram stain of small, non-spore forming, non-motile, aerobic, gram stain negative coccobacilli and positive blood cultures and sensitivities. Advances in polymerase chain reaction (PCR) detection technology identify organisms within minutes. The Navy Medical Research Unit has developed a mobile, 4 box, 300# portable lab combining immune-analysis, PCR, and traditional techniques that can provide onsite BW agent identification in fifteen to twenty minutes. New miniaturization techniques may have already created palm, and even dog tag sized detectors. Although genetic engineering may allow BWs to evade traditional detection, new "canary on a chip" technology will detect classes of organisms (bacilli, cocci, etc.) and warn those in the vicinity to obtain treatment. Once a diagnosis of tularemia was reached, antibiotics would need to be administered on a massive scale, probably overwhelming even national stockpiles. Manning triage sites, warehousing large numbers of casualties, and disposing of the dead would all be challenging logistic issues.

Except for respiratory paralyzing toxins, it is unlikely that specialized equipment or surgical services will be needed. The specific agent will dictate subsequent triage. For example, if the agent is in the incapacitating group, home care may be recommended. If an untreatable lethal class BW agent is disseminated (anthrax), supportive care by non-medical personnel may unfortunately be mandatory. With the exception of rapidly acting toxins (SEB), a bell shaped curve of symptom onset would be expected. Casualties might return home during the incubation period, unless this is contraindicated by cross contamination fears (smallpox, pneumonic plague). As medical care would be spread thin, an information campaign would be necessary to allow casualties to initiate their own care. Large-scale decontamination of materiel would be challenging to impossible (high-rise buildings). A soap and water shower with clothing decontamination by boiling and soaking in hypochlorite seems to be a bare minimum recommendation. Insecticides will be needed to control secondary insect vectors. Many deaths would be expected, especially among the young, the old, and the immunocompromised. A mandatory educational campaign to inform the public that the agent has been identified and that treatment plans are underway would be needed to avoid panic, the true "force multiplier" and goal of the terrorist.

Neutralization of the BW munition, if found, is a necessary but risky task. All munitions have a reservoir of agent and they may still be armed in some manner to continue dissemination. Bomb squad or military munition and BW agent experience is useful here. The response team should be in level A gear (SCBA suit with positive pressure and communications; NFPA 1993). 2 prime functions of the responding team are to sample the agent and to neutralize the threat. Sampling gear is needed while decontamination can frequently be performed with the standard 5% hypochlorite solution delivered from a 10-20psi garden sprayer. Hi pressure sprayers are not recommended as they may aerosolize residual dried agent. Because of the high level of knowledge needed regarding munitions and agents, it is recommended that dedicated teams such as the FBI Hazardous Materials Response Unit (HMRU) or the Chem-Bio Incident Response Force (CBIRF), phone number (301)744-1092, assume munition neutralization responsibilities.

Summary

It is overwhelming to consider the comprehensive picture of a bio-war incident. However, a high index of suspicion and Col. Jeff Cooper's Condition Yellow (relaxed awareness or head on a swivel) mentality will be needed to become aware of a large group of patients with common symptoms to initiate a response plan as soon as possible. Truly, this is one situation where we hear hoof beats and seek zebras.

REFERENCES

1. Jane's Chem-Bio Handbook- Sidell, F. R., Patrick, W. C. III, and Dashiell, T. R., Jane's Information Group, Alexandria, Va. 1998
2. The Ultimate Terrorists- Stern, Jessica, Harvard University Press, Cambridge, Mass. 1999
3. Consequence Management: Domestic Response to Weapons of Mass Destruction- Chris Seiple, PARAMETERS, US Army War College Quarterly, Autumn-1997
4. Emergency Action for Chemical and Biological Warfare Agents- Ellison, D.H., CRC Press, Boca Raton, FL 1999 pp. 117-127.

Medical Threats of Chemical Weapons

Martin Greenberg, MD

"You must have full knowledge (of your situation) to have full confidence of success. It is not enough just to have partial knowledge. A little knowledge will pay just a little dividend... The linkage between knowledge and victory is so complete (that) if you should know not just yourself and your opponent but include all those factors pertinent to victory, then your victory...will be total and complete." Sun Tzu

This reference chapter will present a description of the Chemical Warfare Convention, common chemical warfare (CW) agents, their effects, and treatment. Its goal is to make the law enforcement community aware of and to recognize the Chemical Warfare (CW) threat. Treatment plans for specific problems are included only as reference guidelines and are also available from other sources.

The Chemical Warfare Convention
The Geneva Protocol of 1925, enacted in response to the WW1 chemical warfare ravages of mustard and phosgene gas, prohibited only the use of CWs. The production, stockpiling, and transfer of these weapons remained legal. Geneva Protocol signatories reserved the right to retaliate in kind if attacked, and international corporate assistance of rogue state CW production was permitted. In 1984, because of the Iraqi use of CWs

against Iran, western nations formed the Australia Group to limit the export of member CW materials. At least partially due to this agreement, Iran was prevented from developing nerve agents through 1996. On 4/29/97, the Chemical Weapons Convention (CWC) entered into force. It banned the development, production, acquisition, storage, transfer, and use of CWs. Stringent verification measures were enacted including routine inspection of chemical manufacturers on site. Short notice inspections of all related government facilities, limitation of chemical exports to non-signatories, and penalties for violations were enacted. The CWC banned all use of CWs including retaliatory strikes. Suspect signatories including India, Pakistan, S. Korea, China, and Iran "must" comply with its provisions and hopefully the twenty to twenty-five active CW programs worldwide will be thwarted by its effects.

Weaponization
The process of modifying CWs into an optimal delivery payload is termed *"weaponization."* Stabilizers and thickeners are added to the CW to prevent product degradation and to improve persistence (the length of time the agent remains as a liquid) and dispersion (the area over which the vapor spreads). Chemical munitions have been developed to create a respirable aerosol for widespread dissemination or a larger droplet spray to penetrate skin. Delivery systems may be of the explosive, thermal, pneumatic, or mechanical type. Airborne or ground-based aerosol generators similar to those in pesticide use have also been described. These commercial, dual-use systems may even include underarm deodorant spray cans, and pump spray bottles. Crop dusters or vehicle mounted aerosol generators are used to create an upwind line source that contaminates downwind targets. First responders should be aware of such makeshift delivery systems and be prepared to dismantle them. Military munitions include artillery shells, aerial bombs, missiles, grenades, and mines. Their goal is to

deliver a respirable aerosol mist of less than eight microns that will remain suspended six to ten feet above ground level or a large droplet spray that will persistently contaminate the ground causing casualties from skin contamination and forcing the use of personal protective equipment (PPE). The Limited availability of PPE may quickly cripple CW response. Most munitions contain a "burster" charge. The charge is activated by a fuse and bursts the munition that disseminates the CW. Impact fusing is used with thicker, persistent CWs (for example; VX) in ground burst munitions. Proximity fusing, activated by barometric pressure changes or timers, is employed with agents designed to create an aerosol. The concept of binary munitions was developed to allow safer agent production and storage. Here, two non-lethal compounds are separately loaded into a warhead which mixes them to form the agent upon detonation. This is especially useful for sarin and VX. A standard one-ton container was used for bulk agent storage. The tactical importance of these military delivery systems is that they are representative of weapons available worldwide. In many countries, stockpile security is questionable. For example, in Albania (1997) antigovernment bandits stole CW agents from four army depots. In Russia (1994) CW storage site locations were published in the newspaper Rossiyskaya Gazeta. This raised security concerns by then Soviet army chief of staff General Kolesnikov. The Russian "brain drain" also encouraged impoverished scientists to provide CW consulting services to the highest bidder. Lone scientists could easily start a one-man CW program due to the minimal expense, the dual use precursor availability, and the low level of technical sophistication needed. Jessica Stern pointed out that thiodiglycol, an immediate precursor of the mustard agent, is also used in the industrial production of ballpoint pen ink. It requires only the addition of a simple acid to complete mustard's synthesis. Considering these factors, it is foreseeable that we may encounter a CW domestic scenario.

The Dread of Chemical Weapons
We feel a gut level, almost genetic aversion to poisoning. Risks that are disproportionately feared share certain similarities. They may be uncontrollable, inequitable, and may affect future generations. They have invisible effects; they "inhabit" us. They may be ingested, turning life preserving actions (eating and drinking) into life perverting actions. This cross-cultural aversion has been present throughout history. CW agent effectiveness depends, in large part, upon this evoked horror. The panic and social disorganization CWs cause far outstrips their true lethality. In WW1, only three percent of troops exposed to mustard gas died, while twenty-five percent of those injured by conventional weapons succumbed. Similar statistics were available for the Iran-Iraq war. Iraq attributed its victory mainly to CW provoked terror.

What are these agents and how do they work?

The Chemical Agents
The US army defines a CW agent as "a chemical substance intended for use in military operations to kill or seriously injure or incapacitate humans or animals through its toxicological effects." CW agents are generally classified as blood, nerve, blister, and pulmonary (choking) agents. Each agent has its own NATO designation that differs from its chemical formula. This classification may be confusing. For example, the NATO designation for cyanide is AC, but its chemical formula is CN. The NATO designation for Mace is CN.

Blood Agents
Cyanide: This agent is usually encountered as hydrogen cyanide (AC) or cyanogen chloride (CK). Ingestion of sodium or potassium cyanide salts may be lethal. The industrial materials acetonitrile or acrylonitrile if exploded could cause toxic effects. While "small" amounts of hydrogen cyanide may have no effect, "medium" amounts of AC or CK will cause diz-

ziness, nausea, and weakness. Large amounts will cause loss of consciousness, several minutes of convulsions, apnea (breathing stops) and death within ten minutes. The first effects occur within seconds. Low concentration prolonged exposure may also cause severe effects. To recognize cyanide poisoning, physical exam reveals normal/large-sized pupils and no fasciculations (muscle twitching) under the skin. The skin may appear reddened due to oxygen laden venous blood. Cyanide occurs naturally in some fruit pits and lima beans. It is also a dual-purpose industrial chemical. It is a volatile liquid: it evaporates quickly. AC vapor is lighter than air and rises. CK vapor is heavier than air and sinks to low terrain and basements. AC has the odor of bitter almonds but only about half of the population is genetically able to smell it. AC / CK work by poisoning the cell mechanisms using oxygen. Since arterial oxygen going to the cell is not used, venous blood leaving the cell remains a brighter red. Because the brain is so dependent upon oxygen, central nervous system failure is responsible for cyanide's effects. The amount that kills fifty percent of casualties or LD50 (skin) is 100mg/kg. For vapor, the CT50 (mg/min/cubic meter) is 2,500-5,000. Cyanide can be detected by the ICAD device or the military M256A1 paper. Nitrates in the cyanide antidote kit combine with cyanide to convert red blood cell hemoglobin to methemoglobin. The combined cyano-methemoglobin allows oxygen transfer to occur. Another antidote, thiosulfate, combines with cyanide to form thiocyanate and is eliminated in the urine. Other adjunctive medicines include sodium bicarbonate to treat metabolic acidosis and diazepam (Valium®) for seizure control.

Triage considerations for AC/CK include no treatment for asymptomatic casualties and immediate triage including antidote(s)/oxygen for those with symptoms. Here, nitrate "pearls" may be given through an endotracheal tube (tube in the trachea). Methemoglobin pulls cyanide out of the cell reversing its effects, while thiosulfate inactivates cyanide by combining with it. Delayed triage is recommended for those recovering, unconscious but breathing casualties with the use of oxygen and antidote. Expectant triage includes vigorous resuscitation for those without cardiac activity. If treated, these patients might recover.

Nerve Agents
Nerve agents have been on the world stage since WW2 when Germany produced 12,000 tons of *tabun* between 1942 through 1945. *Sarin* was first synthesized in 1938 while soman, the third classical nerve agent first appeared in 1944. These agents were given a "G" classification in NATO nomenclature. After the war, efforts were focused on the mechanism of action of nerve agents so that better protection strategies could be developed. In 1949, resulting from these studies the more stable "V" group of agents (VX) was formulated by the British chemist R. Ghosh. It was about ten times as lethal as the "G" group. The first scientific article regarding nerve agents was published in 1955 by Ghosh and Newman. Several companies marketed these compounds as insecticides beginning in 1952, but withdrew them when unintended "mammalian" toxicity became an unexpected problem. Large scale VX production was begun by the U.S. in 1961. A famous contemporary use of nerve agents was in the Iran-Iraq war. The U.N. confirmed that Iraq used tabun and other agents against Iran. *The Aum Shinrikyo cult* dispersed sarin in a Tokyo subway on 3/20/95 injuring over 5,500 and killing two people. A previous "Aum" attack had injured 200 and killed seven victims.

All nerve agents are organophosphates and inhibit the enzyme acetylcholinesterase. The effects of the agent are due to the absence of this enzyme. Vapor effects appear immediately while liquid effects appear thirty minutes to eight hours after exposure. A large group of casualties will be affected to varying degrees. To recognize the problem, *the symptom triad of uni/bilateral miosis (pupillary constriction), rhinorrhea (runny nose), and shortness of breath will usually be present.* Examine casualties in the shade to better document miosis. Not every victim will present with the full symptom triad. Convulsions, apnea and flaccid (limp) paralysis then occur. These nerve agent effects are both dose and time dependent. Exposure to a small amount for a long time may be equivalent to a large amount for a short time. Nasal and oral secretions are copious, and fasciculations may be present. *The mnemonic SLUDGE (salivation, lacrimation, urination, defecation, gastrointestinal cramping/hyperactivity, and emesis) describes the early clinical picture.* Remember: victims of AC/CK will NOT demonstrate hypersecretions, miosis or fasciculations. Miosis will not usually occur after isolated skin exposure to nerve agents. Physical exam with a stethoscope will also demonstrate hyperactive (increased) bowel sounds, and chest auscultation (listening with a stethoscope) reveals rales (crackles).

The military nerve agents are tabun (GA), sarin (GB), soman (GD), GF, and VX. They are generally odorless and may be colorless. GA and GD may have a nondescript odor. Since their liquid phase is heavier than water and the vapor phase is heavier than air, they sink into low terrain/basements. VX is oily and persistent. In the presence of excess acetylcholine, because of the lack of its inhibiting enzyme acetylcholinesterase, the target organs acetylcholine affects will be over-stimulated. The facial organs (eyes, nose, mouth, and airways) are affected first. *Even 1 "large" drop of nerve agent on the skin may prove fatal.* The LD50 of sarin is 0.5mg. Nerve agents are twenty-six times more deadly than cyanide gas. Smaller single drops will produce lesser symptoms.

Treatment plans include the use of Level A PPE (Personal Protective Equipment. Move the casualty to an outdoor/upwind location. Remove his/her outer clothing only for vapor contamination but remove all clothing for liquid contamination. Decontaminate the casualty with soapy water or 0.5% hypochlorite solution (Clorox bleach; 1:10 dilution). Of course, always monitor and support the ABC's (Airway, Breathing, and Circulation). Decide on the appropriate triage level. A casualty with seizures, apnea, or multi-organ system involvement requires immediate care. The asymptomatic liquid exposed casualty requires hours of observation. The recovering casualty who has received at least 4 mg of atropine (a treatment drug) may be placed in the delayed category. The ambulatory, talking, vapor only exposed casualty may not need treatment if only miosis is present. Treatment is recommended if this casualty demonstrates any other symptoms. If cardiac activity is present in an apneic (not breathing) victim, aggressive resuscitation is mandatory.

Antidotes for nerve agent poisoning are atropine and pralidoxime chloride (2-PAM). Atropine sulfate blocks the "muscarinic" receptors of target organs reversing bradycardia (slow heart rate), bronchospasm (constricted air passages), bronchorrhea (copious secretions in the airway), vomiting, cramps and miosis. 2-PAM regenerates acetylcholinesterase activity and reverses the toxic "nicotinic" effects of muscle weakness and respiratory depression. Diazepam (Valium®) is used as an anticonvulsant drug. Ocular atropine drops reverse miosis, "dim" vision and even nausea. The military Mark I injector system includes two spring driven injectors. One contains 2mg atropine in 0.7ml diluent, while the second contains 600 mg 2-PAM in 2ml diluent. Treatment recommendations vary depending upon whether mild, moderate, or severe effects are present. The EMS system will triage and treat these victims. Detection of nerve agents is accomplished through the use of the military M256A1, M8, M9 papers, ICAD (chemical agent detector) and digital detectors.

Blister Agents (Vesicants)
This group of strong alkylating (chemical base producing) agents *includes impure sulfur mustard (H), distilled sulfur mustard (HD), nitrogen mustard (HS), Lewisite (L) and phos-*

gene oxime (CX). The mustard agent family has had a long history on the battlefield from WW1 through the Iran-Iraq War. It is an oily liquid heavier than water and its vapor is heavier than air. It smells like onions, garlic or mustard. Its aroma is noticeable only at high concentrations. Liquid mustard is a pale yellow to dark brown color. It is persistent on material and in soil for up to a week. Its vapor is detected by digital sensors or ICAD, while the liquid requires the military M8 paper. The vapor LCD50 (mg. min/cubic meter) is 1,500; the liquid LD50 is 100mg/kg. Mustard enters the body through the skin, the airway and the eye. It damages the skin by forming blisters, which do not form in the airway or the eye. The mechanism by which mustard damages cells is radiomimetic (mimics radiation damage) and injures cell DNA which is responsible for controlling vital cell functions. Interestingly, no free mustard is found in blister fluid. Although mustard damages cells almost immediately, symptoms usually appear in the four-to-eight-hour range. Damage is time and dose dependent. Symptoms appear after liquid exposure sooner than vapor exposure. Warm and/or moist body surface areas are most vulnerable. Tissue damage progresses for days. It may take up to five days for bone marrow suppression infection symptoms to appear. Eyelids may become swollen shut although unlike lewisite, the eyes themselves will not initially be injured. Skin damage progresses like a deep, partial thickness burn (like sunburn) from redness to coalescing blisters. Small mustard doses cause upper airway irritation including sinus pain, sore throat and a cough. Larger doses cause lung irritation with shortness of breath and death if symptoms occur within four hours. The cause of death is usually overwhelming pulmonary infection. The bone marrow produces all blood cell precursors including white blood cells that fight infection. White blood cell damage leads to serious infection problems unresponsive to antibiotics. Gastrointestinal damage may lead to diarrhea with large fluid/electrolyte losses.

Mustard exposure is insidious because it is odorless except at toxic levels and symptoms are delayed for hours. Despite disabling symptoms, mustard is generally not fatal. Again, only three percent of mustard exposed troops in WW1 died. Triage recommendations are the same as for nerve agents. Encountering vapor concentrations high enough to cause pulmonary symptoms within four hours of exposure is unlikely, but if these casualties occur, they must be immediately transported to an ICU. Because of the delayed nature of mustard effects, all potential casualties should be monitored for at least twenty-four hours.

Lewisite and Phosgene Oxime are uncommon blister agents that unlike mustard cause immediate effects. Similar to riot control agents, severe irritation to eyes, skin, and mucous membranes will occur within minutes of exposure. Unlike riot control agents, effects worsen with time. Exposed skin may die and appear gray within minutes. Severe damage to eyes and airways may occur. Lewisite and phosgene oxime do not suppress the bone marrow or its blood forming functions. Immediate triage is recommended for airway symptoms in the first few hours after exposure. Treatment schema or decontamination recommendations for blister agents are the same as for nerve agents.

"Remove contamination from the victim and remove the victim from contamination."

Get outside and upwind. Remove outer clothing only if vapor contaminated, and all clothing if liquid contaminated. Decontaminate with soapy water or 0.5% hypochlorite. Eye symptoms require urgent attention. Delayed triage is appropriate for isolated skin lesions. Lewisite is an arsenical (a heavy metal in the arsenic family) and its antidote is the chelating (heavy metal binding) agent Dimercaprol or British Anti-Lewisite (BAL). BAL decreases the internal effects of lewisite, but does not affect skin, eye, or airway damage. BAL is formulated in peanut oil and must be given IM. General adjunctive care recommendations for blister agents include the use of calamine lotion for skin erythema (redness). Silvadene® cream may also be used for skin irritation and blisters. Wound care for deep partial thickness burns is recommended including 3X/day wound irrigation and generous Silvadene® applications. Unlike burn treatment, significant skin fluid loss doesn't occur and fluid loading is contraindicated because of concurrent pulmonary damage. Eye care includes frequent BSS (basic salt solution) irrigation and atropine eye drops to prevent adhesions. Vaseline on eyelid edges also fights adhesions. The use of steroid eye drops is controversial. Topical analgesics are not recommended. For mild airway problems, cough suppressants and a humidifier are helpful. Severe airway problems require endotracheal intubation (a tube in the airway) and assisted ventilation. PEEP (positive end expiratory pressure) and bronchodilators (asthma medications) may also be beneficial. If possible, antibiotic therapy should be withheld until an infectious organism can be isolated.

Pulmonary Agents
Phosgene, or carbonyl chloride (CG) and chlorine (HC) are the 2 main chemicals in this group and are no longer felt to be CW threats. Phosgene was used in WW1 and is currently encountered as a by-product of methamphetamine production. Pulmonary agents are defined as chemicals that damage the pulmonary membranes separating alveoli (small lung air sacs) from capillaries (small blood vessels). Plasma then leaks from the capillary blood system filling the alveolus and preventing oxygen transfer. The casualty may die of suffocation and for this reason pulmonary agent poisoning may be termed "non-cardiac" pulmonary edema or "dry land drowning." Pulmonary edema takes two to twenty-four hours to develop. Early symptoms suggest severe poisoning. Diagnostic symptoms include exertional shortness of breath and a productive, frothy cough that are the first symptoms to appear and worsen

to shortness of breath at rest. Pulmonary fluid loss may be significant and hypotension (low blood pressure) may result. Only the agent's vapor phase is dangerous and no detection device exists. General triage recommendations are the same as for blister agents. Immediate triage is needed for all short of breath casualties while delayed triage is appropriate for others.

Personal Protective Equipment (PPE)
Personal protective equipment has both respiratory and dermal elements. When wearing full PPE, individual and collective performance is degraded by up to fifty percent. Military and civilian PPE have developed independently. The civilian system uses Occupational Safety and Health Administration (OSHA) or National Fire Protection Association (NFPA) codes as a standard for dermal protection. The military uses the MOPP system. *Civilian respiratory protection is provided by the Powered Air-Purifying Respirator (PAPR) or the Self-Contained Breathing Apparatus (SCBA).*

The PAPR uses ambient air drawn by a power source through a particulate canister to remove particles even of viral size. The purified air is drawn with positive pressure into a facemask or full hood. With the facemask, positive pressure helps to protect against ambient unfiltered air entering the system. A battery pack is worn on the belt while an inflow and an outflow hose connect the canisters to the mask. This system cannot be used in low oxygen or highly contaminated chemical environments.

The SCBA provides complete respiratory protection as it utilizes an independent oxygen source. It may be of closed or open circuit type. The open circuit type vents exhaled air into the environment and is the most commonly used type by fire hazmat teams. Usage limitations of respiratory devices are imposed by the equipment, the wearer, and the air supply.

Equipment limitations include limited visibility, hindered

voice communication with casualties (level A) and personnel (level B and C), increased weight of 25-35#, decreased mobility, the limitations of chemical agent specific cartridges and the need for repeated tank changes. Wearer limitations revolve around adequate physical fitness. Personnel must be cleared for respirator use. Medical conditions such as asthma, emphysema, lung disease, psychological problems including claustrophobia, facial deformities, and intolerance to increased heart rate (tachycardia) are all relative use contraindications. The SCBA system requires a back mounted air tank providing forty to sixty minutes of oxygen. Air supply limitations include variability factors all affecting the rate of oxygen consumption. The EPA, OSHA and the NFPA all recognize 4 levels of dermal protection.

Level A consists of a "moon suit" including SCBA, a completely enclosed positive pressure suit, two-layer chemical resistant gloves, steel toed boots and communications.
Level B replaces the positive pressure suit with full coverage chemical resistant clothing. Here, the CW agent is known and high-level respiratory protection is desired.
Level C substitutes a PAPR as respiratory protection.
Level D is a work uniform and may include a particulate mask. This level doesn't provide CW agent protection.

Chemical protective clothing protects against specific chemical hazards. Manufacturers must specify what chemical protection is compatible with a particular suit. Suits are available in reusable and limited use categories. The former can be used, decontaminated, tested, and re-used. Limited use (disposable) clothing can be reused only if it is not damaged or contaminated. Disposable garments must be decontaminated before disposal. Even reusable clothing has the potential to retain agent which days or weeks later may present a hazard due to agent leaching in or out. The National Fire

Protection Association (NFPA) describes suit performance standards in the following categories: vapor protective suits (NFPA1991) protect against vapor and liquid splash environments. They are designed for use in level A dress. Not all vapor suits protect against all vapors, although they all must protect against a minimal list of seventeen chemicals including acetonitrile, chlorine, and sulfuric acid (seen in cyanide generator booby traps.) Level A suits are hot and require special training above the first responder level. Liquid splash protective suits (NFPA1992) and support garments (NFPA1993) cannot be used inside a CW Hot or Warm Zone, but they may be appropriate for Cold Zone activities. Local and national hazmat regulations will dictate clothing choices.

The Hazmat Site
Any CW scenario mandates a Hazmat response. To date, federal funding has been directed to fire department hazmat for PPE and related gear. Although needed for perimeter control, law enforcement entities cannot respond without appropriate PPE and training. Efforts should be made to obtain locally compatible fire Hazmat PPE so that replacement gear (canisters, oxygen tanks) are readily available. Preplanning and realistic scenario training with involved agencies to promote seamless NIMS interaction cannot be overstressed.

Three *zones* are created in a typical Hazmat site:

The *Hot Zone* is the area directly surrounding the site epicenter (device, building, spill, etc.). The size and shape of this zone depends upon containment factors such as indoor/outdoor location, the delivery vehicle (blast vs. mechanical,) wind speed/direction (wind > 20 MPH may degrade agent; <20MPH may speed dispersal), terrain (open areas=wider dispersal), location of population centers, waterways and other factors. It should generally be 75-3300' from the source and be upwind/upgrade. One *entry control point (ECP)* is created for all entry/exit from the zone. The ECP is outside the directly contaminated area. The *Hot Line* demarcates the border between the Hot and Warm Zones. All material inside the Hot Zone is contaminated, including vehicles. Minimal immediate medical care is rendered inside the zone including airway /life threatening hemorrhage control and antidote administration. EOD and rescue personnel enter this zone.

The *Warm Zone* is uphill/upgrade from the Hot Zone. The Hot Line perimeter is controlled by law enforcement personnel in level A PPE. Rescuers and decontamination teams in level A PPE enter this zone. One ECP exists at the *Warm Line* (Warm-Cold Zone boundary) for personnel and 1 patient transfer point is also present. A log is kept of all personnel and patient movement in/out of the Warm Zone. The Warm Zone should be about 60' long and minimally 15' wide. Size may vary depending upon triage needs. Directly adjacent to the Hot Zone ECP, a *Warm Zone triage point* is established. Casualties are advanced from this point to the immediate care/litter decontamination station, the delayed care/decontamination station, or the ambulatory decontamination station. Again, medical care includes only the basics: airway, hemorrhage, and seizure control. All Warm Zone personnel are deconned prior to Cold Zone Entry.

The *Cold Zone* is separated from the Warm Zone by the *Cold Line*. It is upwind and upgrade of the Warm Zone. PPE should be immediately at hand but need not be worn unless winds shift, or incomplete decontamination is discovered. The cold triage point is adjacent to the Warm Zone ECP and all the standard triage stations (immediate, delayed and minimal) emanate from it. The full spectrum of medical care can be delivered in this zone. Treated patients move to the clean transport area and enter/exit through the Cold Zone ECP. The geography of a site is not set in stone and depends upon all the environmental factors described above. The shape and size of the various perimeters may change as weather or other variables change. An interesting question is what level of force is justified to preserve these perimeters. Nerve agent can certainly cross-contaminate caregivers and zones as twenty percent of exposed international hospital workers in the Aum Tokyo subway Sarin attack discovered. However, no caregivers died there and there are no other reported episodes of lethal cross CW contamination.

It is hoped that this communication will provide the team placed in a CW environment with the basic tools to safely bring order to the havoc that will certainly be present. Realistic NIMS based scenario training is needed. Please note that some information in this article may be time sensitive.

REFERENCES

1. Emergency Action for Chemical and Biological Warfare Agents- Ellison, D.H., CRC Press, Boca Raton, FL 1999 pp. 117-127.
2. Jane's Chem-Bio Handbook- Sidell, F. R., Patrick, W. C. III, and Dashiell, T. R., Jane's Information Group, Alexandria, Va. 1998
3. The Ultimate Terrorists- Stern, Jessica, Harvard University Press, Cambridge, Mass. 1999
4. Consequence Management: Domestic Response to Weapons of Mass Destruction- Chris Seiple, PARAMETERS, US Army War College Quarterly, Autumn-1997
5. Counter-Terrorism for Emergency Responders- Burke, R., Lewis Publishers, Boca Raton, 1999
6. The U.S. Armed Forces Nuclear, Biological and Chemical Survival Manual- Couch, D., Basic Books, New York, 1993
7. Explosives and Demolitions- FM5-25, Headquarters, Department of the Army, p. 104, 1967
8. Terrorism: An Investigator's Handbook- Dyson, W., Anderson Publishing Co., Cincinnati, OH, 2001

Explosions and Blast Injuries

Martin Greenberg, MD

Introduction

Scenario 1: A nine-story high reinforced concrete building is torn apart by a Ryder truck bomb parked in front. A crater thirty feet wide and eight feet deep is left by the blast. Responding fire departments entered a scene resembling a war zone with over 800 surrounding buildings sustaining blast damage; fifty ultimately require demolition. Windows are broken two miles away and the explosion is heard for fifty miles. sixty cars in a parking lot across the street are destroyed; the blast measures 3.5 on the Richter scale in an adjoining state. Property loss is thought to be $250 million. 1,000 firefighters and hundreds of police, EMS, and medical volunteers arrive within minutes. Within sixty minutes, 204 victims are transported to hospitals in 66 ambulances. Communications and rescue are hindered by fear of activating a secondary explosive device. The bomb is later discovered to be a 4000 lb. ammonium nitrate/fuel oil mixture. 169 people eventually die and 600 more are injured. It could have been worse... if chemical or nerve agents were present, over 5,000 citizens may have died. This amazing scenario is not a Tom Clancy fictional account. It accurately describes the bombing of the Oklahoma City Alfred P. Murrah Federal Building on April 19, 1995.

Scenario 2: Four teams of Islamic fundamentalist terrorists hijack four fuel laden, transcontinental, commercial jetliners using only box cutters and plastic knives. Almost simultaneously, the planes crash at full throttle into the New York City World Trade Center and into the Pentagon. The twin towers soon collapsed. A fourth plane crashes into a Pennsylvania strip mine thanks to a heroic passenger insurrection. Over 2753 innocent victims in the World Trade Center perished. Master terrorist Osama Bin Laden is implicated in the attack. The United States officially declares war on terrorism. September 11, 2001, will be forever burned into our memories as the date of the worst domestic terror incident in our history.

How would your community deal with such catastrophic events? This article hopes to present a brief history of conventional terrorism, describe the physical properties of bomb blasts, and summarize the medical aspects and treatment of explosive injuries.

A Brief History of Conventional Terrorism on American Soil

Despite the notoriety given to nuclear, biological, and chemical (NBC) unconventional "WMD" (Weapons of Mass Destruction,) it should be understood that seventy percent of all terrorist incidents are of a conventional nature. Unlike rare NBC attacks, there were over 10,000 bombings worldwide in the years 1990-95! The human toll exacted from these episodes included 3,176 injured and 355 killed. The goal of terrorists to induce panic and apprehension were successfully achieved worldwide multiple times. The terrorist's motivation is multi-factorial. The Oklahoma City Murrah Federal Building bombing was felt to be in retaliation to the Federal management of the Waco, Texas and Ruby Ridge, Idaho confrontations. In 1975, Croatian nationals attempted to draw attention to their plight by bombing LaGuardia Airport in Queens, New York City injuring seventy-five and killing eleven. The terrorist may also be mentally ill, and act alone. The "Unabomber" managed to elude law enforcement agencies for 17 years while completing fourteen successful letter and pipe bomb attacks.

The number of conventional bombings increased dramatically during the 1990s. On February 26, 1993, the World Trade Center in New York City was bombed by an Islamic Fundamentalist cult. The World Trade Center is comprised of two 110 story towers which house about 150,000 people when fully occupied. The attack occurred at 12:17PM when the center was most busy in order to inflict maximal casualties. The goal of the attack was to undermine US support of Israel and to show that our country was not immune to terrorism. The 1,200-pound nitrate/fuel oil bomb created a crater 180 feet deep, 100 feet long, and 200 feet wide that encompassed six levels of the parking garage. Amazingly, the twin towers were destroyed on September 11, 2001 when two teams of Islamic terrorists flew fuel laden commercial jets into their upper structures. Almost 3000 lives were lost. For the first time in history, air travel over the United States ceased, and thus began our first declared war in over fifty years.

There is a very real threat of a secondary explosion directed at responding law enforcement and rescue personnel in terrorist incidents. On January 30, 1998, a bomb exploded near the front door of an abortion clinic in Birmingham, Alabama, drawing the attention of authorities. As the responding personnel gathered, it is believed that the bomber was watching and intentionally detonated a secondary bomb, killing a security guard and seriously injuring a counselor.

Explosive terrorism is still the weapon of choice of the domestic terrorist. Disturbingly, Burke points out that "acts of explosive terrorism almost doubled from 1989 to 1994." For every successful explosive act of terror, many others are narrowly averted. The time, energy, and dollars invested in counter-terrorist activities is staggering.

Physical Properties of Bomb Blasts

What defines an explosion? Most authorities will agree that *an explosion may be described as "a rapid release of high-pressure gas into the environment."* This energy is released as a blast, or shock wave, heat, and flying debris. The rush of air caused by the movement of blast gas is termed the shock wave, or blast wind. *The magnitude of this wave of compressed air can be measured as overpressure, or direct impulse.* The magnitude of overpressure is proportional to the amount of explosive used, and is measured in pounds per square inch (psi.) It can be calculated by multiplying PSI x the duration (milliseconds) of the impulse.

How much blast wave does it take to cause death? The expected injury to the blast victim is dependent upon several factors including the distance from the point of detonation, the duration of the blast (milliseconds), the size of the detonation, and the environment in which the explosion occurs.

Powerful conventional explosives have high overpressures of relatively long duration, while small-arms weapon noise will generate negligible peak overpressures of short duration (<1 atmosphere; <0.5msec).

Closed spaces will magnify the effects of the direct impulse. The shock wave "bouncing" off a hard surface or wall is termed the *"reflected impulse."* This "bounced" blast wave may combine with the direct impulse and may cause injuries at a greater than expected distance from the blast site. An example is the Israeli bus explosion (six kilogram explosive) in Jerusalem that caused more severe injuries in passengers located further away from the explosion. Thirty percent of these blast victims sustained multiple injuries while ten percent died. Blast pressures can be measured. The higher the blast overpressure, the worse will be the resulting injury. An overpressure of 58 to 80 psi is more than ninety-five percent lethal. Overpressures of only 0.5 - 1.0 psi break windows and "knock down" people. 5 psi may rupture eardrums while 7-8 psi from a sizable explosion may overturn rail cars and shear brick walls.

How does compressed air cause all this damage? The molecules of all types of gases in our atmosphere are in constant motion. At sea level, there are thirty million, billion molecules in each cubic millimeter of air, traveling at 300 meters/sec. They strike each other 100 million times each second, although each molecule has traveled only 0.001 mm! When an explosion occurs, molecules of air are "bumped" outward by the release of explosion energy. Moving at the speed of sound, molecules bump into each other over a very short distance. The energy is transferred outward as a "ripple" or ring-like effect away from the blast epicenter. This causes tissue damage as compressed air strikes the victim and stretches, tears, and ruptures tissues inside the body. The injuries produced by this blast wave are termed "primary blast injury."

What are the differences between "high and low explosives?" *Explosives are described as "high" or "low" depending upon the speed of reaction and the psi generated. HIGH EXPLOSIVES change from a solid to a gas almost instantly (microseconds), and generate 50,000-4,000,000 psi at the immediate blast site. LOW EXPLOSIVES incompletely burning over a period of time (milliseconds or longer, termed a deflagration), can generate <50,000 psi.* Low explosives such as black powder are used as propellant charges and powder trains (fuses), while high explosives, such as trinitrotoluene (TNT) create a blast wave that creates a shattering effect and can move large objects. Only a detonation creates a true blast, or shock wave. The pressure and heat waves travel equally in all directions at supersonic speed (>1,250 ft. /sec.) and may carry deadly shrapnel. Blast wind speeds in a detonation may actually reach 20,000 mph. The yield of a material describes the rate at which an explosion involving the material occurs. When high yield explosives detonate, including TNT, dynamite, detchord, semtex, C3 and C4, the blast wave may destroy objects it strikes.

Blast wave pressure can also be described in two *phases*. *The POSITIVE PHASE* occurs as the blast wave travels in an outward direction away from the blast epicenter. In a detonation, the blast will travel equally in all directions. A partial vacuum is then created near the epicenter due to the outward movement of air, and the consumption of oxygen by the burning process. This vacuum sucks smoke, gases, and debris back towards the epicenter and is termed the *NEGATIVE PHASE*. The negative phase may last three times as long as the positive phase and is described by a "standard" waveform termed the Friedlander Waveform. The thermal wave then carries explosion products up vertically and downwind. A detonation blast wave will usually be preceded by a thermal wave that may ignite local combustible material. Explosive devices, which contain *nails, screws, flechettes or other debris are termed 'anti-personnel munitions.'* The injuries caused by flying debris (pipe bomb metal fragments, nails, glass, rocks, etc.) are called secondary blast injuries. *Secondary blast injury is the most common cause of death in explosions.* The use of ballistic vests will greatly protect the officer from flying debris. During the Vietnam War, soldiers who wore their "flak vests" had a much greater statistical chance of survival from artillery, grenade, and mortar shrapnel. Explosives have been mixed or attached to unconventional hazardous materials and used as "hybrid" weapons that disperse radioactive material, or biological/chemical agents. In larger explosions, nearby victims may actually be "blown away" and physically hurled through the air by the blast wave. Injuries resulting from being thrown are termed tertiary blast injuries. When responding to an explosive incident, it is very important to remember to screen the site with a Geiger counter, and carefully observe for signs of chemical agents or other potential threats. Secondary explosive devices should be sought and expected; thus, only essential personnel should be allowed near the explosion site.

Types of Conventional Explosives

Conventional explosives are compounds of nitrogen, oxygen, carbon, and hydrogen. They may exist in any physical state (solid, liquid, or gas). There are two categories of materials used in explosive devices. *Primary explosive materials are sensitive to heat or pressure.* They include substances such as lead azide or mercury fulminate. They are difficult to handle for this reason. *Secondary explosive materials are less sensitive* to prevent unintended explosions, and can be handled relatively safely. These include compounds such as trinitrotoluene (TNT), pentaethyltrinitride (PETN) and C4 plastic explosives. These less-sensitive explosives are not usually affected by high temperatures. Most military munitions consist of a fuse (a sensitive primary explosive), a booster (a less sensitive secondary explosive) and a main charge (an insensitive explosive). Most conventional terrorist weapons are improvised or assembled from individual dual use components. For example, ammonium nitrate is an agricultural fertilizer, but it is also the oxidizer in an ammonium nitrate/fuel oil bomb. These materials were used in the New York and Oklahoma City attacks and were transported to the sites as Vehicle Borne Improvised Explosive Devices (VBIEDs.) These bombs are usually large and destructive. Rental trucks were used in both cases. *The most common type of improvised explosive is the PIPE BOMB.* This bomb has been used in about one-third of all conventional terrorist attacks made by filling a pipe, or metal "Mag-light" style flashlight with black powder. Alternately, a simple cannon-type fuse may be lit, or a timer may be used. The flashlight switch itself may serve as a booby trap! As flashlights are an increasingly popular pipe bomb booby trap, do not disturb flashlights encountered at a bombing scene but consider them to be bombs until proven otherwise. According to the BATF (Bureau of Alcohol, Tobacco, and Firearms), 20 such devices have been discovered in the years 1997-98. The ubiquitous backpack is a convenient method of concealment that was successfully employed at the Olympic Park bombing in 1976.

Medical Aspects of Explosive Terrorism
The severity of blast injury is dependent upon characteristics of the blast, the surroundings, and the victim. Blast intensity is directly proportional to the level of inflicted trauma. Hybrid elements of the explosion will also adversely impact victims. Characteristics of surroundings include the size and magnifying effects of the enclosure. A small enclosure will greatly magnify the reflected impulse and create a large, combined impulse (direct plus reflected impulse). The reflected or combined impulse may injure victims distant from the epicenter. Victim characteristics include the distance from the epicenter, body orientation to the blast, and clothing factors such as the use of body armor or a bomb suit. Even the use of a bomb suit will not completely protect against blast wave effects. In fact, the use of a bomb suit/ballistic vest may actually slightly worsen the severity of blast lung injury, but the benefits of protection from shrapnel and penetrating trauma override this risk.

Body positioning in relation to the advancing blast wave is also important. The end-on position (lying down with the head or feet pointing towards the blast) offers the best protection against blast injuries. For example, "the threshold for lung injury is about 12 psi. in blast waves of 20-30 msec. duration... Subjects end-on to the blast would require an incident shock of 12 psi....to cause this lesion. If the subjects are oriented side-on, an incident shock of 10 psi.... would cause equal damage." Adding a nearby wall to "bounce" the blast wave into the body would also cause more damage, thus decreasing the injury threshold to 5 psi.

Repeated exposure to explosive blasts dramatically increases tissue damage. For example, a blast that causes a one percent mortality when experienced once, will cause a twenty percent mortality when experienced twice and a 100% mortality when experienced three times.

Blast injury is described as primary, secondary, and tertiary. Primary blast injury (PBI) is caused by the physiological effects of the blast wave upon the human body. Primary blast injuries occur through three basic mechanisms. *SPALLING* describes the tissue injury caused when the blast wave rapidly changes velocity as it moves through tissues of different densities. The lungs are prone to this type of trauma. *IMPLOSION* is the result of the air-filled intestines (the gastrointestinal track) rapidly stretching beyond its elastic limit and rupturing after being compressed by the passing shock wave. *INERTIAL EFFECTS* describe the injury occurring when connected tissues of different densities move at different velocities such as the bowel on its mesentery (connective tissue and blood vessels attaching the bowel to the abdominal wall).

If the victim is close to the explosion, skin burning may occur. Fortunately, this is rare unless materials such as gasoline or organic chemicals are used.

An eight-year study of over 500 victims of bomb blasts in Northern Ireland revealed different injury constellations in survivor and non-survivor groups. The fatal injury constellation included brain damage (66%), skull fracture (55%), blast lung (47%), ear drum (tympanum) rupture (45%) and liver laceration (34%). Interestingly, brain damage frequently occurred without skull fracture. Survivor's injuries included fractures (18%), burns (15%) and concussions (15%). Blast lung is a severe form of pulmonary contusion (lung "bruise") where lacerated, crushed lung tissue fills with blood and cannot exchange oxygen.

Medical Blast Treatment
When responding to the explosion scene, the first consideration of the first responder is self-preservation! Ask yourself: Is the scene safe for me to enter? Are radiation, biological

and/or nerve agents present? Are the victims the result of the actual explosion or are their secretions, tears, and vomit the result of a nerve agent release? Do not enter the scene unless you have a definite role, and only then after you are certain you won't be joining the ranks of victims.

The blast victim should have his "ABCs" (Airway, Breathing, Circulation) evaluated. Make sure the victim can breathe through an open airway, check pulses, and treat for possible shock. Remember that penetrating trauma (secondary blast injury) causes most injuries. Attempt to stop major bleeding. Victims with altered mental status, in shock or having sustaining penetrating torso trauma require immediate transportation to a Level 1 Trauma Center. The victim may have suffered spine or extremity fractures. An EMS backboard, stretcher or even a wooden door may be used for transportation.

In a disaster with multiple victims, most or all of the "walking wounded" will likely be gone by the time you arrive. Therefore, most of the blast victims remaining on-site will be dead or critically injured. *Triage* should occur during the initial evaluation and repeated often during subsequent care and transport. A fact to remember is that victims with blood or reddish fluid coming out of their ears (ruptured eardrums) have a fifty percent chance of life-threatening internal injuries. The overriding triage rule is "to do the most good for the greatest number of victims."

For patients who have severe lung or brain injury, intubation (breathing tube placed in their trachea) will be required. If heat injury or burns occur to the throat or trachea, the victim's airway may rapidly swell and close. Therefore, early intubation should rapidly be performed if difficulty talking or swallowing is present.

Hemorrhage needs to be controlled. If bleeding continues without success in using pressure bandages, then the previous dressings should be removed and the wound re-inspected. Get a good look at the wound, remove the old dressings, apply direct pressure with a fresh pressure dressing and you should be able to stop *non-pulsatile extremity bleeding* in most circumstances. If *pulsatile bleeding* occurs, consider the use of an approved tourniquet.

Penetrating trauma to the chest may be treated with a bandage called a chest seal. This device is easily applied and allows rapid treatment that may prevent a tension pneumothorax (high pressure developing in one half of the chest). Several hemostatic agents are also commercially available in the form of a powder, impregnated gauze or tampons. Please review the self-aid/buddy-aid chapter for a more complete discussion of this topic.

Burns may be encountered in caring for blast victims and if the skin or material is still hot cool water / non-flammable liquids should be applied to prevent further skin damage. Care should be taken to avoid hypothermia (low body temperature). Once the skin is at body temperature, non-adherent burn dressings or dry loose sheets/clean blankets may be used. Transportation to a burn center should then occur.

Summary
The blast victim will likely survive if his airway and breathing are maintained, bleeding is stopped, shock is treated, and rapid transportation to a Level 1 Trauma Center occurs. The mechanisms of injury include primary (shock wave) blast injury, secondary (flying projectiles) blast injury and tertiary (blunt trauma from being thrown by explosion) blast injuries. The first responder may be required to manage blast injury victims. Their survival may depend upon your blast injury knowledge and the rapid application of appropriate medical skills you employ.

REFERENCES

1. The Ultimate Terrorists- Stern, Jessica, Harvard University Press, Cambridge, Mass. 1999
2. Consequence Management: Domestic Response to Weapons of Mass Destruction- Chris Seiple, PARAMETERS, US Army War College Quarterly, Autumn-1997
3. Counter-Terrorism for Emergency Responders- Burke, R., Lewis Publishers, Boca Raton, 1999
4. Explosives and Demolitions- FM5-25, Headquarters, Department of the Army, p. 104, 1967
5. Terrorism: An Investigator's Handbook- Dyson, W., Anderson Publishing Co., Cincinnati, OH, 2001

Canine (K-9) Considerations

Martin Greenberg, MD

Scenario
Your tactical team is called out to apprehend an armed suspect known to be in a large warehouse. It is night. The warehouse is poorly lit and intelligence about its interior is scant. After establishing an outer perimeter, the decision is made to release the team's canine officer. Several "stacks" are assembled for multiple entries. Before the stealth entry can be initiated, screams and growls from the building's interior make it clear that the dog has isolated and subdued the perpetrator, greatly simplifying the tactical mission.

Why Are We Drawn to Canines?
"I think we are drawn to dogs because they are the uninhibited creatures we might be if we weren't certain we knew better. They fight for honor at the first challenge, make love with no moral restraint, and they do not for all of their marvelous instincts seem to know about death. Being such wonderfully uncomplicated creatures, they need us to do their worrying." From the Illinois Police Work Dog Association (ILPWDA).

Introduction to the Canine Officer
The police dog, or K-9, has been an invaluable asset to tactical teams since their inception. Although no statute in law exists

defining their role, canines are frequently considered officers and are informally "sworn in," issued badges and become part of the agency and handler's family. They are partners, not merely living tactical tools. The type of dog chosen for this special role depends upon the niche it will be expected to fill. A general-purpose patrol dog will frequently be a German Shepherd or Belgian Malinois. Other breeds may be considered if tasks such as drug or Explosive Ordinance Device (EOD) detection are foreseen. The dog is trained from puppy hood to follow scents and in obedience while being evaluated for possessing the proper temperament and intelligence for the job. Formal training may begin from nine to twelve months of age and the canine may not be placed into police service until even two years of age. The agency will spend at least $7500-$10,000 on a trained canine depending upon the type of training needed. These dogs may hail from the United States or from Europe. Some trainers feel that European bred and trained dogs have purer bloodlines and are thus more reliable and less susceptible to genetically transmitted disease. Maintenance costs are about $1,000-$1,500/year. Add the cost of a specially outfitted squad car, gear, and housing. The initial investment then becomes even more substantial, easily reaching the $40,000 range. It takes about a year for a true bond to form between the dog and its handler. The canine may remain in service based upon its ability to maintain performance qualifications and to remain healthy. The canine's effectiveness in performing law enforcement activities is well documented. A canine team may effectively perform the job that might typically require the services of many police search officers. In terms of drug detection, numerous studies have shown that trained canines are generally ten times better than any instrument. Canine teams have excelled in the area of bomb detection with a "ninety-six percent surety rate." (1) Regarding building searches, "police canine teams ... represent a considerable benefit to police agencies... As the building size increases, the canine teams' time savings, accuracy, and subjective reported certainty far surpasses that of searching officers' teams." (2) Currently, no mandatory retirement age is generally prescribed for police dogs. It would be unusual, however, to see a canine remain in service past age ten years (human age seventy). Upon retirement, the dog will usually continue to live with the handler who may purchase the animal from the agency for a nominal fee. The police canine has earned a valued, permanent place in police work and deserves the respect of the law enforcement community.

Canine Physiology
Normal physiologic values of a 30-38 kg German Shepherd police dog are as follows:
  Temperature: 38.5 degrees C. (101.5 degrees F.).
  Pulse: 120-130/min. during exercise. Young dog's heart rate (HR) is 110-120 beats/min. HR is less than 90/min. at rest in a large breed adult dog. A small breed adult dog may have a HR of 80-120/min. HR may normally be irregular.
  Respiration: 15-40/min. at rest. Panting may increase respiratory rate to several hundred/min.
  Mucous membranes: generally pink.
  Water Intake: 15-30 ml./kg./day = about 35 oz. /day.
  Weight: 30-38 kg.
  Caloric Requirements: min. 15 Kcal/lb./day = 1050 Kcal/day. At work, requirements may rise to over 60 Kcal./lb./day = >4200 Kcal.
  Approximate Calories in Food: 450 Kcal/can; 350 Kcal/cup of dry dog food. (3)
  The dog's respiratory system provides oxygen to its body. It inhales through the mouth and nose by expanding the diaphragm. Air then travels through the bronchi to the lungs. Minute bronchioles transfer oxygen to capillary sized arterioles for transfer to the body through the circulatory system. The thoracic (chest) cavity is filled by the heart and lungs.

The heart is the body's blood pump. The endocrine (hormonal) and nervous systems control the distribution of blood to the dog's organs. Twenty percent of the circulatory system's blood remains in the brain at all times. Increased blood flow to the heart and large extremity muscles groups occurs during exercise and stress.

The digestive system is comprised of the mouth, esophagus, stomach, and small/large intestines. Chewed food passes through the esophagus to the stomach. The stomach is especially thick and muscular, allowing the dog to swallow large items. Digestion of food begins in the stomach mixing with acids and enzymes. The pH of stomach hydrochloric acid (HCL) is only about 1.0 and is therefore extremely acidic. Food moves by muscular contraction (peristalsis) through the pyloric sphincter (valve) into the first part of the small intestine called the duodenum. It mixes with enzymes from the liver and pancreas in the small intestine. Nutrients are also absorbed here into the bloodstream. In the large intestine, fluid is absorbed and residual waste products are broken down. Toxins are removed from the bloodstream by the excretory system.

Dogs' and humans' senses differ significantly. A dog's eye is covered with a tough layer called the sclera. Dog's eyes are more sensitive to movement and light but less sensitive to color and shapes than ours. The average German Shepherds' hearing is four to ten times as sensitive as human hearing. The senses of smell and taste also vary from ours. Moisture on the dog's nose "dissolves" molecules traveling in the air and they eventually are converted to electrical impulses sent to the brain's olfactory (smell) center. This center is over forty times the size of ours and the dog's sense of smell is on average 10-100 times as acute as ours (www.uspcak9.com). For selected scents (butyric acid) this acuity difference may be even 1,000,000 – 100,000,000 times more effective than human's. (4) Interestingly, dogs possess a *vomeronasal organ* in the roof of the mouth. This organ allows the dog to "taste" selected smells and then transmit the information to the brain's limbic system that controls emotional memory. Taste and smell are thus closely linked. Taste buds are clustered at the tip of the dog's tongue and can discriminate between bitter, sweet, salty, and sour tastes. Their sense of taste is relatively worse than ours since they possess only one sixth the number of taste buds compared to humans.

Thermoregulation
The dog's normal body temperature is about 101.5 degrees Fahrenheit. Canine thermoregulation has many unique features. The primary method of cooling is through evaporation with rapid, shallow breathing termed panting. Increased airflow occurs over the moist surfaces of the respiratory tract. When panting begins, the respiratory rate suddenly rises ten times from its basal level of about thirty to forty to 300-400 breaths/minute. This rate is maintained periodically depending upon the heat load. The elastic nature of the respiratory tract allows it to oscillate at a natural frequency and facilitates breathing with little muscular effort. Blood flow to the dog's tongue is controlled by arteriovenous anastomoses (AVAs). They are present more at the tip than at the tongue's base and are only about 100-150 microns long (one micron = one millionth meter=one tenth millimeter= 1/250 inch). These anastomoses are usually open and allow blood to travel directly from arteries to veins. When body temperature rises, AVAs constrict and force blood into the tongue's superficial capillary network where heat is dissipated. Core body heating of the hypothalamus gland also causes dilation of the lingual arteries and increased tongue blood flow. (5)

The fur coat provides insulation against heat and cold. The thicker the dog's coat becomes, the greater is its resulting insulation effects. Dogs shed their coat in the spring to lose excess hair and also in the fall to prepare for growth of a thicker winter coat. Dogs living primarily indoors may shed more continuously.

Cutaneous blood flow regulation in less hair bearing areas (ears, abdomen, and genitals) plays only a minor role in thermoregulation. Vasodilation increases blood flow and heat loss while vasoconstriction decreases it. These effects are under control of the autonomic (automatic) nervous system and the hormones adrenaline and noradrenaline. We are all familiar with the "fight or flight" reactions occurring with sympathetic nervous system stimulation. Alpha adrenergic sympathetic stimulation decreases cutaneous blood flow and retains heat. Beta adrenergic parasympathetic stimulation has the opposite effect.

Sweating is the major form of thermoregulation in humans but is negligible in canines. Sweat glands are present only in the dog's footpads and ear canals. Well-hydrated dogs can tolerate heat stress better than their dehydrated counterparts.

The Canine Primary Survey
The medic and the dog handler should be viewed as a team providing canine first aid. The first step in providing canine medical care is to recognize that a problem exists. Just as in the human patient, a primary medical survey or "once over" may reveal treatable medical problems. It's important to partner here with the dog's handler as this officer knows best how his partner normally behaves. Remember that your demeanor is very important when dealing with an injured or ill canine. Only six percent of communication is verbal. The medic's anxious or aggressive body language or physical behaviors are definitely appreciated by the dog that will negatively react to them. Assume a firm but gentle approach. Be cautious! The canine officer is an attack dog who may not know you and who doesn't feel well. Muzzle the dog prior to providing care. Obtain the handler's assistance every step of the way. Check the familiar First Aid Airway, Breathing and Circulation. Are the dog's vital signs normal? After assessing these basics, check the capillary refill time by pressing on the dog's gum above its

teeth. Push down until the gum is white and see how long it takes for color to return. It should return within one to two seconds. Dogs' gums may vary in color dramatically, so the handler's input is important. When taking a rectal temperature, make sure it's accurate. Pulse is measured by gently pressing at the groin crease. If in doubt, take the temperature/pulse again. You'll definitely need to obtain the handler's assistance in all phases of the canine medical evaluation!

Other common sense questions to ask yourself are:

Is the dog limping?

Is the dog in pain? Is he/she biting or pulling at a certain body area? Are other pain or unusual or pain behaviors present?

Is there an obvious laceration or wound present?

Is an extremity deformed?

Is the dog alert, responsive and mobile?

What does the handler think?

The Secondary Survey

The secondary survey is a quick canine physical exam. Drs. Heiskell and Tang point out that making a specific diagnosis through this exam is crucial to providing appropriate care. They present the mnemonic *"A CRASH PLAN"* summarizing the organ system evaluation.

A is for Airway; (Is the airway patent and is adequate air exchange occurring?)

C is for Cardiovascular; (Is a groin pulse present? Is the heart rate normal?)

R is for Respiration; (Is the dog breathing normally and effectively? Is breathing labored? Are breath sounds symmetrically present?)

A is for Abdomen (look for signs of obvious trauma and use your stethoscope to listen for bowel sounds.)

S is for Spine (Is the dog moving all its extremities? Are obvious spinal deformities present?)

P is for Pelvis; (Is the pelvis stable to manipulation?)

L is for Limbs; (Are the limbs symmetric or deformed? Are they being protected or are they used normally?)

A is for Arteries; (Is bleeding present? Is a groin pulse present?) (6)

Canine First Aid

It is the responsibility of the dog handler and the medic to provide first aid care to their injured canine partner. This dog isn't just a pet. He is usually an unofficially "sworn" officer in whom a greater departmental financial and training investment has been made than in his human counterparts! The canine officer deserves the same level and commitment to medical care as afforded to other officers. Your transport vehicle will be the K-9 squad car that also contains a muzzle and possibly the restraints you may need to treat the canine officer.

Shock- Shock is a reversible, life-threatening medical problem resulting from inadequate circulatory system function. The most common cause in canines is blood loss or hypovolemic shock. Other much less common causes include neurogenic shock (a loss of vascular tone from poisoning) and septic shock (low blood pressure due to overwhelming infection.) Cardiogenic shock or hypotension due to heart pump failure may rarely occur due to the ill effects of congenital cardiac anomalies suddenly affecting the canine officer.

Symptoms of shock include:
- *Pale mucous membranes* including gums and eyelids with capillary refill time over two seconds;
- *Dehydration;*
- *Excessive drooling* in selected poisonings;
- *Weak, rapid femoral pulse (tachycardia);*
- *Cool extremities;*
- *Respiratory rate >25/minute;*
- *Confusion, restlessness;*
- *Weakness.*

Advanced symptoms include: unresponsiveness, dilated pupils, capillary refill time over four seconds, white mucous membranes and rectal temperature < 98 degrees F. (7)

Treatment is based upon supporting the dog's airway, breathing, and circulation and correcting shock's underlying cause. This will usually include intravenous (IV) fluids, keeping the dog quiet, calm, warm and controlling any source of bleeding if possible. Elevating the hind quarters may have the beneficial effect of increasing brain blood supply. Remember that a dog in shock may not recognize familiar humans. It may bite unpredictably. Muzzling the dog is a good idea but may not be possible if difficulty breathing or vomiting occurs. A muzzle must be monitored and possibly removed with the same care you would devote to observing a limb with an applied tourniquet.

Major Lacerations and Bleeding- Bleeding can be a life threatening problem and should be promptly controlled if possible. Treatment is the same as for humans with direct pressure applied over the wound. If unsuccessful, apply more direct pressure, elevate the extremity, and even consider using a tourniquet if this is within your medical standing orders. Tourniquet application times should not exceed one hour. You may be risking limb viability by applying a tourniquet but this risk may be acceptable if you truly feel that exsanguination (bleeding to death) is the alternative. Apply a compression dressing, splint the extremity, restrict movement, calm the dog, and verify adequate distal circulation. Obtain prompt veterinary intervention.

Fractures- Symptoms include: Pain, deformity, not using the limb, limping (closed fracture), or an obvious bone protruding through the skin (open fracture). It may be impossible to differentiate a dislocation (a joint out of alignment) from a broken bone (author's note-fractures and broken bones are synonymous). Treatment of a closed fracture should be to apply a full extremity splint. If the fracture is open, leave the bone fragment exposed and apply an antibiotic soaked 4 x 4 inch gauze dressing over the wound if available and then a full extremity splint. Elevate the extremity. Treat bleeding and prevent shock. Transport as soon as possible.

Gunshot Wounds (GSWs) and Stab Wounds- These problems are treated as in humans with the application of an antibiotic dressing or chest seal. Shave the area as needed. Splint an injured extremity and control bleeding. Monitor the first-aid "A, B, C s" and intervene as needed. This is a load and go situation. Please review the Self-Aid/Buddy-Aid chapter for a more detailed discussion.

Heat Stress (Heatstroke)- This medical emergency occurs when the canine loses its thermoregulatory ability. When the dog's respiratory track cannot adequately dissipate heat, its temperature rises. The normal body temperature is less than 103 degrees F. When body temperature rises above 105 degrees, metabolic problems arise and when the temperature reaches 108 degrees, multi-organ system failure and death can occur within minutes. Risk factors for police dogs include high ambient temperature, enclosed spaces with poor ventilation, high humidity, high activity level, large size, short nosed (brachycephalic) and heavy coated breeds, dehydration, and multiple medications including anti-histamines and anti-emetics. Symptoms of heat stroke include a muddy pink or brick red gum color, elevated temperature (the top of the dog's head will feel hot), rapid panting, confusion, and prostration. Emergency treatment includes submerging the dog in cool (not ice cold) water. If submersion isn't possible, wet them down all over and run water especially over the groin area as superficial blood vessels there will effectively cool him. Don't cover them with a wet towel as this decreases evaporation. Transport emergently in the air conditioned K-9 vehicle and start IV fluid replacement if possible. If transport is not possible, place the dog in a shaded, ventilated area. Be aware of heat stress problems occurring in the spring and fall seasons as well as during the summer months.

Heatstroke prevention is better than treatment! (8)

Poisoning- Quite a few poisons may affect the canine. Symptoms are generally vague and include difficulty breathing, unusual behaviors, digestive upset, abnormal heart beat, shivering, drooling, and/or convulsions. Know your local poison control phone number or call 1-800-548-2423, the ASPCA Animal Poison Control Center. Do not induce vomiting if the poison is caustic or unknown.

Rodent Poisons (Rodenticides)-Anti-coagulants: Warfarin (Coumadin) is an anti-coagulant (blood thinner) commonly used in humans that kills by causing spontaneous bleeding. Effects are dose dependent and are delayed by hours or longer. Treatment is to induce vomiting and to transport to the veterinarian a.s.a.p. with the poison sample.

Other rodenticides include ANTU, Thallium, Pindone, Strychnine, Sodium Fluoroacetate (1080), and Zinc Phosphide. This group may cause seizures, liver/kidney failure, hemorrhagic gastroenteritis (bleeding in the gut) or fatal pulmonary edema (fluid in the lungs). Induce vomiting if the dog is conscious.

Pesticides- This group includes Arsenic, Chlorinated Hydrocarbons, Organophosphates (the military form is sarin, tabin, VX), Carbonates, Rotenone and Metaldehyde.

Glycols/Antifreeze- The dog may appear "drunk." Fatal effects may occur hours later. Rinse the dog's mouth, feet, or other contact points. Induce vomiting.

Transport the poisoned canine to a veterinary hospital as soon as possible in all cases!

Seizures- Seizures may be of either a focal or global nature. Unlike global seizures, focal seizures don't involve a loss of consciousness. They may be a symptom of other medical problems such as poisoning, heatstroke, head trauma, infection, or even a brain tumor. Alternatively, they may occur spontaneously as an isolated finding. Seizures may resolve spontaneously or they may require treatment. *Valium*® (Diazepam) is the drug most commonly used to temporarily control seizures. It is administered intravenously or rectally. Treat the underlying cause of the seizure if possible. (9)

Selected Canine Medical Problems
1. *Internal Parasites*- Heartworm disease is caused by parasite Dirofilaria immitis. It lives in the right side of the dog's heart and great vessels. The female worm produces microscopic heartworms that circulate through the blood stream. It takes about 190 days for an infected dog to become able to transmit infection. Through mosquitoes, the worms may be passed after about two weeks to other dogs. The microfilariae (microscopic heartworms) eventually travel to the heart to mature and may reproduce in about three weeks. Heartworm disease is usually diagnosed by examining a blood smear for microfilariae. Untreated heartworm disease results in multi-organ system failure and death.

2. *Hip Dysplasia*- Congenital Hip Dysplasia (CHD) is the most common canine orthopedic problem. CHD is a hip arthritis problem due to poor alignment of the femoral head (hip ball) under the acetabulum (hip socket). It is transmitted genetically in unclear ways and is one reason that pure, traceable bloodlines in canines are important. During the puppy's growth spurt from birth to 2 months of age, for whatever reason, the connective tissue growth around the hip can't keep up with bony growth resulting in laxity (looseness) around the joint. The hip ball is then partially out of its socket or *subluxed*. Symptoms in young, pre-arthritic dogs include an audible and palpable click when walking and a "bunny-hop" gait pattern. Older dogs will develop stiffness when arising and a painful limp. The presence of congenital hip dysplasia would disqualify a dog from police service (https://www.uspca.com).

3. *Ocular Problems*- These issues are common in service

dogs. The tactical environment may be dirty or dusty. If the dog squints or has red, tearing eyes, flush with sterile saline eyewash. Small corneal abrasions incurred while pursuing a scent may be invisible to gross inspection. If eyewash doesn't resolve the problem, seek prompt veterinary consultation as abrasions can become infected with permanent consequences. Penetrating eye wounds require emergent care. Don't remove the foreign body and transfer the dog to your veterinarian or veterinary ophthalmologist immediately (Canine Field Trauma and Emergency Manual, Arboretum View Animal Hospital).

4. *Bloat- "Bloat" refers to the two gastrointestinal medical problems of gastric dilatation and gastric dilatation volvulus (GDV).* Bloat may occur in any breed but larger service dog breeds are more prone to this problem. For whatever reason, gas is suddenly retained in the stomach and is not expelled in the usual manner. Abdominal pain, panting, and restlessness occur in the gastric dilatation stage. The stomach may the twist on its supporting structures and cut off its blood supply along with the small intestines and spleen in the volvulus stage. This may ultimately lead to cardiac (heart) abnormal rhythms and arrest. The treatment is emergency surgery to untwist the stomach and restore its blood supply before any abdominal structures die. In this surgery, called *gastropexy*, the stomach is sewn to the abdominal wall to prevent further volvulus (twisting) problems. GDV is a medical emergency requiring emergency surgery. If too much dead bowel is encountered at surgery, euthanasia may be needed. A good relationship and close communication with your animal care facility is especially important in this situation.

5. *Dental Disease-* Bad breath in dogs (halitosis) may be due to problems inside or outside the mouth. Intra-oral causes include decaying food between the teeth, periodontal (gum) disease, and even rare oral tumors. Extra-oral problems include respiratory and sinus infections, tonsillitis, lip infections,

and even generalized problems such as diabetes, kidney, and liver failure. The normal dog's mouth has 750 million bacteria/cc. of saliva. Harmful bacteria including the "gram-stain negative" rods, a virile rod-shaped group of bacteria including Bacteroides, Fusobacterium and Actinomyces adhere to teeth forming *plaque*. Odors result from the bi-products of their bacterial sugar metabolism. The gum problem resulting from this inflammatory process in dogs and humans ranges from *gingivitis* (gum inflammation) to frank *periodontal (gum) disease*. As in humans, treatment lies in prevention. The first doggie dental exam should be done by one year of age. Dental decay may lead to infections causing potentially fatal multi-organ system failure. This is not intuitively obvious as it is not as serious a problem in humans. Dental cleaning with a home maintenance program is recommended including regular brushing. (10)

6. *Snake Bites*- Snake bites are uncommon in Illinois but may be encountered elsewhere in our country. Pit vipers are the largest group of poisonous snakes in the U.S. that includes rattlesnakes, copperheads, and cottonmouth water moccasins. The coral snake is not a pit viper but may also be deadly. (11) Heiskell and Tang recommend catching and/or killing the snake for identification purposes. Symptoms may include a bite wound, pain, lethargy, vomiting, diarrhea, salivation, thirst, local swelling, and even shock. Seek immediate veterinary care! In transport, immobilize the involved extremity and consider watchfully applying a venous tourniquet (a loosely applied tourniquet allowing arterial inflow but limiting venous drainage). Keep the dog muzzled, wrapped in a blanket and calm during transport. (12)

The Basic Canine First Aid Kit
There is no limit to what might be included in a K-9 basic first aid kit. The following modified basic kit is recommended by the United States Police Canine Association: (13)

1. 1 tourniquet
2. Kling ®-2 inch roll (2) and 4 inch roll (2)
3. Elastoplast ® dressing- 2 and 4 inch rolls (elastic plaster roll)
4. porous adhesive tape-1" and 2" rolls
5. vet wrap- non-adhesive bandage- 2" and 4" rolls
6. sterile Telfa pads (5)
7. sterile 4 x 4" gauze pads (1 box)
8. antibacterial ointment tube (any type)
9. antiseptic soap prep pads
10. hydrogen peroxide bottle
11. .sterile blunt scissors
12. sterile tweezers
13. sterile hemostat
14. rectal thermometer (digital preferred)
15. .saran wrap, chest seal for chest wounds
16. sterile gloves
17. SAM ® Splint (short)
18. wire cutters
19. muzzle
20. restraints
21. razor prep blades
22. suture tray
23. IV administration kit incl. large bore IV catheter (14-20G.)
24. airway kit available in the general medic's back pack.

Police Dog Support Information

Several excellent resources exist for police canine support.

The United States Police Canine Association (USPCA) can be reached on the internet at www.uspcak9.com. It has been in existence since 1971 and is currently the largest police canine association in the country. It holds a yearly summer meeting and again at the National Police Dog Trials. Its goals are to serve as a forum for canine police agencies, to develop minimum working canine standards, to maintain a legal assistance fund and to disseminate police canine information.

The North American Police Work Dog Association (NAPWDA) is a second national organization devoted to police canine issues. Their website is www.NAPWDA.com. The goal of this organization seems more oriented towards the training and certifying of police dogs.

No one would argue that it is important to know the capabilities of the hospital to which we transport injured officers. It is equally important to know the capabilities of the veterinary facility to which we bring the injured canine officer. It is incumbent upon care providers familiarizing themselves with canine first aid to acquaint themselves with the veterinarians and the veterinary facility they may be using. Some relevant questions to ask here include:

Is the facility full service or are some aspects of canine care referred out?

Does a special interest exist at the animal facility regarding police dog care?

Are the veterinarians there amenable to developing programs directed towards teaching canine first aid?

Selected Canine Wellness Issues

Ballistic/Stab-Resistant Vests- Preventing canine gunshot and stab injuries should be as high a priority as treating them. Ballistic and ballistic/stab resistant combination vests are currently in common police canine service and are produced by several manufacturers in a variety of NIJ threat levels. Remember that ballistic resistant vests are not puncture resistant unless so specified. The British West Yorkshire Police Operations Support Unit, Carr Gate, Wakefield County even reported the use of canine fire resistant vests and booties. (14)

Regular Veterinary Maintenance Exams- At least yearly veterinary exams are suggested to screen the police canine for early treatable problems. Basic screening blood studies including minimally a heartworm test, complete blood count (CBC) and chemistry panel are also valuable.

Summary
The police dog is here to stay in law enforcement operations. He is more than an important tactical tool; he is a partner. As a partner, the police dog deserves the same respect and attention medics offer their human teammates. This includes a familiarity with the dog, his medical history, and his handler. Appropriate application of first aid skills may save a canine life. This chapter has not discussed every canine medical problem the provider may encounter. However, a team approach to canine first aid including the medical care provider, the canine handler and the resource animal care facility will likely optimize treatment decisions. Many local and national resources are available to assist your delivery of this valuable service.

REFERENCES

1. https://www.uspcak9.com
2. Ibid. www.uspcak9.com
3. Ibid. www.uspcak9.com
4. http://www.bio.davidson.edu/Courses/anphys/2000/Hatfeld/Hatfeld2.html
5. Thomson et al.-Arch. Eur. Jour. of Physiology, 387: 161-166, 1980.
6. Heiskell, L. and Tang, D.-Medical Management of K-9 Emergencies-Part Two, The Tactical Edge, Winter, 1996 p.44
7. http://www.k9forensic.org/k9firstaid.html
8. https://www.workingk-9vet.com Working K9 Veterinary Consultation Services

9. Canine Field Trauma and Emergency Manual, Arboretum View Animal Hospital, Downers Grove, Illinois
10. Ibid. www.uspcak9.com
11. Op. Cit. Heiskell, L. and Tang, D., The Tactical Edge, Winter 1996 p.51
12. http://www.k9forensic.org/k9firstaid.html
13. http://www.uspcak9.com/medical/emergency.html
14. Police Magazine Feb., 2004 vol. 28 No. 2, p. 90

About the Author

Dr. Martin (Marty) Greenberg has recently retired after a forty-year career as an orthopedic trauma and hand surgeon at a level one trauma center in Chicago. He was born in Brooklyn, New York and resided there until his graduation from Brooklyn College with a Magna Cum Lauda Bachelor of Science degree in Psychology. During high school and college, he was Captain of his schools' Rifle Teams which were varsity sports in New York at the time. His high school team captured the New York City championship in 1968. He then attended Loyola University Medical School in Maywood, IL and subsequently entered an orthopedic surgery residency program at that institution. He then began an orthopedic surgery practice in the Chicagoland area until his retirement in 2021. Dr. Greenberg was motivated by the 9/11 tragedy and the Colombine High School mass casualty incident in Littleton, Colorado to help develop the field of Tactical Emergency Medical Support (TEMS) whose goal was to provide medical care inside the inner perimeter of critical incidents. EMS protocols generally did not allow medical care to be rendered inside an inner perimeter until "the scene was safe." Tactical medicine potentially allowed trauma victims to receive life saving care during the first "golden hour of trauma" after their injuries. The critically needed emergency medicine subspecialty of tactical medicine was embryonic at that time and didn't formally exist in the State of Illinois. Dr. Greenberg spearheaded the formation and licensure of the subspecialty in the state and helped popularize it locally and nationally. He was then recruited by a large multijurisdictional SWAT team to develop a TEMS program and became a state certified part time police officer and SWAT operator while continuing his orthopedic trauma and hand surgery practice for the next 20 years. Marty currently lives in the Chicago suburbs with his wife Julie, who as a spine surgeon, has also been his practice and life partner for all of this time. They have 4 wonderful, grown children and 6 young grand children. Martin hopes that he has brought his medical and practical experience both as an orthopedic trauma surgeon and as a tactical police officer and medic to these chapters.

www.ingramcontent.com/pod-product-compliance
Lightning Source LLC
Chambersburg PA
CBHW052027030426
42337CB00027B/4901